Decolonizing Israel, Liberating Palestine

"It is fashionable to say that the two-state solution to Israel-Palestine is dead. Jeff Halper thinks it was never born. In this brave, thought-provoking and highly original book, he presents both a searching critique of Zionist settler colonialism and a compelling case for one democratic state with equal rights for all its citizens."

—Avi Shlaim, Emeritus Professor of International Relations at Oxford and author of *The Iron Wall: Israel and the Arab World*

"Strikes at the core of the political revolution boiling under the surface in Israel/ Palestine. Halper serves a generous helping of hope for anyone who cares about the future of this land."

—Shir Hever, political economist and author of *The Political Economy of Israel's Occupation*

"An important chapter in the development of a conversation that will form the foundation of a just regime for the inhabitants of the country and the refugees."

—Eitan Bronstein Aparicio, founder and former director of the NGO Zochrot and co-founder of De-Colonizer, a research/art laboratory for social change

"Jeff Halper harnesses his extremely sharp and original mind alongside his prophetic voice to change the international debate. A gem for both the novice as well as the expert, his book offers a brilliant analysis of Israel's colonial project and outlines what a decolonial horizon might look like."

—Neve Gordon, author of *Human Shields: A History of People in the Line of Fire*

"This is the first serious contribution in drawing a path to the project of liberating Palestine."

—Awad Abdelfattah, former Secretary General of the Balad/Tajamu Party and Coordinator of the One Democratic State Campaign (ODSC)

"Helps us to see light at the end of the tunnel. At a time when Israel is seeking to legalise its apartheid regime and colonisation of occupied Palestine, it is vital to imagine and discuss alternative futures."

—Haidar Eid, Associate Professor of Postcolonial and Postmodern Literature at Gaza al-Aqsa University and the author of *Countering the Palestinian Nakba: One State for All*

"A powerful and convincing case – a must read for anyone looking for fresh ideas of how to end the long and bloody conflict in Palestine."

—Ilan Pappe, Professor of History and Director of the European Centre for Palestine Studies at the University of Exeter

T0133412

"With informed lucidity, political sophistication and moral integrity Halper depicts the path from here to there. What is most unexpected, given present realities, is that this manages to be a book of realistic hope, the finest work of advocacy scholarship I have ever read."

—Richard Falk, Professor Emeritus of International Law at Princeton University, was the UN Special Rapporteur on Palestinian Human Rights and author of *Palestine's Horizon*

"Those seriously engaged with the search for justice in Palestine have for many years benefitted from Jeff Halper's contributions as both a serious scholar and committed activist. This is a serious work that deserves to be widely read. Halper is among the few who not only understands that we are at a critical historical juncture, but is also able to analyze its multiple dimensions and offer a transformative plan of action."

—Mouin Rabbani, Co-Editor of *Jadaliyya*

"Amid a raft of failed policy choices, Halper's book is a cathartic practical vision of one possible way out of the protracted Israel-Palestine conflict."

—Sophia Akram, *The New Arab*

"A perceptive analysis that should be read by anyone interested in excavating the entwined futures of Palestinians and Israelis."

—Thomas Abowd, Department of Race, Colonialism, and Diaspora, Tufts University and the author of *Colonial Jerusalem: The Spatial Construction of Identity and Difference in a City of Myth, 1948–2012*

"Halper's book is informative, offering an in-depth perspective that is lacking and addresses the concept of memory within the political framework of decolonisation."

—*Middle East Monitor*

"An extremely convincing and persuasive argument that the only conceivable future for justice and peace necessitates a process of decolonization and equal rights for all."

—*Electronic Intifada*

"He doesn't pretend that creating one democratic state will be easy but he contends that it is the only way for Palestinians and Israelis to gain long-term security and a viable way of life."

—*Jordan Times*

"[Halper] reframes Israel as a settler-colonial state necessitating a clear oppositional political strategy with an end-game of actively decolonizing the whole political structure."

—*Counterpunch*

Decolonizing Israel, Liberating Palestine

Zionism, Settler Colonialism, and the Case for One Democratic State

Jeff Halper

Foreword by Nadia Naser-Najjab

PLUTO PRESS

First published 2021 by Pluto Press
New Wing, Somerset House, Strand, London WC2R 1LA

www.plutobooks.com

British Library Cataloguing in Publication Data
A catalogue record for this book is available from the British Library

ISBN 978 0 7453 4340 2 Hardback
ISBN 978 0 7453 4339 6 Paperback
ISBN 978 0 7453 4343 3 PDF eBook
ISBN 978 0 7453 4341 9 EPUB eBook

This book is printed on paper suitable for recycling and made from fully managed and sustained forest sources. Logging, pulping and manufacturing processes are expected to conform to the environmental standards of the country of origin.

Typeset by Stanford DTP Services, Northampton, England

Simultaneously printed in the United Kingdom and United States of America

Contents

Foreword

Nadia Naser-Najjab

Institute of Arabic and Islamic Studies,
University of Exeter

On first receiving Jeff's proposed solution to the Palestinian-Israeli conflict, many readers will undoubtedly reflexively dismiss it as "utopian." It is considerably less likely that they will acknowledge that it only appears this way when perceived from the confines of a pernicious orthodoxy that refuses to acknowledge, let alone engage with, possible alternatives. This is increasingly recognized by the Palestinian and Israeli peace activists who are seeking to retrieve the one-state solution and explore its possibilities and potentials. They have not necessarily accepted this solution on its own merits but have instead realized that Israel's ongoing colonization of the West Bank makes the two-state solution impossible.

Jeff's willingness to engage with the one-state solution clearly distinguishes him from those Israelis who are reluctant to renounce the privileges and entitlements that derive from the colonial state. These Israelis are at some level aware that their privilege was attained through various forms of oppression, and this creates a deep cognitive dissonance that they have never managed to fully resolve. Accordingly, their mentality, words and practice remain deeply, and perhaps irredeemably, colonial.

Jeff therefore stands apart from the Israeli mainstream. This was not the case when he emigrated to Israel (from the US) in 1973, with the aim of finding his Jewish roots in the Zionist state. Although he was a Leftist and peace activist from the beginning, it was only after he saw a Palestinian house being demolished in Jerusalem that he began to comprehend the colonial and irreversible nature of the Zionist project. In 1997 he co-founded the Israeli Committee Against House Demolitions (ICAHD), which rebuilds Palestinian homes demolished by Israel as acts of *political resistance*, not humanitarian gestures. Jeff has been arrested on several occasions for attempting to stop demolitions, as well as for other resistance activities (like sailing into Gaza with the Freedom Flotilla in order to break the siege).

It was in this context that he realized that the issue at hand was settler colonialism, not a "conflict of nationalisms" or merely occupation, and that the establishment of a Palestinian state alongside Israel was never in the cards. After initially opposing and resisting occupation – a place where most Israeli Leftists remain – he shifted to becoming an anti-colonial activist, committed to transforming colonial relations between Palestinians and Israeli Jews. With a view to this end, he holds up coexistence between Christians, Jews and Muslims in Arab countries as a model for the single state.

Although Jeff and I have not always agreed when discussing the one-state solution, I have always been impressed by his insistence on Palestinian rights, including the Right of Return, and recognition of their central role in any future solution. He is also clear (in this book and on other occasions) that he cannot speak on behalf of Palestinians, and that their voices must be foremost. He knows that he is a privileged colonizer. But he simultaneously accepts and rejects this status and this confirms him, to borrow Albert Memmi's phrase, as the "colonizer who refuses."[1]

As a "refuser," Jeff can speak to Palestinians, while as a "colonizer" he can engage with Israelis on issues of identity, national narratives and nationalism. The "colonizer who refuses" is therefore not conflicted but is instead uniquely well placed to challenge and undermine colonial power. In addressing the Right of Return, Jeff accepts that it is not fair to expect Palestinians to live alongside those who were responsible for their expulsion and subsequent suffering. He proposes that this injustice could be addressed by the redistribution of resources and land. I believe, however, that such questions of justice can only be answered by those who were dispossessed. Jeff, throughout the book, underlines and reiterates his commitment to live alongside Palestinians on the basis of an equality that actively seeks to address and resolve past injustices. This vision is embodied in the One Democratic State Campaign (which he co-founded) and its specific commitment that "no group or collectivity will have any privileges, nor will any group, party or collectivity have the ability to leverage any control or domination over others."

Jeff's book helps the reader to think about how Palestinians and Jews can live alongside each other in a single state that upholds human rights and the broad principle of equality. He makes it clear that one of the elements of a shared life is reconciling narratives that do not seek to negate "the [o]ther's narrative and aspirations." Palestinians may be disconcerted by this proposed reconciliation when they think back over years of dispossession, oppression and humiliation, but I believe it will help them to sustain a constructive and productive debate of the past, present and future.

Jeff's book is more than just a vision or open proposition, as it also sketches out a clear and concrete plan for future action that will work towards decolonization. He does not therefore just wish to apologise for the past and present actions of the settler state but instead sets out a clear program for the dismantling of the colonial structure and the establishment of an alternative grounded in pluralism and equality.

I view his book as the starting point of a discussion that will work towards, and ultimately produce, a genuinely inclusive alternative to a deeply pernicious status quo.

Acknowledgements

My analysis is informed by my interaction with "real world" comrades and insights gathered from struggles "on the ground." It is to my partners-in-crime in the Israeli Committee Against House Demolitions (ICAHD), especially Linda Ramsden of ICAHD UK, and the One Democratic State Campaign (ODSC), headed by Awad Abdelfattah, that I owe the intellectual and political interaction out of which this book's analysis emerges. To the thousands of ICAHD supporters and political activists who hosted my many speaking tours throughout the world over the years – my equivalent of students and professional colleagues – I owe a great intellectual debt as well. I must also acknowledge the families of Salim and Arabia Shawamreh and of Ata and Rudeina Jabar, Palestinians whose homes ICAHD has rebuilt and who have become significant friends and comrades in every sense of the term.

I owe a debt of gratitude as well to a few academic comrades who made available to me their own thoughts on this work and even some academic resources. In particular, Ilan Pappe, with whom I have worked closely on the one-state project and who arranged two small-group conferences around issues of decolonization and the one-state program at the European Centre for Palestine Studies at the University of Exeter, and Nadia Naser-Najjab, a Research Fellow at the Institute of Arabic and Islamic Studies at the University of Exeter. Nadia played a key role in organizing the conferences at Exeter. She also read this book, made valuable comments, and kindly wrote the Foreword. No less important for an activist/scholar with limited access to university resources, she even arranged a library card for me from the university.

Several friends whose opinions I value read the manuscript and gave me valuable feedback: Robert Herbst, Jonathan Kuttab and an anonymous reader in particular. I also thank my editor David Shulman and the people of Pluto Press, for whom this is my third book. Finally, of course, I must acknowledge my wife and partner Shoshana – her wisdom and criticism infuses all my work. The book is dedicated to our children, Efrat, Yishai and Yair, and our grandchildren, Zohar, Alex and Nora, in the hope that this book may contribute to their living in a just and inclusive future state and region.

Introduction:
The Colonist Who Refuses,
the Comrade in Joint Struggle

The philosophers have only interpreted the world, in various ways; the point is to change it.

– Karl Marx

The times, they are a-changin', even when it comes to the interminable Israeli-Palestinian "conflict." No less than the *New York Times* has taken notice. On January 5, 2018, it ran a piece entitled: "As the 2-State Solution Loses Steam, a 1-State Solution Gains Traction." Mustafa Barghouti is quoted as saying: "It's dominating the discussion."

Certainly the latest flurry around Israeli Premier Netanyahu's plan to annex up to 30 percent of the West Bank, taking advantage of the opening offered by Trump's "Deal of the Century," has changed the equation, whether or not it actually happens. It has forced liberal Zionists like Peter Beinart and Gershon Baskin, two leading lights of liberal Zionism, to confront Zionism's inability to reconcile its exclusive claim to the Land of Israel with the national rights of the Palestinian people. "Now Prime Minister Benjamin Netanyahu has vowed to annex parts of the land that Israel has brutally and undemocratically controlled for decades," Beinart writes.[1]

And watching all this unfold, I have begun to wonder, for the first time in my life, whether the price of a state that favors Jews over Palestinians is too high. The painful truth is that the project to which liberal Zionists like myself have devoted ourselves for decades – a state for Palestinians separated from a state for Jews – has failed. The traditional two-state solution no longer offers a compelling alternative to Israel's current path. It is time for liberal Zionists to abandon the goal of Jewish – Palestinian separation and embrace the goal of Jewish–Palestinian equality.

He followed his piece with another in the *New York Times* (July 8, 2020) entitled plainly: "I No Longer Believe in a Jewish State" (although he followed that with an interview in *Ha'aretz* (July 22, 2020) proclaiming that he is still "a Zionist." Gershon Baskin, too, published in the right-wing newspaper *The Jerusalem Post* (June 3, 2020) a piece entitled "With the Two-State Solution Dead, We Must Build for a New Future."

Such sentiments seem to reflect a fundamental shift in the views of young Jews abroad towards Israel, and their concerns with the human rights of Palestinians. The Jewish Voice for Peace, one of the largest and fastest-growing Jewish organization in the United States, issued an explicitly anti-Zionist position paper in 2019. Entitled "Our Approach to Zionism,"[2] it states:

> Jewish Voice for Peace is guided by a vision of justice, equality and freedom for all people. We unequivocally oppose Zionism because it is counter to those ideals .... Through study and action, through deep relationship with Palestinians fighting for their own liberation, and through our own understanding of Jewish safety and self-determination, we have come to see that Zionism was a false and failed answer to the desperately real question many of our ancestors faced of how to protect Jewish lives from murderous antisemitism in Europe. While it had many strains historically, the Zionism that took hold and stands today is a settler colonial movement, establishing an apartheid state where Jews have more rights than others. Our own history teaches us how dangerous this can be.

The prospect of annexation also shook the international community, for whom the notion of two states is essential for perpetuating an eternal "peace process," its strategy of cost-free conflict management. Heads of State from Boris Johnson and Angela Merkel in the West to Xi Jinping of China urged Israel not to annex. The European Union (EU) warned that it

> will spare no diplomatic efforts to help Israel understand the risks of proceeding with the unilateral annexation of parts of the West Bank .... Annexation would constitute a violation of international law; it will cause real damage to the prospects for a two-state solution; it

would also negatively influence regional stability, our relations with Israel, the relations between Israel and Arab states and, potentially, the security of Israel.[3]

Tellingly, while annexation disquieted a few Israelis – mainly liberal *Ha'aretz* readers – for the vast majority it came off as a non-issue. For all its potential political significance, few could see how annexation of the major settlement blocs on the West Bank would change Israel's ongoing occupation in any fundamental way. Although such a move would garner the approval of 103 of the 120 members of the Israeli parliament (all the parties except the Joint Arab List and Meretz), it was (and is) considered a cynical attempt by Netanyahu to distract public attention from his criminal trial. Yet even the readers of *Ha'aretz*, as liberal as Israelis come, took the comments of Beinart and others who question whether the two-state solution is still viable as "utopian dreaming." Anshel Pfeffer, a senior *Ha'aretz* columnist, dismissed Beinart's views as, indeed, "utopian," but for a particular reason that will concern us as we move towards visions, programs and strategies for achieving a single democracy between the River and the Sea. Beinart, says Pfeffer,

> isn't talking to anyone who will actually live in "Israel-Palestine." He's having an internal conversation with a handful of Palestinian American academics and, with their blessing, has created a utopian half-Jewish state which can serve as safe space for a section of young American Jews … who are trying to reconcile their Jewish identity, their inherent affinity with Israel and their progressive values, in a period of ideological and racial turmoil in the U.S.

In other words, so disconnected are Israelis from both the moral and political concerns raised by Beinart that they dismiss his concerns, if not his analysis, with a sense of bemusement at the naivete of American Jews and other foreign critics. Israeli Jews have removed themselves as political actors. Convinced that only they "know the Arabs" and that the international community will in fact do nothing to sanction them, they perceive the status quo as more or less permanent and sustainable. In fact, two-thirds of Israeli Jews don't believe the West Bank is occupied at all.[4] Having dumped Palestinians, the occupation,

3

Iran, Hezbollah and related issues into the bag of "security" which is better left to the army, the Israeli Jewish public has moved on to more pressing matters such as the economy, religious-secular relations, the Covid virus (as of this writing), the latest political scandal and consumerism. When asked what issues concerned them most, Israeli Jews ranked the occupation and their "conflict" with the Palestinians seventh out of eight.[5]

All this creates an anomalous situation. The more the Israeli-Palestinian "Conflict" disrupts regional and even international stability, contributing to the polarization and militarization of an unstable yet geo-politically crucial region of the world, generating intensive initiatives for peace over the past five-and-a-half decades, the less of a concern it is to the Israeli public. And so, as urgent the need for a resolution is – for Palestinians first and foremost – the less the chance that that resolution will come from Israelis themselves. The fact that Israel has succeeded in reducing one of the world's great conflicts to a "non-issue" domestically does not mean that it is any less urgent or critical, however. There are at least four good reasons why we must concern ourselves with what happens in Palestine/Israel:

1. The suffering of the Palestinians calls out for our intervention. Indeed, the Palestinians living in historic Palestine labor under a hybrid regime of triple repression: settler colonialism since the turn of the twentieth century, the occupation of the West Bank, East Jerusalem and Gaza since 1967 and, country-wide again, an ever-tightening regime of apartheid. Much of this book details that hybrid regime and its implications for Palestinians.

2. We must not lose track of the fact that only half the Palestinians remain in the country. Massive waves of expulsion and displacement, particularly in 1948 and 1967, have generated a refugee population of 7.2 million people: 4.3 million Palestinian refugees and their descendants displaced in 1948 live mainly in United Nations (UN)-sponsored refugee camps in Lebanon, Jordan and Syria (where many have been displaced once again by the civil war); 1.7 million refugees of 1948 live outside of the UN system; 355,000 Palestinians and their descendants remain internally displaced inside present-day Israel; with another 834,000 persons displaced in 1967. In addition, Israel continues to generate new

refugees every day. Almost 60,000 homes and livelihood structures have been demolished by Israel in the Occupied Territory since 1967 according to the UN, B'tselem and the figures my organization, the Israeli Committee Against House Demolitions, have collected; 15,000 have been displaced by the construction of Israel's "Separation Barrier"; and tens of thousands more (Arab) *citizens of Israel* have had their homes demolished on an ongoing basis.[6] The refugees must be brought home (or given the choice to remain in the countries where they found refuge or emigrate somewhere else) and provided with equal rights and adequate, secure housing.

3. The Israeli-Palestinian "Conflict" ("Conflict" in quotes because, as we will discuss later, the "conflict" is actually unilateral colonialism) disrupts the entire Middle East and beyond, preventing any movement towards stability, democracy and development. It is not the only cause of instability in the region, of course, but its role as a surrogate of American interests, pursued through the export of arms and technologies of repression to repressive American-allied regimes throughout the region and occasionally by their actual use makes it a major (and not constructive) player. Not only would resolving the Israel-Palestine "conflict" go a long way towards reducing militarization and polarization in the region, it would give more progressive Palestinian and Israeli voices an opportunity to link up with progressive forces throughout the Middle East to produce genuine change – something that is today foreclosed by the "conflict."

4. Israel is exporting not only weaponry, surveillance systems and tactics of militarized policing throughout the world, technologies and structures of repression perfected on its Palestinian guinea pigs in its West Bank and Gaza labs, but a broader model of a Security State. As I detail in my book *War Against the People: Israel, the Palestinians and Global Pacification*,[7] Israel is universalizing, weaponizing (literally) and exporting its model of a militarized democracy based on the permanent repression of Palestinians. Defining them as "terrorists" gives Israel the ability to "sell" a sophisticated police state driven by the logic of permanent war, in which the demand for "security" trumps all democratic protections. Whether a government and its military/police structures are already police states who merely need the weaponry and justification that

Israel provides – unfortunately the case in much of the Global South – or are democracies who feel besieged by crime, immigration or restlessness on the part of its working poor or young people increasingly excluded from the job market and seeking internal "security" and pacification, Israel's concept of a Security State holds great attraction. Israel's exporting of its militarized Security State to *your* country directly threatens *your* civil liberties. Dismantling Israel's laboratory would send a strong message that Israel's model of militarized democracy is unacceptable.

The problem, then, is that this untenable and repressive hybrid regime of settler colonialism, occupation and apartheid, which threatens us all, whether locally or globally, seems immune from resolution. By making itself useful to the world's hegemons, employing skillful lobbying, the strategic use of the massive financial resources, manipulation of the Holocaust and strategic accusations of anti-Semitism, Israel fears no international sanctions from any quarter. Having marginalized the Palestinians politically and militarily, it feels it has rendered the "conflict" to the sidelines, among the Israeli Jewish public as well as internationally (although, as I argue later in this book, this need not be true). And it has done so in large part through conniving with governments to keep the "two-state solution" alive as an effective means of perpetual conflict management, by separating the process of (seeming) negotiating from its actual resolution. In addition to all this, because the Zionist/Israeli settlers have become so deeply embedded in the country, having worked to marginalize the indigenous Palestinians and so Judaize the country, they have rendered Zionist settler colonialism difficult to dismantle.

But this is not a book about settler colonialism or Zionism *per se*. It is a book about summoning power and *decolonizing*, about dismantling a settler regime and replacing it with something more equitable. The two-state solution has always been merely a cynical tool of conflict management never intended to actually resolve the "conflict." The good news is, as Beinart's articles, JVP's anti-Zionist manifesto and appreciation of what annexation all imply, that the two-state solution is becoming less and less tenable, even among "pro-Israeli" supporters. People aware of how important it is to actually resolve this issue are therefore asking: So where do we go if the two-state solution is no longer viable and the current regime of growing Israeli apartheid is unacceptable? The only just and workable alternative appears to be transforming Israel's apartheid regime into a single democracy for all the country's inhabitants, including refugees and their descendants who choose to return. A one-state solution. It is this position that this book argues for.

While the one-state solution might, indeed, be "in the air," it is not yet a viable alternative. No one has really thought through the entire process of decolonization, very different from conflict resolution but the only way out of a colonial situation. What does decolonization entail? What replaces a colonial regime? How do we overcome Israeli opposition to a single state (and no less Israeli indifference to the entire issue), as well as the unconditional support Israel receives from the world's governments? What is our strategy for reaching a just, post-colonial reality? Without a long-term vision and a political end-game, without organization and strategy, and without the active leadership of Palestinians supported by their critical Israeli Jewish allies, those of us who seek justice and peace in Palestine/Israel are not political actors. We are simply not in the game.

This book attempts to "think through" the process of decolonization and suggest ways of actually getting there. Since the anti-colonial political analysis and program set out in the book was written by a settler and not an indigenous Palestinian, some contextualization is necessary before we start. As Patrick Wolfe said so clearly: in settler societies there can be no innocent academic discourses about Indigenous knowledge and experiences.[8] Positionality is critical if my remarks are to be properly understood.

POSITIONALITY: ACTIVIST/SCHOLAR, COLONIST WHO REFUSES, COMRADE

I am an engaged academic who has researched and written about Palestine/Israel for many years.[9] My political activity "on the ground" since 1997 has been as the head of the Israeli Committee Against House Demolitions. ICAHD is an Israeli organization that fights Israel's policy of demolishing Palestinian homes – some 55,000 in the Occupied Palestinian Territory (OPT) since 1967, more than 130,000 in historic Palestine since 1948. It is one of the cruelest, most superfluous aspects of Zionism. But ICAHD also takes what it's learned from house demolitions to address major political questions. Why is Israel demolishing homes throughout the country? What is Israel's intent towards the OPT and the Palestinian people? How is the occupation being constructed and how does it operate? What is the human cost of colonization, occupation and apartheid? That work has led me into involvement as a founding member of the Palestinian-led One Democratic State Campaign, about which more later.

I am not a Palestinian (although my friend Uri Davis would characterize me as a "Palestinian Hebrew),[10] and I certainly cannot speak for Palestinians – or for 98 percent of Israeli Jews, for that matter. I am an anti-Zionist Israeli Jew, a settler/immigrant from the US, a White cis-male, whose political commitments were forged in the 1960s. For our purposes here, what defines me most appropriately is a "colonist who refuses."[11]

I settled in/immigrated to Israel in 1973, for many reasons I will not go into here. I did so with my eyes open, believing I could reconcile my desire to become an Israeli with my readiness to work for "peace" with the Palestinians. I was active on the Palestine/Israel issue on campus in the US. Upon my arrival as a settler/immigrant (I had not yet understood the difference), I became involved in *Siakh*, the Israeli New Left. Over the years, as my political awareness has grown along with Israeli apartheid, I have accepted my colonial status – although I still identify myself as an Israeli. I have entered into the anti-colonial struggle with my Palestinian victims/comrades, in the hope of "redeeming" my Israeliness, giving it expression within a post-colonial society in which the Palestinian refugees return and we all share a common society and citizenship in equality. But I am faced with the fundamental dilemmas of every settler colonial, as expressed eloquently by the late Tunisian Jew Albert Memmi:

> Once he has discovered the import of colonization and is conscious of his own position ([vis-à-vis] that of the colonized and their necessary relationship), is he going to accept them? Will he agree to be a privileged man, and to [merely] underscore the distress of the colonized? Will he be a usurper and [still] affirm the oppression and injustice to the true inhabitant of the colony? Will he accept being a colonizer under the growing habit of privilege and illegiti-

macy, under the constant gaze of the usurped? Will he adjust to this position and his inevitable self-censure?[12]

Even after answering these questions "no," after years of inner struggling and political growth, yet other critical questions remain. Should I simply leave, as some suggest, or focus on changing Israeli society, policies and attitudes? Or (the path I chose) become a co-resister, a (junior) partner in a joint Palestinian/Israel struggle for decolonization. I reached the latter conclusion out of the conviction that decolonization of a settler state like Israel is possible, must be an inclusive endeavor, and that in a post-colonial reality I can find a just and meaningful place as an Israeli Jew in a new, inclusive civil society – in which I will integrate my present political identity with the new one of my new country. I can do this, I believe, through establishing political and personal relationships predicated on joint struggle. Anti-colonialism divides the "sides" differently from conflict resolution: not Jewish versus Palestinian, but anti-colonial versus colonial. As Palestinian activist Muhannad Abu Gosh phrased it, we are in a "common liberatory struggle; ... everyone is welcomed to join it as long as they renounce the privilege of being a 'Jewish side in Palestine.'"[13]

The next question becomes: How does a settler, one of the dominant, oppressive population, properly engage with the colonized? On one level, what is the political agenda? What does coexistence entail, and is it really possible? And how do we, the ever-privileged settler/activists, enter into the political equation? "Solidarity should be directed to decolonization," writes Clare Land of her work with the Indigenous of Australia, "and the way solidarity is undertaken needs to be decolonized."[14] On another level, how do we, the powerful, establish genuine working relations across power differentials? A new relationship must emerge. Those aspiring to surmount their colonial position, like me, must adopt a mix of critical self-reflection and a willingness to submit to, or at least accept, the agenda of the colonized, their priorities, their decisions, even their ways of working. The goals are three-fold. Agency and sovereignty must be restored to the Indigenous. The colonial structures of domination and control must be dismantled. And the settlers themselves must be liberated, indigenized in a post-colonial society after they relinquish their privileges and become citizens of the new polity, but without having to sacrifice their own identities, collective memories, symbols or associations. "This new way of relating," says Land,[15] "includes non-Indigenous people seeing their interests as linked in with those of Indigenous people, though not in a way which appropriates Indigeneity."

These were the personal and political considerations that went into my political work. We, the Israeli Jewish activists who founded ICAHD a quarter-century ago, have, over the years, managed to forge close working relationships across the power differentials by "being there" for the Palestinians. We physically resist Israel's demolition of Palestinian homes, and we have rebuilt almost 200 homes that have been demolished. Through our work "on the ground," we have developed a powerful political analysis which we share, including such useful concepts as the Matrix of Control. We produce maps, brochures, booklets, books, films, PowerPoint presentations and other informational materials, bringing them to the international community through our strategic advocacy. And we are actively engaged in anti-colonial work with our Palestinian partners, endeavoring to transform a settler colonial regime into a democratic state of all its citizens. Through all this we have focused on decolonization ourselves and our methods of working with Palestinians and other oppressed peoples. The fact that we, as Israelis, have managed to sustain our close working relationships with our Palestinian partners despite the strains of ever-greater Israeli repression and violence speaks well to our attempts to be relevant, sincere partners in decolonization. Although we remain colonists-who-refuse until the conclusion of the process of decolonization, the decolonization project must be a shared one between the Palestinians and their Israeli Jewish allies. We must become comrades in a joint struggle – and I believe our Palestinian colleagues have come to see us in that light.

I have tried to take my critical abilities as a colonizer-who-refuses into my work with the One Democratic State Campaign, from which this book emerges. Being an Israeli Jew has its advantages in the struggle for decolonization. I am a stakeholder in the process, an ally coming from the oppressor's side. I can bring to the table an intimate and critical understanding of Israeli society, its history and ideologies, its internal differences and its aspirations and fears. These can make a crucial contribution in our collective effort to end the Zionist settler project and transform the country into an egalitarian polity. As a trained anthropologist with extensive experience in both research and activism, I am well placed to contribute to communicating both the issues at stake and an inclusive way forward – to harness the power of knowledge production for liberation, instead of as a tool of control.[16] The program of decolonization and reconstruction I present in this book reflects the discussions we have had within the One Democratic State Campaign. It is augmented by my own academic analyses and views gained through my years of "being there." The process of "thinking it through" must be a collective one in the end. It is to that task that this book – really a kind of working paper – is offered.

FOCUSING ON DECOLONIZATION

In terms of the intent and focus of this book, it is not meant to be "academic," that is, a book whose main purpose is theoretical analysis, although it does apply critical theory to the task at hand: decolonizing Zionism and establishing a single democracy between the River and the Sea. As the book's subtitle indicates, its purpose is to "makes a case" for a particular political program. To that end, I ground my analysis in the academic literature, taking from it what serves my purpose, but careful to respect the substance of the analyses and the views of their authors. Because my purpose is to "make my case" in a clear and focused way – my intended audience is more activists and the informed public than fellow academics – I try to apply theory, analysis and concepts in ways that are comprehensible and accessible to my readers. I also validate non-academic sources of knowledge and analysis; the views of my Palestinian and Israeli Jewish comrades with whom I have been politically engaged over the past half-century, whether "on the ground," in political forums or in personal interactions. My own experience as an engaged anthropologist is certainly reflected in the ways I put together this book and in the analysis and political program it presents. I have thus gone beyond purely academic sources to "make my case" for a single state, especially as works dealing with the form of decolonization Palestine/Israel calls for are sorely lacking.

The book is divided into three sections. Part I: Zionism as Settler Colonial Project (Chapters 1–2) describes settler colonialism in theory and then shows why Zionism is best understood in that light. Strategies for dismantling Zionist colonial structures and then reassembling a truly liberatory post-colonial reality require us to examine how settler colonialism works, how it is structured and in what ways a program for summoning focused power may decolonize it. Towards that end I suggest focusing on what I call Zionism's Dominance Management Regime.

Part II: Three Cycles of Zionist Colonial Development (Chapters 3–5) traces the development of the Dominance Management Regime through its cycles of expansion and development: the pre-state cycle (1880s–1948), the Israeli state cycle (1948–67), and the occupation cycle (1967–present). This part reveals the governing "logic" of Zionist settlement and shows that decolonization, not conflict resolution, is the only way out of colonization towards genuine liberation.

Part III: Decolonizing Zionism, Liberating Palestine (Chapters 6–10) focuses on the process of decolonization, of summoning power through popular international mobilization and effective strategy revolving around a comprehensive political program, and the completion of the liberation project through the establishment of a democratic polity, a common civil society and, ultimately, a shared political community. It is to that undertaking that this second half of this book is devoted.

A book that attempts to "make a case" for a democratic state between the River and the Sea must set out clearly its terms of reference, its theory and its analysis before moving on to possible ways of getting there. Some readers may prefer to get the theory and overview in Part I and then jump to the nitty-gritty of a political program in Part III, skipping (or skimming) over the history and structural details of Zionist colonialism in Part II if that is of less interest.

So as to ground my discussion as much as possible in "real" political terms, I take the One Democratic State Campaign's 10-point program as the starting point of my discussion of decolonization. I do this for two reasons. First, it is the product of a two-year process of intensive deliberation by a core group of some 50 Palestinian intellectuals, academics, political figures and activists representing all the Palestinian communities, including Palestinians involved in researching and resisting Zionist colonialism and in formulating previous one-state programs – although initiated by Palestinian citizens in Israel. Their labor was supported by the active participation of 20 or so Israeli

Jewish comrades, myself included. Thus the Palestinian voice in all its diversity (gender included) was paramount in formulating the political program that forms the basis of this book's analysis.

Second, I am keenly aware that, as the author, an Israeli voice occupies a disproportionate space. The original intent was to write this with a Palestinian colleague, but as we approached the work we understood that a joint analysis should come at a later time. Not that we disagreed in our analysis, but we thought it better that an Israeli analysis of Zionist settler colonialism should stand separately from an analysis by a Palestinian, since we would raise different but no less important issues from our different perspectives. As an Israeli I can't approach settler colonialism as a Palestinian would, and if I tried I would suppress elements of Zionism I would otherwise consider critical. And vice versa. This work, then, is but a step towards a shared analysis somewhere down the line. Still, my engagement with Palestinian sources and my reliance on a political program produced by Palestinians in the consideration of decolonization means that a meaningful amount of integration took place (although I acknowledge that there is a large literature in Arabic to which I have access only through translations). This is not a book a Palestinian would write, but hopefully it is one a Palestinian would find useful, containing insights that might otherwise be lost. In the end I take umbrage as an anthropologist in the comparative method: it is clear that no ethnography can be complete and that no one researcher, Indigenous or not, can cover everything. It is in our collaboration that the best and most effective analysis emerges.

Just one word about the seeming inconsistency in capitalizing – or not – the terms "Indigenous" and "Native." I tried to follow the *Indigenous Peoples Terminology Guidelines for Usage*,[17] which specifies: "Always capitalize Indigenous, Aboriginal, First Nation, Inuit, Métis as a sign of respect the same way that English, French, Spanish, etc. are capitalized." There's one complication, however. Unlike "English," etc., "indigenous" or "native" can also be adjectives (e.g., indigenous rights, native peoples) that apply to a category of people but not to a specific one, or a generic description (my Israeli kids are indigenous to Jerusalem, where they were born, but are not part of the country's Indigenous population). So I tried to capitalize when referring to particular populations but not when referring to indigenous people generically. I know this creates some apparent confusion – in fact, the line gets very fine sometimes and I might make a misjudgement based on context – but the usage attempts to be consistent with the *Guidelines*.

PART I

ZIONISM AS SETTLER COLONIAL PROJECT

1

Analysis Matters: Beginning with Settler Colonialism

Sometimes, the very name you give to a phenomenon determines how it is understood and what can be done about it. Since 1948, we have spoken of the "Arab-Israeli Conflict." This term well describes the six major wars Israel has fought with its Arab neighbors: the 1948 War of Independence, the Sinai Campaign of 1956, the 1967 war, the 1973 war between Israel and Egypt, and the two wars fought in Lebanon (1982, 2006). It may also apply to "informal" wars between Israel and its Muslim neighbors. The "war of attrition" waged between Egypt and Israel from 1967 to 1973 is a case in point. So are the slew of "dirty wars" involving special operations units, targeted assassinations, sabotage, cyber-attacks, terrorism and regime change. Then we have all the diplomatic intrigues and, occasionally, negotiations and "peace processes." Since 1987, when the first Intifada catapulted Israel's long-standing occupation into public view, we speak also of an "Israeli-Palestinian Conflict."

The terms "war" or "conflict" conceal a deeper struggle, however: the colonization of Palestine by the Zionist movement, culminating in a state of Israel ruling over the entirety of the country. To be sure, colonization *generates* conflict. But "conflict" did not simply erupt for one reason or another. Jews, in fact, had lived in peace with the local Arab population for centuries, if not millennia. They were known in Arabic as *yahud awlad 'arab* (Native Arab Jews), *al-yahud al-'arab* (Arab Jews), *al-yahud al-muwlidun fi Filastin* (Palestine-born Jews) or *al-yahud al-'aslin* (Native Jews), *abna al-balad* (Sons of the Land) or, in Hebrew, *Bnei Ha'aaretz* (Children of the Land).[1] Zionism shattered this historic relationship.

Driven by persecution and the rise of nationalism in Europe, it was European Jews with little knowledge of Palestine and its peoples who launched a movement of Jewish "return" to its ancestral homeland, the Land of Israel, after a national absence of 2000 years. In their newly minted nationalist ideology, they were the returning natives. In their eyes, the Arabs of Palestine were mere background. They had no national claims or even cultural identity of their own. Palestine was, as the famous Zionist phrase put it, "a land without a people." The European Zionists knew the land was peopled, of course. But to them the Arabs did not amount to "a people" in the national sense of the term. They were just a collection of natives – though not *the* Natives, a status the Jewish claimants reserved for themselves. They played no role in the Zionist story. Having no national existence or claims of their own, the Arabs were to be removed, confined or eliminated so as to make way for the country's "real" owners.

This form of conquest – for that is what it was – took the form of settler colonialism. Zionists felt a deep sense of historical, religious and national connection to the Land of Israel.[2] But in claiming Palestine for themselves alone and rejecting the society they found there, they chose to come as settlers – or more precisely, their choice of settler colonialism rested on formative elements in both Jewish and European societies,[3] such as the notion of biblical "chosenness" and a Divinely sanctioned ownership of the Land; a self- and externally enforced ethno-national existence in the European "Diaspora": embeddedness in the rise of European nationalism, primarily the "tribal" nationalism of Eastern Europe and European experiences of settler colonialism (particularly of Germans in Slavic lands); immediate pressures of economic and religious persecution; and more, which we will discuss presently. The upshot is that Zionists intended to displace the local population, not integrate into it as immigrants would. And displacement is by definition a violent process. Zionist ideology justifying the displacement of the Indigenous population. The "logic" of settler colonialism worked itself through nationalist ideology.[4] Early Zionist leaders presented the "conflict" as one ethno-religious nationalism against another so as to deflect attention from settler colonialism, garner the support of the Jewish people and stifle diasporic Jewish opposition. They also used arguments of self-defense to win support of non-Zionist Jews, especially allies in Britain and the US. As the only legitimate national group, the Zionists reduced "the Arabs" into a faceless, dismissible enemy Other. Zionist ideologues like David Ben-Gurion and Golda Meir knowingly altered the framework from one of settler colonialism to that of conflict between an aggressive (and foreign) Arab "Goliath" and the peace-loving (native) Jewish "David."[5]

Whatever its justification, the Zionist takeover of Palestine resembled other instances where foreign settlers, armed with a sense of entitlement, conquered a vulnerable country. The European conquest of North America from the Native Americans is perhaps the best-known case of settler colonialism, not to ignore the settlement of Spanish and Portuguese in the Caribbean and parts of Latin America – all of which imported slave labor. The violent settlement of Australia and New Zealand is well known. So is the subjugation by Dutch Afrikaner and British settlers of South Africa, of Kenya and Rhodesia by the British, of Angola and Mozambique by the Portuguese, of Algeria by the French, and of Tibet by the Chinese. Lesser known cases include the Russians in the Kazakh Steppe, Central Asia and Siberia, the Tswana and Khoi-San peoples of southern Africa, the Indonesians in New Guinea, and the Scandinavians among the Sami.[6]

Now, as we've said, settler colonialism generates conflict between the colonist usurpers and the Indigenous population. No population is willingly displaced. But if a conflict involves two or more "sides" fighting over differing interests or agendas, then a colonial struggle is not a "conflict." Colonialism is unilateral. One powerful actor invades another people's territory to either exploit it or take it over. There is no symmetry of power or responsibility. The Natives did not choose the fight. They had no bone to pick with the settlers before they arrived. The Indigenous were not organized or equipped for such a struggle, and they had little chance of winning, of pushing the settlers out of their country. The Natives are the victims, not the other "side." Nor, to be honest, are they a "side" at all in the eyes of their conquerors. At best they are irrelevant, a nuisance on the path of the settler's seizure of their country, an expendable population, one that must be "eliminated," if not physically annihilated then at least reduced to marginal presence in which they are unable to conduct a national life and thus threaten the settler enterprise.[7] Such a process of unilateral, asymmetrical invasion that provokes resistance on the part of Native peoples threatened with displacement and worse can hardly be called a "conflict." Rather than the "Israeli/Palestinian/Arab Conflict," we must speak of Zionist settler colonialism.

Why does this matter? Because it has everything to do with arriving at a just resolution, and you can only do that if you have a rigorous analysis. The conflict paradigm has led us to reduce a century-long process of colonial expansion over all of historic Palestine into a limited struggle to "end the occupation" over only a small portion of it (22 percent). By focusing solely on the Occupied Palestinian Territory (OPT) – the West Bank, East Jerusalem and Gaza – the conflict model leaves Israel "proper" out of the picture altogether. In so doing it legitimizes, or at least ignores, Zionist colonialism over the vast majority (78 percent) of Palestine.

If the problem is a dispute between two countries or a civil war between two nationalisms, as the Palestinian/Israeli "conflict" is often phrased, then a conflict-resolution model might resolve it. But it cannot resolve a colonial situation. That requires an entirely different process of resolution: decolonization, the dismantling of the colonial entity so that a new, inclusive body politic may emerge. This is not to say that the OPT is not occupied according to international law. It is, and after 50-plus years the occupation should be ended. It is only to point out that occupation is a *sub-issue*. It must be addressed, but only as one element in a much broader decolonization of the settler state of Israel. Only that will end "the conflict," not limited Palestinian sovereignty over a small piece of their country.

Before moving on to decolonization – or to "resolving the conflict," as most people say – let us revisit the origins of the Zionist project so that we may understand its basic character. Let's begin by asking:

WHAT IS SETTLER COLONIALISM, AND HOW CAN IT BE ENDED?

In broad strokes, settler colonialism is a form of colonialism in which foreign settlers arrive in a country with the intent of taking it over. Their "arrival" is actually an invasion. The settlers are not immigrants; they come with the intent of replacing the Native population, not integrating into their society. The invasion may be gradual and not even recognized as such by the Indigenous. And as in the case of Zionism, it is not necessarily violent, at least in its early stages. In the end, a new settler society arises on the ruins of the Indigenous one. A "logic of elimination" which Patrick Wolfe suggests is inherent in all settler colonial projects "disappear" the Indigenous through

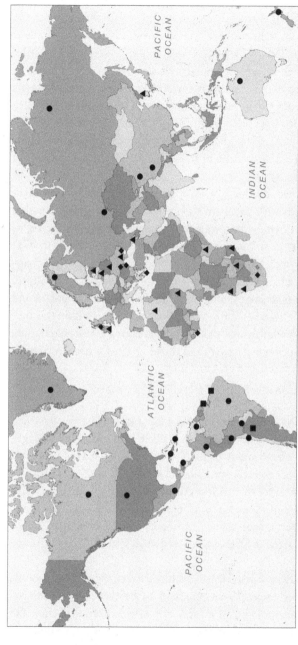

Colonialism: Control over a country by an external metropole for purposes of extracting the country's resources. Settler colonialism: When a foreign settler population comes to take over a country. The natives are eliminated, displaced, marginalized, disappeared, assimilated. The colonists seek to normalize their regime.

Decolonization: ▲ Settlers leave (though not their "legacy"): British in Ireland, Kenya and Rhodesia (Zimbabwe); French in Algeria; Portuguese in Angola and Mozambique; South Africans in Namibia. In former USSR republics, native populations reassert sovereignty.

■ Settlers eliminate the indigenous population: Spanish in Argentina; or ● reduce it to marginality, often with "reconciliation" and "integration," as in Brazil, Mexico, and much of Latin America, the US, Canada, Tibet, Taiwan, Australia, and New Zealand.

◆ Settlers establish an independent polity, deny indigenous sovereignty, but unable to defeat the Natives. Only solution is decolonization: acknowledging indigenous sovereignty, dismantling structures of domination, establishing a shared civil society, constructing a new national/native narrative, moving to postcolonialism. Apartheid South Africa; Israeli settler colonialism over Palestine.

Figure 1.1   Types of Settler Colonialism

displacement, marginalization, assimilation or outright genocide.[8] Through myths of entitlement, the settlers validate their right to the land. They claim to be the "real" Natives, whether "returning" to their native land or because only they love and will "develop" it. Settler narratives either ignore the Indigenous population or cast them as undeserving, unassimilable, menacing and unwanted. The Indigenous cease challenging the normalcy of the settler society only after they disappear, remaining at best "exotic" specimens of bygone folklore.

Settler colonialism is both an ancient and modern phenomenon. It is also widespread, as the map of settler colonialism in the modern era shows (Figure 1.1).

As we've noted, this book is less concerned with settler colonialism per se than it is with decolonization – ending the colonial situation and replacing it with a more equitable system that restores the rights and sovereignty of the Indigenous. But the form that decolonization takes depends upon the forms of the settler regime it seeks to dismantle and supersede, as well as its own history, resources and political situation. The map surveys the major types of settler colonialism and suggests possibilities and forms of decolonization. It is within this theoretical framework that we can locate and analyze Zionist colonialism, Palestinian oppositional agency and the prospects for decolonization.

The Settlers Leave (But Not Their "Legacy")

Perhaps the most definitive end to a colonial regime occurs when the settlers simply pack up and leave, albeit after prolonged struggle, and hand the country over to its Native inhabitants. This happened in cases of classic extractive colonialism (the British in India, for example, or the French in West Africa or the Dutch in Indonesia), and it happened in a few cases of extensive settlement (French Algeria, for example, Portuguese-controlled Angola and Mozambique; Kenya, Rhodesia and Ireland, all colonized by British settlers; South Africans in Namibia).

Decolonization, however, is a matter of degree; it is a process, not a one-time event. What appeared to be the end of colonialism most often turned into a form of neo-colonization. Either the colonial power continued to dominate its former colony, a condition anti-colonial campaigners derisively called "flag independence," or

the post-colony found itself trapped on the periphery of the capitalist world system, unable to develop and unable to give its formal
independence any meaningful political, economic or social content.
Mahmood Mamdani,[9] who writes of "the institutional legacy of
colonial rule" which lasts long after the colonists have departed, notes
that the political institutions most likely to collapse after independence are precisely those that had been imposed by the colonial power.
Indeed, colonial "mentality" and institutions whose purpose had been
to subordinate and exploit the Native population became embedded in
the "decolonized" state's very foundations.[10]

The Settlers "Eliminate" the Indigenous Population, Reducing It to Marginality

In the vast majority of settler colonial cases, however, the settlers stay
and gradually take over the country, their settler state and society
ultimately "superseding" the social and political systems of the Indigenous population. Here is where Wolfe's "logic of elimination" comes to
inform all settler regimes. Because the settlers covet the Natives' land
– after all, there is no settler state without land – they must be removed
and their return foreclosed forever. Some measure of physical elimination is the norm in most settler projects, especially in the early stages of
colonization when the settlers are attempting to assert their domination and carve out ethnically "pure" spaces of their new homeland. In
the case of colonial Argentina, elimination took on its literal meaning,
the almost total extermination of the Native population. In most
cases, as the settlers take possession of the land, strategies of elimination range from genocide to displacement, expulsion, segregation
and collective confinement; other strategies of marginalization include
miscegenation, religious conversion, incarceration and bio-cultural
assimilation.[11] It all depends on the situation at the time, the settlers'
ambitions and the opportunities that arise. The purpose, again, is not
only to marginalize the Native presence, but to foreclose any possible
return to their lands (or, we might add, any possibility of decolonizing)
by destroying their systems of life. To this end, and to lend the settler
project a veneer of "civilized" legitimacy, policies of elimination are
embedded in legal systems employing racialized categories.[12]

To such a degree do settlers become embedded in the colonized
land that, in the vast majority of cases, they cannot be dislodged. The

Native population is left with no choice but to try and decolonize its country while allowing the settlers to remain. This is especially the case where the Indigenous constitute what has been called Fourth World peoples. These consist of relatively small and marginalized communities, often hunter-gatherers, pastoral nomads or subsistence farming peoples, living in established and internationally recognized settler states. They therefore have no choice but to acknowledge the political reality of the settler state in which they live and, while struggling for their cultural rights and lands, integrate into the dominant society. This is the case of Native Americans in Latin and North America and the aboriginal peoples of Australia, New Zealand/Aotearoa, Taiwan and Scandinavia.

These settler societies have normalized, the settler project having "triumphed" in that it has been recognized, locally as well as internationally. The settler population retains its dominant political, economic and social positions even though it has "integrated" in one way or another the Indigenous population. In such cases, decolonization is not even seen as an option, except in that Native peoples struggle to carve out a cultural space for themselves, ideally on their ancestral lands. As Glen Coulthard phrases it: in the struggle for self-determination, "Indigenous peoples tend to view their resurgent practices of cultural self-recognition and empowerment as permanent features of our decolonization projects."[13] Whether or not the settler state grants such space to the Indigenous, it certainly rejects the notion of decolonization, since it implies that the state is not legitimate, a claim the settlers worked hard over the years to erase. Instead, they employ a "logic of inclusion" to serve the logic of elimination. By granting the Indigenous citizenship and, to one degree or another, allowing or forcing their individual assimilation into the wider civil society, settler state authorities strive to eliminate their cultures and therefore their demands for collective sovereignty.

The Settlers Establish an Independent Polity, Deny the Indigenous Their Sovereignty, But are Unable to Defeat Their Aspirations for National, State-Level Self-Determination

Palestine/Israel, like apartheid-era South Africa and perhaps Tibet and Chechnya, represents yet another form of settler colonialism, one in which the Indigenous constitute not small Fourth World peoples but major national groups who not only refuse to surrender their sovereignty and right of self-determination to the settlers, but demand that the settler state itself be superseded by a completely new polity in which their national rights are restored. Here the settlers and the Indigenous have arrived at a draw. The former are strong enough to establish a state of their own and marginalize the latter, but are not strong enough to decisively defeat them. For their part, the Indigenous are strong enough to mount a major challenge to settler dominance, preventing the "triumph" the settler state realized over Fourth World peoples. Even if they should succeed in overthrowing the settler regime, however, as in fact happened in South Africa, they cannot expel the settler population, which is too large and embedded. Decolonization in this case is only partly achieved by the rise of a new polity. The Indigenous may achieve self-determination, but they must share their sovereignty with the settlers. An additional phase of decolonization is thereby called for. Together with an inclusive polity and civil society, and in tandem with a process of reckoning with the settler past, a new, shared political community must emerge that gives meaning to the new layer of national identity that "thickens" joint citizenship.

THE LOGIC AND STRUCTURE OF SETTLER COLONIALISM

In his seminal book *Settler Colonialism: A Theoretical Overview*,[14] Lorenzo Veracini has set out the logic and progression of settler colonialism, which I have elaborated and adapted to Palestine/Israel. Settler projects differ in their historical details. They never progress smoothly and inexorably along a linear path, and often end up far from where the settlers intended. Settler projects are also subject to resistance, which alter their forms and progression. Nonetheless, five stages of settler progression may be discerned from the "inner logic" and structure of settler projects:

(a) *Impetus.* For whatever reason, voluntary or not, settlers and their colonial sponsors (the metropole) set their sights on a foreign land. Often they fantasize it as barren, undeveloped, in need of their civilizing mission or "belonging" to them by Divine or historical right.

They then construct stories of entitlement, narratives invented to legitimize their right to seize the land.

(b) *Settlement Invasion.* The arrival of settlers intent on conquering the country and displacing the Indigenous population constitutes an invasion, even if it takes place over time. "Invasion" begins by acquiring land. Indeed, the need for territory was what turned Zionism from a national into a colonial project.[15] Since the settlers aim not only to conquer a country but to make it permanently their own, invasion requires means of maintaining control. It creates a *regime* to sustain settler dominance while suppressing the Indigenous population.

(c) *Foundational Violence.* The process of establishing a settler society is necessarily a violent one. It must be imposed by force because the Native population can never accept their own elimination. The foundational stages of the settler project resemble military campaigns to displace and pacify the local population. And since Indigenous resistance becomes more organized as the scale and intent of the invasion becomes clear, "security" becomes a central preoccupation of the settlers. Since the settlers cannot acknowledge the national claims of the Indigenous lest they legitimize them, they criminalize all resistance. Portraying Native resistance as "terrorism" is a quintessential colonial practice. Casting the Indigenous as "terrorists" also disconnects the Native peoples from the land, as if their only aim as "bad people" is to attack an innocent settler community that only wants to cultivate "its" land.

(d) *Establishment of a Dominance Management Regime.* Until it actually takes over a country and normalizes its control, the settler enterprise must rely on a Dominance Management Regime to sustain and expand its control. This Regime has four functions. It deploys militias, military and police forces to take control of the land. It acts to expel, suppress and manage the Indigenous population. It provides ongoing security necessary to ensure settler dominance. And it disseminates the settlers' narrative in order to legitimize their rule.

(e) *The "Triumph" of the Settler Regime.* Over time, as the Native population is driven out, killed, marginalized and pacified, a "normal" state and society emerge, one which obviously "belongs" to the settlers-as-natives. The Indigenous population disappears from both the national narrative and the landscape, except as folklore. The settlers' claims of entitlement are now confirmed and become "historical fact." Settler colonialism has achieved its ultimate goal: replacing the former society.

Figure 1.2 depicts the progression of settler colonialism from its initial impetus to its "triumphant" culmination.

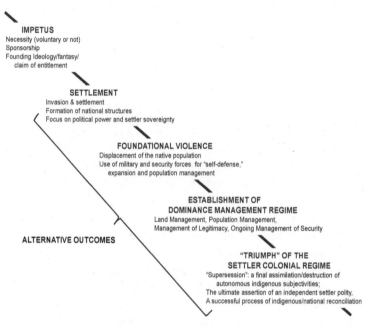

IMPETUS
Necessity (voluntary or not)
Sponsorship
Founding Ideology/fantasy/
    claim of entitlement

SETTLEMENT
Invasion & settlement
Formation of national structures
Focus on political power and settler sovereignty

FOUNDATIONAL VIOLENCE
Displacement of the native population
Use of military and security forces for "self-defense,"
    expansion and population management

ESTABLISHMENT OF
DOMINANCE MANAGEMENT REGIME
Land Management, Population Management,
Management of Legitimacy, Ongoing Management of Security

ALTERNATIVE OUTCOMES

"TRIUMPH" OF THE
SETTLER COLONIAL REGIME
"Supersession": a final assimilation/destruction of
    autonomous indigenous subjectivities;
The ultimate assertion of an independent settler polity,
A successful process of indigenous/national reconciliation

Figure 1.2 The Logic of Settler Colonialism

This model of settler colonial progression helps us get a proper grasp on the problem: settler colonialism itself and not merely "conflict." Understanding settler colonialism's workings – its goals of displacing and then replacing a Native society, its self-serving ideology and language, its logic and the structures of domination and control it engenders, its systemic evolution, its strategies and policies – is a necessary first step towards this book's actual goal: "thinking through" the process of decolonization that must begin in the colonial situation itself. Specifically, the decolonization of Zionism. Despite the vast literature on settler colonialism, the issue of decolonization has not been analyzed extensively. This is especially true of the type of settler colonialism represented by Palestine-Israel, one that involves two or more peoples aspiring to a state of their own, in contrast to the struggles for a different kind of decolonization by Fourth World peoples. This book, then, takes up a challenge posed by Veracini, who notes that "Discontinuing settler colonial forms requires conceptual frames and supporting narratives of reconciliation that have yet to be fully developed and narrated. Nation-building in formerly colonized contexts can be difficult, but at least it can be conceptualized; enacting genuine post-settler passages in white settler nations is another matter."[16]

THE ROLE OF INDIGENOUS AGENCY

Although he overstated the case, Patrick Wolfe advised a separation between analyses of settler colonialism as a system and Indigenous agency striving to dismantle it. He feared what he called "ethnographic ventriloquism," in which academics and non-indigenous activists come to represent the indigenous voice, thus "reproducing settler invasion."[17] Clare Land, who explores the problematics and sensitivities of settler/non-Indigenous/Indigenous collaboration in *Decolonizing Solidarity: Dilemmas and Directions for Supporters of Indigenous Struggles*, nonetheless concludes that it is possible for non-Indigenous people to collaborate with Indigenous people, although not in a way which appropriates indigeneity."[18] Svirsky, too, proposes "collaborative struggles" whereby Indigenous agency leads and finds ways, in collaboration with settlers-who-refuse, to transcend settler formations.[19]

This book adopts both perspectives. This chapter and the following ones focus on the structure and dynamics of settler colonial systems, Zionist colonialism in particular. Such a focus is necessary if we aspire to understand how this settler form of colonialism works, if only to know better how to dismantle and reassemble it, a project of decolonization to which we turn in Chapter 8, a project utterly dependent upon Indigenous agency, particularly what I call (following Svirsky and Ben-Arie)[20] "summoning power." My analysis certainly subscribes to the view of Svirsky and others: "To exclude resistance from the analysis of the settler Zionist formation is tantamount to excluding Palestine and the Palestinians from the analysis altogether. Resistance, whatever its sources and operations, always plays a part in the shaping of the developing oppressive structure. That is, resistance is a structure, not an event."[21]

Going a step further, although settler colonialism *does* possess a logic and a structure (discernable across cases despite specific historical differences) and *tries* to be totalizing in its control of the land and the Indigenous population, in the "real world" it falls far short. Indeed, as numerous students of settler colonialism show, its control is invariably incomplete; Veracini points to "permanent movement" among settler and Indigenous forces,[22] and Svirsky notes that "structures" are actually combinations of practices, institutions, subjectivities, imaginations and more[23] – always containing the possibility of decombining (or being decombined) and being reassembled in new formations. "What the structure fails to capture, discipline and codify," says Svirsky, is what defines its thresholds, its limits, or more exactly, the limitations of its functions."[24] For that reason, Indigenous resistance has the power to fundamentally "unsettle" the settler project,[25] whether that means carving out indigenous space and asserting rights as in Native American struggles in defending and even recovering their ancestral lands, or in defeating it as in South Africa, Algeria, Ireland or Mozambique. Our task, as researchers and activists alike, is, in the words of Marcelo Svirsky, "to trace the forces that cause the settler structure to fail and remain incomplete"[26] – and then as political activists to develop strategies to direct those forces at the colonial structure's most vital yet vulnerable areas.

Indigenous agency "unsettles" the colonization process so that it can never be fully normalized and the potential for decolonization, be it complete or partial, is never suppressed.[27] For Indigenous agency refuses to die or surrender. The Indigenous scholar Kauanui posits that "indigeneity itself is enduring – that the operative logic of settler colonialism may be to 'eliminate the native'... but indigenous peoples exist, resist, and persist."[28] Agency, whether of the Indigenous or of other opponents of settler colonialism, acquires through struggle its own logic, structures, ideologies, strategies and resources. While both the settler project and resistance to it contain patterns of organization and evolution, a focus on agency prevents the internal "logic" and its structures from being "inexorable," inevitable.[29] Responding to often-expressed concerns that the determinism inherent in a structural approach runs the risk of becoming mechanistic, Uri Ram contends,

Actual events explain history better than appeals to a supporting ideology. A sovereign Jewish state in the whole of Palestine might have been the plan of the Zionist settlers, but its outcome was by no means inevitable. Zionism's clear goals and its ability to take advantage of political conditions and opportunities account for its success, not some disembodied 'inexorable systemic logic.'[30]

The point, I think, is to view *both* settler colonialism and the Indigenous agency applied against it as being structured (though not always consciously). We are able to perceive broad patterns of development that are evident across settler cases, but at the same time understand that they are subject to the forces of agency and process that often lead to different forms of colonialism and outcomes.

Chapter 6 delves in depth into the issue of the role of Indigenous/Palestine resistance and of "summoning power," strategically deploying forms of agency that have the potential to actually decolonize. In the meantime, let's "bracket" resistance as we examine the logic, structures and processes of settler colonialism, and Zionist colonialism in particular. This is done for purely analytical purposes, in the understanding, as reflected in Figure 1.3 (and later in Figure 2.1), that

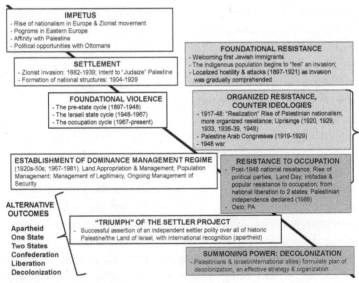

Figure 1.3 The Process of Zionist Settler Colonialism and the Evolution of Palestinian Agency Against It

settler colonialism and Indigenous agency (including non-indigenous forms of decolonization it is able to muster) form one intertwined whole. Figure 1.3 enables us to keep Indigenous agency in mind as we examine the historical development of Zionism's Dominance Management Regime.

Equipped with this holistic theoretical framework, let us now delve more deeply into the workings of Zionist colonization so that we have a clear and detailed idea of what exactly has to be decolonized and how to go about it.

2

Zionism: A Settler Colonial Project

Any approach to ending settler colonialism in historic Palestine must begin with Zionism. Palestinian history, after all, would have played itself out completely differently if it had been left to its own devices. As it was, settler Zionism landed on the Arab population out of the blue. Although Palestinian resistance has had its effect on the Zionist project, the colonial system was conceived and executed exclusively for the benefit of the Jews, with no consideration for the those already living in Palestine. As Frantz Fanon noted, "The settler owes the fact of his very existence ... to the colonial system."[1]

Zionism embarked on its settler colonial venture with only a partial idea of what that would entail. Its initial impetus came out of its European experience; it had little, if anything, to do with the "real" Palestine and its people. For its Central European originators – Theodor Herzl, Max Nordau, Chaim Weizmann, delegates to the various Zionist Congresses, the early functionaries of the different Zionist organizations – Palestine was more an ideal than a geographical reality. Perceived as a barren wasteland (a quintessential colonial trope), the "real" Land of Israel would be redeemed by Jewish settlement. As an extension of Eastern and Central European nationalism, Zionism shared the idea that a state "belonged to" the people "owned it." Rather than settling a foreign country, they perceived their national movement as merely *transferring* a legitimate and familiar form of nationalism to what everyone knew was their own historical homeland – and which anyway was barren and "waiting" for them.[2]

Jews, like many other peoples, did not see themselves as a "nation" until Zionism emerged in Europe at the turn of the twentieth century. Historically, they have been described as an ethno-nation, a people "living apart." This was especially the case in Eastern Europe, where they existed as an "internal colony" in ghettos or the Pale of Settlement.[3] Vicious pogroms in Russia and Eastern Europe in the last two decades of the nineteenth century caused mass displacement and flight. So when Zionism arose in the context of modern European nationalism, it had a fertile ground from which to sprout. Indeed, Zionism *was* a Central/Eastern European form of ethno-nationalism. The *nation*-states of Russia, Poland, Hungary and Germany saw themselves as "tribes" set off from, often hostile to or threatened by, other nation-tribes. They needed to create a "pure" racial space reflecting "the authentic spirit of the nation," ethno-nations enclosing themselves within an exclusive nation-state.[4] This was the world of romantic nationalism in which the vast majority of Jews lived. It is no wonder that Zionism adopted this form of ethno-nationalism, and exported it to Palestine.

Ethno-nationalism found additional confirmation in the biblical account of God "giving" the Land of Israel to the Jewish people. All the ethno-nations of Europe sought their "authentic" ancient roots, a fascist element that had a great influence on Zionist thinking.[5] The persecution they were experiencing fed into this need for a space of racial and ideological purity and security. From there it was a simple step to extend that primordial enmity to the Arabs, Amalek, the ancient enemy that tried to prevent the Israelites from entering the Promised Land. Palestinians were "ideologized" from the start. They were never an actual people with a history, culture and national claim of their own to "our" country.

All this makes understandable, if not acceptable, the emergence of a Jewish settler colonial movement intent on "reclaiming" or "redeeming" its national space in Palestine, unwilling to share it or recognize other national claims.[6] The ethno-nationalism that gave rise to Zionism fed into the logic of settler colonialism, which became a zero-sum game.[7] Still, as massive waves of Jewish emigration to the New World shows, ethno-nationalism was not the dominant force in Eastern European Jewish life, and nothing in the Jewish experience made the shift to Zionism and settler colonialism inevitable.

We should also not overstate the actual tie between the Jewish people and Palestine/the Land of Israel, which forms the basis of Zionism's claims to entitlement in Palestine. Zionism, after all, attracted but a tiny fraction of the world's Jews in its formative years. Only 3 percent of the 2 million Jews who left Eastern Europe between 1882 and 1914 went to Palestine, and many of those subsequently emigrated to other countries. Zionism reflecting a kind of "diaspora nationalism"[8] that threatened the claim to citizenship and national belonging of many Jews to the countries in which they lived. "The country for which I have worked ever since I left the university – England," grumbled Edwin Montagu, a Jewish minister in the British government, "the country for which my family have fought, tells me that my national home … is Palestine."[9]

Depicting Zionism as a settler colonial project is therefore fair and useful. It is not to deny the historical, religious and even political connections the Jewish people genuinely felt for the Land of Israel. Nor that it served as a place of refuge for Jews in times of persecution, as it did, for example, for Jews from Poland before and during the Holocaust as well as during the Communist era leading up to their expulsion in 1968. Pappe characterizes Zionist thought and praxis as motivated by a national impulse but acted as pure colonialists.[10] Regardless, once Palestine became the object of settlement, Zionism, a foreign national movement, took on a settler colonial form with all the dire consequences to the indigenous Palestinians. No matter what the Jews were experiencing in Europe or the genuineness of their national claims to the Land of Israel, the local Arab community was under no obligation to forfeit its own country and national aspirations to them. "There is no inherent logical or empirical contradiction between a settlement movement being national and its being colonial at the same time," the Israeli political scientist Yoav Peled contends.

> Different national movements employed various ideological platforms for achieving their nationalist aims, such as liberalism, socialism, even fascism, and there is no a-priori reason to preclude the possibility that the Zionist movement used a colonial strategy to achieve its national purpose. Moreover, an examination of the Zionist discourse at the early stages of settlement reveals that a colonial terminology and colonial analogies were used openly by the Zionist settlers and by their sponsoring organizations.[11]

Peled, Shafir and Pappe all label Zionism a "national colonial movement." Peled notes that the Hebrew name of the Labor Movement, which gave rise to Labor Zionism and the dominant Labor Party, was *hityashvut ovedet*, the Labor *Settlement* Movement.[12]

All this has great implications for the process of decolonization addressed later in this book.[13] Israeli Jews, like other settler colonialists, do not conceive of themselves as such. The very term "settler" arouses antagonism because it implies that Israeli Jews are foreigners who have no claim to the Land. It stands in stark contradiction to their own view of themselves as "returning natives."[14] For all that, Zionists never denied the colonial nature of their enterprise, describing themselves as colonists and settlers and their institutions as well. One Zionist historian notes that "colonialism was still considered legitimate" before and after World War I.[15] Understandably, Zionists continue to resist this framing. They prefer to see it as "a conflict between two nationalisms."

NATIVES, BUT NOT *NATIVES*

Zionism began, as in Europe, as a Jewish national movement that had little if anything to do with the actual country of Palestine. "Jewish nationalism was primarily conditioned by the peculiar diaspora situation of the Jewish people that it claimed to represent and regenerate," noted the historian Eric Hobsbawm. "The modern territorial ingathering of Jewish exiles into Palestine has no connection with the age-old religious yearning for Zion among diaspora Jews."[16] It was the construction of a national narrative of "settler nativism,"[17] founded on admittedly invented history and "traditions" that enabled them to transit from Europe into Palestine.[18]

Indeed, the "cultured" German/Austrian Jews who invented Zionism never saw themselves as part of the "unwashed" Jewish masses or as candidates for emigration to "Asia." Their view is summarized as follows:[19]

First, the majority of Europe's Jews are described [by Hess, Herzl and other early Zionist figures] as semi-Asiatics who would be led by an entirely modern elite, which had absorbed and internalized German culture, and which thus would be an "element of German culture" on the shores of the Mediterranean. Second, the Orient is described as a backward, neglected part of the world. And third, the Jews' return to the land of their forefathers in the Orient was intended to enable them not to shed their Europeanness, but to be European by choice. Not only did European Jews, whom Europe perceived as strangers, not perceive European culture as oppressive and wish to cast it off, but they undertook the mission of disseminating agents of European culture throughout the Orient.

Zionists, then, defined themselves both as "returning natives" *and* as settlers and colonists. "We have come here as Europeans," said David Ben-Gurion. "Although our origin is in the East, and we are returning to the East, we bring with us European civilization and we would not want to sever our connections and those of the country with the civilization of Europe .... We do not see a better representative of western civilization than England [Zionism's chief metropole at the time]."[20] This set up a strange hierarchy of "nativeness." While claiming to be the genuine Natives returning to their ancient homeland, the Zionists and the British alike referred to the local Arabs as "the Natives." This seeming contradiction can only be appreciated if we grasp the colonial tone of the term. "Native," observes the anti-colonial psychologist Frantz Fanon, referred to people who were primitive, on a lower human rung, underserving of self-determination and unable to handle political independence. Colonists routinely referred to colonized people as animals (parasites, dogs, sheep, apes), diseases (a cancer in the *colonists'* body), parts of the landscape ("biblical" Bedouin, "as unchangeable as the pyramids," or a reversal: "a land without a people"), or as inveterate criminals ("eyes like a thief," "terrorists"). They were rendered invisible or at best exotic background ("folklore").[21] Indeed, the differentiation between settlers and the Indigenous is fundamental to the colonial enterprise. "The colonized world is a compartmentalized world," writes Fanon.[22]

> The dividing line, the border, is represented by the barracks and the police stations.... The "native" sector is not complementary to the European sector. The two confront each other, but not in the service of a higher unity. Governed by a purely Aristotelian logic, they follow the dictates of mutual exclusion. There is no conciliation possible, one of them is superfluous....
>
> This compartmentalized world, the world divided in two, is inhabited by different species.... Looking at the immediacies of the colonial context, it is clear that what divides this world is first and foremost what species, what race one belongs to.... In the colonies

the foreigner imposed himself using his cannons and machines. Despite the success of the pacification, in spite of his appropriation, the colonist always remains a foreigner.... The ruling species is first and foremost an outsider from elsewhere, different from the indigenous population, "the others."

Settler colonial theory also sees the settler/native binary as crucial for maintaining settler privilege. The settlers covet the land and wish to "eliminate" the presence of the Natives, there is "the absolute need to at once distinguish between settler self and indigenous."[23] Setting off the settler narrative, with all its entitlement, from the "(non)-story, non-history" of the Native justifies the settlers' claim of entitlement and their elimination practices. The line separating settler and Indigenous may be approached – but is never to be crossed. True, Indigenous and settler identities are often interactive, mutable and ambivalent,[24] not always wholly binary and hostile. Early Zionist militias adopted the *kafiya* and prided themselves on "knowing" Arabs (albeit in the spirit of "know thy enemy").[25] A few figures of the Palestinian elite tried to "make peace" over the years, there were a few mixed neighborhoods and even a few cases of intermarriage. (Although some settler societies encourage or force assimilation as a strategy of elimination, the Zionists did not, and Jewish religious law forbade intermarriage.) Certainly, members of the Israeli and Palestinian "peace camps" tried dialogue and a few joint resistance activities, like rebuilding homes demolished by the Israeli authorities.

Erecting an unbridgeable binary might be a structural weakness of the settler colonial paradigm, but in the case of the Zionists and the Palestinians the view that the settler/native line might be approached but never crossed holds true. Palestinian citizens of Israel can *approach* the status of "Israeli" (e.g., "Israeli Arabs"), but only if they publicly downplay their national Palestinian one and adopt the dress and demeanor of Israeli Jews, a situation that has been described as "internal colonialism."[26] That this oppositional relationship *can be* breached is a crucial contention of decolonization, but only after the settler/native relationship is replaced by equal citizenship in a new civil society and a fundamental redistribution of resources.

As it stands, the settler/native polarity is necessary for a settler project; otherwise, how can the rights and privileges of the former be distinguished from the subversive claims of the latter? And so, at a meeting with Arabs in Jerusalem, Chaim Weizmann declared: "I am no stranger in this country, even if I was born and bred in the far north." But during the drafting of the Mandate document, he cautioned the British *not to* refer to the Jews as the "native population," since that term meant the Arabs.[27]

Even Vladimir Ze'ev Jabotinsky, the fiercest of Zionist nationalists, the beloved founding father of the present-day Likud party in Israel, placed Zionism squarely in a colonial frame. He referred to the local Arabs as the "Natives." But he also granted them the status of a nation, something that would be unthinkable today on the part of Jabotinsky's followers. "Except for those who were born blind," he wrote in his seminal piece "The Iron Wall" in 1923,[28]

[the moderate Zionists] realised long ago that it is utterly impossible to obtain the voluntary consent of the Palestine Arabs for converting "Palestine" from an Arab country into a country with a Jewish majority.... My readers have a general idea of the history of colonisation in other countries. I suggest that they consider all the precedents with which they are acquainted, and see whether there is one solitary instance of any colonisation being carried on with the consent of the native population. There is no such precedent. The native populations, civilised or uncivilised, have always stubbornly resisted the colonists, irrespective of whether they were civilised or savage....

Every native population, civilised or not, regards its lands as its national home, of which it is the sole master, and it wants to retain that mastery always; it will refuse to admit not only new masters but, even new partners or collaborators.

This is equally true of the Arabs. We may tell them whatever we like about the innocence of our aims, watering them down and sweetening them with honeyed words to make them palatable, but they know what we want, as well as we know what they do not want. They feel at least the same instinctive jealous love of Palestine, as the old Aztecs felt for ancient Mexico, and the Sioux for their rolling Prairies....

Every native population in the world resists colonists as long as it has the slightest hope of being able to rid itself of the danger of being colonised. That is what the Arabs in Palestine are doing, and what they will persist in doing as long as there remains a solitary spark of hope that they will be able to prevent the transformation of "Palestine" into the "Land of Israel."

The country's Arab inhabitants – then, as today, Zionists refrained from using the national term "Palestinian" – were thus thought of as little more than a thinly dispersed population of primitive nomads and peasants. "Savage, culture-hating Asians," as the Zionist essayist Ahad Ha'Am characterized them. The "Arab problem" was manageable. Some would be "spirited away" to an Arab country (Herzl's formula). Others would be absorbed into the superior European culture the Zionists brought; we may even grant them a measure of cultural autonomy. Overall, though, they could be ignored. In early Zionism the problematic issue of Arabs in the Land of Israel was called the "Hidden Question." It was best left alone.[29]

The early Zionists thus framed their national movement as a settler colonial project. They then had to contend with the same issues confronting all settlement projects: How to reconcile their foreign origin with their claim of entitlement to the country? How to carry out and legitimize their own political agenda while rejecting the claims, rights and well-being of the Indigenous community? How to motivate and organize settlement itself? How to manage, if not resolve, the "native problem"? How to normalize and legitimize their settler status, in the eyes of their own population as well as internationally?

These issues differ fundamentally from those of "normal" nation-building. There the questions are: How do we promote equal citizenship and civil rights? How can we extend the notion of national self-determination to all our citizens ("nation" now being defined by the state and its citizenry, not by any particular group)? How can we integrate immigrants and minorities? How do we ensure equal access to political, economic, cultural and natural resources? And the like.

Zionism, like other settler projects, is preoccupied with the dilemma of promoting the claims of one group, the settlers themselves, over those of the others in their pluralistic society. How to justify and legitimate discriminatory rights and policies? How to claim exclusive "ownership" over and control of the country and still project an image of a normal, legitimate democracy?

As it was, the overarching aim of Zionism from its inception until our present day is clear and unchanging: to "Judaize" Palestine, to transform an Arab country into a Jewish one, Palestine into the Land of Israel. This, in turn, set in motion a political logic and set of policies that by necessity placed Zionism at complete odds with the indigenous Arab population. Its spawning of an anti-colonial movement among Palestinians was inevitable. As Jabotinsky himself put it, no people can be expected to agree to its own elimination. Resistance to displacement, armed or not, cannot be compared to the colonists' military campaign of conquest. It is a false equivalency, even if it is so useful to those who would cast colonialism as a "conflict" between two equal sides. Adopting a settler colonial perspective threatens, even destroys the settler narrative. But it also opens up new possibilities for decolonization.

HOW DOES ZIONIST SETTLER COLONIALISM WORK?

Turning from the broad development of settler Zionism, let's look at the specific ways in which it is structured and operates. Only by identifying just what mechanisms of domination and control must be dismantled can we progress to an effective plan of decolonization.

Decolonization is no easy matter. We are not merely "making peace" or reforming existing political, economic and social structures. We need a complete transformation. New institutions must be created that ensure collective as well as individual equality. Each citizen must enjoy equal access to the country's land and resources. Membership in society, civil rights and access to economic resources must be deracialized. A new civil identity must be forged. But more than all this, an entirely new post-colonial *relationship* must be realized, what we have called a new political community. Decolonization goes beyond mere dismantling and reconstruction of foundational political, legal, economic, social and ideological structures; it must challenge and effectively neutralize the biopower reflected in those structures and relationships that constitute the colonial legacy – what Wolfe refers to as "traces of racialism," Foucault's "governability."[30]

Let's begin our discussion of what decolonization entails by looking at the basic structure of settler colonization. This will give us a "map" of what needs to be dismantled in decolonization's initial phase.

ZIONISM'S DOMINANCE MANAGEMENT REGIME

Patrick Wolfe,[31] one of the early theorists of settler colonialism, called attention to the structures that anchored that enterprise at every stage. What are those structures? Taken together as a system of control and governance, we might best conceptualize them as a Dominance Management Regime (Figure 2.1). In this chapter we will examine the broad features of this structural regime – the settler invasion and its foundational violence, population management, land management, the management of legitimacy, and ongoing management through securitization – and in the next three chapters trace how the regime is applied, how it changes and how it is resisted by Palestinians over three cycles of development: the pre-state cycle (1880s–1948); the Israeli state cycle from 1948 to 1967, still ongoing within the Green Line; and the occupation cycle (1967–present).

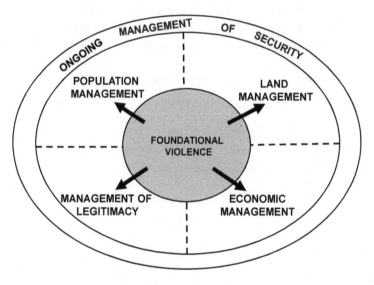

Figure 2.1 The Dominance Management Regime

Settler "Invasion" and Foundational Violence

Frantz Fanon begins his epic *Wretched of the Earth*[32] with the assertion: "decolonization is always a violent phenomenon." The same may be said, of course, for the colonization process itself. All forms of colonialism begin with foundational violence: an invasion, be it sudden and massive or taking place peacefully over time. This was true of "classic" colonialism where a powerful metropole came to exploit the resources and labor of another country. The British in India are one example, the Belgians in the Congo are another. And it is true of settler colonialism as well. When a population arrives in a country with the intent of taking it over, that is an invasion. It happened with varying degree of violence and speed in North America, Algeria, South Africa, Australia, Palestine and elsewhere. Settlers, notes Mamdani,[33]

> are made by conquest, not just by immigration. Settlers are kept settlers by a form of the state that makes a distinction – particularly juridical – between conquerors and conquered, settlers and natives, and makes it the basis of other distinctions that tend to buttress the conquerors and isolate the conquered, politically. However fictitious these distinctions may appear historically, they become real political facts for they are embodied in real political institutions…. Settlers and natives belong together. You cannot have one without the other, for it is the relationship between them that makes one a settler and the other a native. To do away with one, you have to do away with the other.

Since settlers "come to stay," foundational violence marks the start of the Dominance Management Regime, akin to what Jabotinsky meant by an Iron Wall. It is thereafter enforced by an ongoing regime of "security."

Once in place, the Dominance Maintenance Regime carries out four main functions, described below.

1. *Population Management.* Settler colonialism is at root an ethno/religious/national enterprise – all the more so when a country is defined as "belonging" to one particular group. The US, Australia and South Africa are examples of a settler colonial country. Like most other such regimes, however, they defined the settler/immigrant population broadly. So while excluding and "eliminating" the natives, they all allowed people from varying backgrounds to become part of the new society. Zionism is a kind of doubly exclusive regime. Not only do settlers claim exclusive rights to an Arab country, but they then restrict

even the kinds of settlers who can come; they all have to be Jews. Perhaps the form of settler colonialism closest to Zionism are transfers of populations in order to ethnicize a particular territory, often forced. The "Russification" campaigns into the Russian interior in the nineteenth and early twentieth centuries, and later into Eastern Europe are one example. Or the massive population transfers of Chinese into Tibet and, today, into Uighur Xinjiang.

Once the colonial project had established itself, it was able to shift from foundational violence to "proper" administration. Population management ensured the domination of the colonizers over the colonized, and produced a system of Native "elimination." A first step, then, was to separate the two populations, physically but also administratively. Racialized legal codes provided different categories of inclusion and exclusion. Each category defined the rights that population enjoys, which rights are denied them and with whom they can associate, marry and work. The "conquest of labor" and the "conquest of land" were more than Zionist slogans. They defined in the pre-state period who could be a part of the Yishuv and who not. Zionist regulations allowed allocation of land to Jews alone, and a separate state-within-a-state emerged.

As the settler enterprise expands and takes more land, the process of "eliminating" the Natives proceeds. But, stresses Wolfe, "not in any particular way."[34] While the elimination of the Natives in order to take their land sets up a zero-sum game, the process of elimination, a key to population management, takes different forms. Whatever works, and each additional step in its time. Genocide, displacement, marginalization, confinement, assimilation and even symbolic self-determination – it all depends on demography, opportunity, the ability of the Indigenous to resist, the stage of settlement, the political atmosphere (internally and externally) and much more.[35]

Then comes the problem of ensuring that the settler state and society replacing that of the indigenous Arabs is "Jewish." Even in the pre-state period when the Yishuv was wrestling with the British authorities over immigration, the Jewish Agency and other Zionist institutions vetted the immigrants by their Jewishness. With the establishment of Israel, the Law of Return applied solely to Jews. Now Israel had another problem: How to present itself as a liberal European democracy while preventing the return to their homes of 720,000 Palestinian refugees from the 1948 Nakba? Population management in the form of technical legalisms provided a solution. The Citizenship Law of 1952 permitted everyone who had Palestinian nationality to return, but with a caveat: they had to have been registered residents of Israel in *1949*. With that sleight of legal hand all the refugees were "legally" barred from returning to their homeland. Those that remained – 150,000 out of more than a million – were subject to some 184 laws that limited their civil rights. Some were symbolic, like the Jewish Nationality Law of 2019 that demotes Arabic from an official language to one of "special status." Others more disenfranchising. Palestinian citizens of Israel, for example, are forbidden to buy, rent, lease or reside on land or buildings on land that are defined as "Jewish" – lands on 94 percent of their own country.

Since 1967, of course, Israel rules over 4.6 million Palestinians in the Occupied Territory. It cannot extend them citizenship lest it endanger the Jewish character of the country. So Palestinians living under Israel rule possess six administrative statuses, each with its own set of limitations: citizens of Israel; permanent residents of East Jerusalem (whose residency can be revoked at any time); residents of Area C of the West Bank, with no civil protections at all; residents of Areas A and B who live under the Palestinian Authority but are *de facto* ruled by Israel; residents of the Israeli-controlled enclave H-2 in Hebron; and residents of besieged Gaza.

Now the categories can be expanded or constricted for purposes of population domination. Upon the establishment of Israel, an immigrant needed to have a Jewish mother to gain citizenship. In order to accommodate the Russian immigration of the 1980s and 1990s, that was expanded to a person who had a Jewish grandparent or who was married to a Jew. It is estimated that a third of the million Russians who immigrated to Israel in the 1990s were "non-Jews" or "the unclarified," another racialized category).[36] Ethiopian Beta Israel/Falashas were "Judaized" by the Zionist rabbinate but are not accepted as Jews by the anti-Zionist ultra-orthodox.[37] But what to do with Arab Jews coming from Arab lands? Yet another invented racialized identity had to be invented, Mizrahi, or Oriental Jews. To do that it became necessary to lump all Jews from Morocco to Yemen and on to Iraq, Kurdistan and even non-Arab countries like Iran, Turkey and India into the same category – and then endeavor to de-Arabize them.[38]

2. *Land Management.* A main goal of settler colonialism is to take control of the land. Says Wolfe, "Whatever settlers may say – and they generally have a lot to say – the primary motive for elimination [of the natives] is not race (or religion, ethnicity, grade of civilization, etc.) but access to territory. Territoriality is settler colonialism's specific, irreducible element."[39] Land management is intimately connected to population management. Settlers expand onto the coveted land in any way possible. They may simply seize it or conquer it. They may purchase it, then expel the local population. They may expropriate it by legal means. The methods depend upon the strength of both the settler enterprise and of Indigenous resistance. Racialized rationales justify the taking of the land. The need to "tame the frontier" and "make the desert bloom" is set against the barrenness caused by native "neglect." The conquest of the country is framed as "self-defense." Entitled settlers pitted against unworthy, right-less but intractable, irrational and inherently violent natives. Indigenous resistance itself is cast as their "misunderstanding" of how farming and the settlers' "development" of the land is good for the country as well as the displaced themselves.

The land *will be* taken. How the Indigenous fare depends on the land's availability, so interconnected are population and land management. As long as territory is available for expansion, the settlers may remove the Indigenous but leave their communities and cultures intact. But remember that the settlers claim dominion over the entire territory, even if they have not yet taken possession of it. As the Indigenous are pushed or transferred into other parts of the country, they may even be "given" lands. The US did that to the Native Americans before the Civil War. But their tenure is only temporary. Once the colonial project catches up with them, the land – which has always "belonged to" the settlers by entitlement – will now be taken. Indeed, a settler project does not want to determine its final borders until all the "unbounded territory" is finally incorporated physically and legally. The exercise of territoriality, writes Hughes,

> requires that the territorial extent of control be clearly bounded and communicated. In settler colonial contexts, however, the frontier is that territory which has not yet been formally claimed or annexed, but which will eventually (and inevitably) be part of the

settler polity. Therefore, the form of territorial control operating in settler colonial contexts runs counter to traditional conceptions of territoriality. Settlers exercise *unbounded territoriality*, a strategy of territorial control best exercised by *not* delimiting boundaries, by not making clear the extent of sovereign authority.[40]

Witness Israel's settlement but not yet sovereignty over the "disputed territory" – the "unbounded territory" – of the West Bank and Gaza.

During settler expansion, the Indigenous are "eliminated" in one way or another, be it physically or through various forms of "transfer." What happens, though, when all the territory has been conquered and settled? Elimination must take more definitive forms, since there is now only one body politic, one territory. The US, Canada and Australia employed two polar extremes, genocide and forced assimilation, often in tandem. But other options exist as well. In Algeria, where the settlers were far outnumbered and tended to be more urban-centered, they became the thin ruling stratum of the country. In Kenya, they ran the government but were content to confine themselves to certain prime agricultural areas. In South Africa, they took control of the land but contained the Black majority in Bantustans. In each of these cases, the settler minority left the colonized majority collectively intact. Israel, as we shall see, resembles most South Africa.

In Israel-plus-the-OPT, genocide has proven impossible, though not mass displacement, as a form of cultural genocide. Assimilation, however, is equally intolerable, since Greater Israel is to be a "Jewish" country despite its Palestinian majority. Creating delineated spaces for "Arabs" appeared the most practical option. By classifying the natives generically as "Arabs" instead of using the national term "Palestinians," Israel de-territorialized them. They lived in the country, but did not belong to it. Instead, they "belonged to" the Arab world outside. "Let them go live in an Arab country" is a frequently heard phrase. It also permitted their fragmentation into the six categories we mentioned earlier, placing them into more easily governable units of different rights.

Having de-territorialized the Arabs – the West Bank has long been termed "Judea and Samaria" by Israeli Jews, and Trump's Deal of the Century recognizes it is now Israeli territory – Zionism's settler project appears on the cusp of completion. As we will see presently, it still has to overcome resistance from the Palestinians and the international community alike. And the prospect of decolonization raises for the first time a political challenge to apartheid.

3. *Economic Management.* Settler colonialism is less concerned with exploiting Native labor in order to extract raw materials than is classic or "franchise" colonialism. The thrust of settler economies is to develop them as stand-alone enterprises that serve the settler population – often with a view to linking to the metropole's economy, but not dependent upon it – while marginalizing the local population, economically as well as physically and socially.[41] They become the dominant economy in part because, in most cases in modern times, they represent branches of industrialized European economies.[42] The Zionist economy benefited, of course, from being an extension of and supported by that of the British Mandate, as we will see, a form of dependence that was considered contingent: until the British left, their economy served as a vehicle for developing the Zionist one, supporting the construction of a "Hebrew" economy but not seeking to control it. The British left a highly developed "Israeli" economy intact and not dependent in any way upon Arab labor (a self-sufficiency that arose from the large waves of Jewish immigration into the country and the support of Jews abroad).

Because the British managed the economy of Palestine before 1948 (again, giving the Zionists both the protection and the space to develop their own), and because the Palestinians had been "eliminated" as a significant economic community after the Nakba (including losing the vast majority of their lands), economic management of the indigenous Palestinian population became an issue only after 1967, when Israel assumed the governing of a million Palestinians in the Occupied Territory. It is at that time they are integrated into the Matrix of Control, the extension of the Dominance Management Regime in the West Bank and Gaza.

4. *The Management of Legitimacy.* The Zionists have always had a lot of "explaining" to do, which is the literal translation of the Hebrew term *hasbara*. Because it is unjust and violent, settler colonialism must conceal its own intentions and operations – from its own practitioners,

as well as from the outside world. "Settler colonialism obscures the conditions of its own production," says Veracini.

> The settler hides behind the metropolitan colonizer (the settler is not sovereign, it is argued; "he is not responsible for colonialism" and its excesses), behind the activity of settlers elsewhere, behind the persecuted, the migrant, even the refugee (the settler has suffered elsewhere and "is seeking refuge in a new land"). The settler hides behind his labor and hardship (the settler does not dispossess anyone; he "wrestles with the land to sustain his family"). Most importantly, the peaceful settler hides behind the ethnic cleanser (colonization is an inherently non-violent activity; the settler enters a "new, empty land to start a new life"; indigenous people naturally and inevitably "vanish"; it is not the settlers that displace them ...).[43]

Despite the often intolerable conditions where they lived, the European Zionists had to explain and justify why they had the right and even the impulse to settle Palestine. How could they claim to represent the return of the Jewish people to Israel when fully 97 percent of the Jews who left Europe did not choose that option? How, given their own history, could they justify – or conceal – the violence of their settlement project, the scale of destruction of Palestinian society and property? How could they explain away decades of displacement, resistance, war and oppression that an expanding Zionism generated? Ultimately, how could they reconcile their claim of Israel democracy with ongoing occupation and apartheid? Not only to the world, not only to a Jewish community abroad known for its liberal politics and dedication to human rights, but to its own population? *Hasbara* emerged, as it had to, from the very nature of the Zionist enterprise.

The term *hasbara* was coined at the turn of the twentieth century by Nahum Sokolow, a future president of the World Zionist Organization. He used it interchangeably with the term "propaganda."[44] He did not see *hasbara*, however, as manipulation. Sokolow merely believed that the Zionist movement should explain itself to the European Christian public and its governments so as garner their support. He stressed the biblical narrative they all shared. Later generations began to employ sophisticated methods of public relations and public diplomacy, with varying degrees of sincerity.

Viewed from a settler colonial perspective, the task of *hasbara* is clear: conveying a narrative. That meant, first and foremost, casting the Zionist settlers as indigenous "pioneers" "returning" to "their" country to "redeem" it. It also meant presenting a constructed history and exclusive narrative that displaced the Arabs actually living in Palestine, casting them as intruders. Perhaps the most difficult of *hasbara*'s tasks was to conceal the foundational violence that accompanied Zionism. Since it could not deny the violence, it simply turned the tables. Zionist *hasbara* did what other colonial powers have done, it criminalized the Arabs and their resistance. Jewish victims only wanting to return home, bringing the benefits of European civilization, met by terrorists and gangs. Anti-Semitic pogroms worthy of the Cossacks. *Hasbara*, ever evolving, proved an effective vehicle for the Zionist's management of legitimacy.

The Ongoing Management of "Security"

Foundational violence begins as soon as the settlers land in the country they covet. Since conquest takes time, there may be cycles of foundational violence. In the Zionist case, as we will soon discuss, we identify three, the pre-state cycle, the Israeli state cycle and the occupation cycle. But as the settler regime strives to transform itself into a more institutionalized, "legal" and *normal* polity, the volume of violence seems to decrease – or at least be rendered more "officially" sanctioned and less visible. This is often hard to do. We have seen how preoccupied settlers are with security. And since resistance – defined as "violence" or "insecurity" by the settlers – is endemic to a colonial venture, it seeks ongoing security measures that are no less violent but can be concealed as police or routine army operations against terrorists, criminals or subversives. Domestic security agencies, the courts and the prison system are parts of this ongoing management of security. So, too, are unofficial agents of the state, settlers and collaborators, for example, who do much of the dirty work with which the state does not want to be associated.[45]

THE THREE CYCLES OF ZIONIST EXPANSION

In reality, of course, it is impossible to separate the stages of the settler colonial process. Although processes are clearly visible, we cannot cling to a rigidly linear progression. Zionism has been expanding across Palestine over the past century and a half. It has encountered resistance every step of the way, meaning that that expansion has been violent. Nonetheless, taking a step back, it is useful to divide Zionist colonization into three major cycles: a pre-state cycle (1880s–1948); an Israeli state cycle from 1948 to 1967, still ongoing within the Green Line; and an occupation cycle (1967–present). Each has been accompanied by fine-tuned sets of laws, policies, structures, narratives and actions that comprise the Dominance Management Regime best suited to the needs of the time.

In the next three chapters we will trace the evolution and workings of the Dominance Management Regime. Focusing on its primary elements – foundational violence, population and land management, the management of legitimacy (*hasbara*) and ongoing security (adding economic management in the occupation cycle) – we will see how settler colonialism actually works. That is important in itself, of course. But our aim, again, is to understand its workings so as to dismantle it in a process of decolonization.

PART II

THREE CYCLES OF ZIONIST COLONIAL DEVELOPMENT

3

Settler "Invasion" and Foundational Violence: The Pre-State Cycle (1880s–1948)

As we discussed earlier, endemic violence and insecurity by nature accompany a settler colonial project. Any settler regime must be imposed by force. No Indigenous population can ever willingly accept their own displacement. "Foundational violence" begins at the moment in which the settler invasion begins dispossessing the Indigenous population.[1] Settlers, their militias and the metropole countries all engage in it. Over time, foundational violence may appear to ease as the colonial regime "settles in" and tries to normalize itself. Indeed, denying and concealing foundational violence is at the center of a settler regime's attempt to normalize.[2]

FOUNDATIONAL VIOLENCE: THE PRE-STATE CYCLE

From the earliest days of Zionism, settlement was accompanied by what Uri Ben-Eliezer[3] calls The Military Way. From the proto-Zionist settlement in the 1880s until today, Zionism has viewed organized violence as the optimal approach – legitimate, reasonable and desirable – for dealing with "the Arabs." The process of Judaization requires The Military Way, but not in the sense of absolute conquest and victory of the natives. The ideal, of course, often expressed by the Zionists, is a Land of Israel populated solely by Jews. But even the most extreme – Vladimir Ze'ev Jabotinsky in his Iron Wall doctrine, for example – assumed that a substantial population of Natives would remain. The problem, then, was how to manage them.

As I described in my book *War Against the People*,[4] The Military Way adopted a strategy of "sufficient" pacification. This was (and is) a mix of expulsion from the country, internal displacement, violent repression and the confinement of the Arab population to small enclaves. It began with the founding of the Bar-Giora "self-defense" organization in 1907.[5]

In 1920, Yitzhak Tabenkin, a Labor Zionist leader, concluded: "all the force in the world will not enable us to reach a compromise solution with the Arabs, but only our strengthening in this Land on the basis of national strength."[6]

Indeed, The Military Way offered many avenues to sufficient pacification besides military conquest. "Transfer by conceptual displacement" was (and is) one of the most effective: simply deny Palestinian indigeneity and national rights. Replacing the term "Palestinian" with that of the generic "Arabs" implicitly denies their very existence as a people. This form of transfer was employed most notoriously by Golda Meir in her (in)famous question and assertion:

> When was there an independent Palestinian people with a Palestinian state? It was either southern Syria before the First World War, and then it was a Palestine including Jordan. It was not as though there was a Palestinian people in Palestine considering itself as a Palestinian people and we came and threw them out and took their country away from them. They did not exist.[7]

Veracini[8] lists 26 forms of transfer, of which Zionism has employed 20. Together, they amount to "sufficient colonization," the Judaizing of Palestine to the point where it is considered "Israel," even by many of the Indigenous themselves. "Sufficient pacification" has proven adequate over the years for managing the Palestinian natives and their incessant resistance.

Such a strategy avoided the Zionists having to make significant compromises over land and power. "Labor Zionists did not believe that the Palestinians had national aspirations that had to be acknowledged," writes Ben-Eliezer. "Moreover, the Zionists never believed that Arab opposition to their movement should deter them from their efforts to accomplish their national aspirations. Once they had formed this position, the path to the establishment of an armed Jewish force was short."[9] Yosef Haim Brenner, one of the early Hebrew writers (who was killed in a clash with Arabs in Jaffa in 1921), recognized the enmity and violence intrinsic to colonialism already in 1913, just four years after he arrived in the country. "Why should we talk about love towards our neighbors who live in this country, if we are mortal enemies?" he asks.

> Yes, enemies …. In the Land of Israel there are only 70,000 Jews and no less than seven hundred thousand Arabs who are, despite their inferiority and lack of culture … the lords of the land. There is already hatred between us, and there has to be – and there will be …. We are surrounded by hatred and we are filled with hatred, yes, full of hatred.[10]

After the Young Turk revolution in 1908, Arab nationalism began to rise in the Ottoman Empire. The Zionists could no longer ignore Palestinian nationalism – or the growing resistance to their systematic purchasing of land.[11] It was then that the foundational violence of the Zionist colonial venture became more organized and ideologically justified. Guard members hired themselves out to evict the Arab tenant farmers who had long farmed those lands and to protect the Jewish settlers who replaced them.[12] The Guard dressed in flamboyant costumes mixing Bedouin, Circassian and Cossack motifs. Taking as their battle-cry "In blood and fire Judea shall rise again!", they set out on The Military Way, initiating reprisal raids when the Arabs tried to resist eviction.[13] The Guard's activities mark the beginning of the "Israel-Arab Conflict," the first phase of foundational violence.

The Military Way became more organized, however, only after the British conquest of Palestine in 1917. It was then that the Palestinians fully realized Zionism's settler agenda.[14] Suddenly, Palestine had been severed from Syria. No sooner had the British begun governing than they issued the Balfour Declaration in which the British government declared its support for "the establishment in Palestine of a national home for the Jewish people."[15] To be sure, the British added a proviso: "it being clearly understood that nothing shall be done which may prejudice the civil and religious rights of existing non-Jewish communities in Palestine." But by referring to the Palestinians as merely "non-Jewish communities," the British effectively deprived them of their national rights.

Even more significantly, the pro-Zionist wording and spirit of the Balfour Declaration were then incorporated into the League of

Nations' Mandate over Palestine, which the British received in 1922. The Mandate's Preamble repeated the Balfour Declaration's support for a Jewish national home in Palestine but made no provisions for Palestinian national aspirations. The Mandate went on to specify the policies and structures necessary for the establishment of a Jewish "national home" – an innocuous phrase used by the Zionists to conceal their aspirations for establishing the Jewish state in Palestine.[16] Article 4 of the Mandate permitted the establishment of a Jewish agency, a keystone national institution of the settlers' "state-in-the-making." No parallel Palestinian national institution was mentioned or approved. Article 7 provided a process of Jews receiving Palestinian citizenship.[17]

While warnings of Zionist intentions were raised since the 1880s, the British reneging on their promise of an Arab independence and the imposition of the Mandate brought home to the Palestinians that they were losing their country[18] – and they were. In 1919, President Woodrow Wilson, who has just articulated the principle of national self-determination in the post-World War I era, dispatched the King-Crane Commission to Palestine to ascertain just what the people of that country wanted. After extensive interviews throughout the country, the Commission reported: "The non-Jewish population of Palestine – nearly nine-tenths of the whole – are emphatically against the entire Zionist program .... There was no one thing upon which the population of Palestine was more agreed upon than this."[19]

By March 1920, armed hostilities had broken out between Arab villagers and Zionist colonists in northern Palestine. In April, fighting reached Jerusalem. That year the Zionists established the Hagana, their "self-defense" force. The British gave them freedom to conduct limited offensive actions as long as they didn't challenge their authority.[20]

The following years witnessed repeated Arab uprisings – in 1921, 1929 and 1933 – with some 10,000 incidents recorded over the next decade. Thousands died, the vast majority of them Arabs.[21] All this culminated in the Great Arab Revolt of 1936–39, downplayed as "disturbances," "riots" or mere "events" in Zionist historiography.[22]

POPULATION MANAGEMENT: THE PRE-STATE CYCLE

Foundational violence enabled the Zionist settlement project to root itself in the uncompromising hostile environment of Palestine. Only

the construction of a Dominance Management Regime could translate the localized swagger of The Guard into a well-organized colonial
regime. Settler projects revolve around acquiring land, *all* of the land.
They must also retain control of the land and its resources, particularly
if its former tenants try to reclaim it.[23]

The Zionist project faced a Palestinian population that matched
its attempts to overwhelm it with Jewish settlers. True, the Jewish
population of Palestine grew steadily in the pre-state period. Jews represented about 8 percent of the population at the turn of the century,
growing to 14 percent by 1914, 17 percent by 1931 and 32 percent
by 1947. It nevertheless remained a distinct minority.[24] In terms of
land acquisition, the picture was even more extreme. For all their
financial and political resources, by 1947 the Zionists had managed
to acquire less than 6 percent of the country's land, and much of that
in malarial swamps.[25] Add to that increasingly fierce resistance to
Zionist colonization on the part of the Palestinians, and the necessity
for population management becomes clear. Settler colonialism constitutes a form of biopolitics. It must regulate all human life within
the territory it aspires to rule.[26] Making Palestine "Jewish" required
importing as many Jewish settlers/immigrants as possible. Jewish
demographic dominance required an ability to control and repress the
Native majority as well. And since that majority population was over-
whelmingly a peasant one, managing the population and land they
were being displaced from overlapped with foundational violence and
an ongoing preoccupation with security.

Enforcing categories of exclusion[27] is key to the management of
the Palestinian population. It realizes what Veracini[28] calls "transfer
by conceptual displacement," one of the many forms of elimination.
The Indigenous are "disappeared" through denying their indigeneity, and therefore their national rights, their claims to the country or
even a history and culture of their own. Rather than enacting laws
and policies that discriminate against "non-Jews," it is enough to enact
laws and policies that merely affirm Jewish rights and entitlements.
Non-Jews are excluded by implication. Neither the Ottomans nor
the British had ever found it necessary to offset "Arabs" with other
exclusive categories, like "non-Jews." After 1948, Zionists invented
yet more categories of exclusion: "absentees," "refugees," Druse versus
Arabs (depending on service in the Israel Defense Forces, IDF), Israeli

citizens and *real* (Zionist) citizens. The most "Zionist" election ever took place in March 2020, where *all* the Jewish parties agreed to exclude the Joint Arab List from government because only "Zionist Jews" were acceptable political partners.[29] Categories of inclusion play a complementary role. Although most ultra-orthodox Jews are anti-Zionist, do not recognize the secular state of Israel and refuse to serve in the army, as Jews they cannot be denied equal civil, political or economic rights or political legitimacy.

Exclusion extends into outright segregation. "The principle of segregation was accepted by all parts of the Zionist movement," writes the Israeli historian Tom Segev.[30]

> The principle of segregation guided the Zionists' strategy of purchasing land to create a single contiguous area of Jewish ownership.... Segregation had led to the establishment of Tel Aviv.... Segregation was at the heart of a fight over the orange trees of Petach Tikva....
>
> The Histadrut was caught in an awkward situation. It was fighting to protect the Jewish workers' wages and safeguard their political interest, but socialism did not condone discrimination against Arab workers. Histadrut leaders had already been forced to decide whether to accept Arab workers into the labor federation. If the union was open to all, the Jews would quickly lose control, they reasoned, and this would be counterproductive, since the struggle of the Jewish laborer was identified with the struggle for national independence.... Thus segregation won out over socialism.

This, too, conforms to the logic of settler colonialism worldwide. "The colonized world is a compartmentalized world," Fanon informs us, it is a world "inhabited by different species."[31] This does not always mean racial compartmentalization, as in South Africa. Zionism never presented Jews and Arabs as different races. Instead, personal relationships tended to be functional. Arabs worked for Jews (seldom the opposite). Normal friendships or daily interactions were rare. Indeed, equality was to be avoided lest the Native "raise his head" (Judges 8:28). "The line separating settler and Indigenous must be approached but is never finally crossed," observes Veracini.[32] "[D]ifference is a necessary prerequisite of the absolute need to at once distinguish between settler self and Indigenous and exogenous Others."

In *The Flame Trees of Thika*, her classic book about growing up in colonial Kenya, Elspeth Huxley describes how these power differentials work and must be preserved even in situations of close personal contact:

> "No more words," Tilly said snappily. Juma [the family's African "houseboy"] had a patronizing air that she resented, and she doubted if he was showing enough respect.... Indeed respect was the only protection available to Europeans who lived singly, or in scattered families, among thousands of Africans accustomed to constant warfare and armed with spears and poisoned arrows, but had themselves no barricades, and went about unarmed. The respect preserved them like an invisible coat of mail, or a form of magic, and seldom failed; but it had to be very carefully guarded. The least rent or puncture might, if not immediately checked and repaired, split the whole garment asunder and expose its wearer in all his human vulnerability. Kept intact, it was a thousand times stronger than all the guns and locks and metal in the world; challenged, it could be brushed aside like a spider's web. So Tilly was a little sensitive about respect, and Juma was silenced.[33]

LAND AND MANAGEMENT: THE PRE-STATE CYCLE

By folding population management into land management, the Indigenous population may be alienated from the land without it appearing discriminatory or oppressive. The twin Zionist doctrine of "conquest of the land/conquest of labor" reflects the intertwined nature of these forms of management. Establishing a separate, viable Jewish society and economy could not wait on the conquest of the land. That would take time. Since demographic domination depended on immigration, and the ability to attract and keep immigrants depended on their employment, the "conquest of labor" took priority. Now employment by itself did not need land; it could be generated in the urban areas. By the end of the 1930s, a third of the Jews lived in Tel Aviv, with significant populations in Haifa, Jerusalem and other cities as well.[34] But Palestine could not be conquered through urban settlement alone.

It was the need to conquer land that extended the conquest of labor outward to the rural kibbutz and moshav settlements.[35] This is what the Israeli architect Eyal Weizman points to as the "military logic" of settlements.[36] It found its most graphic expression in the "Stockade and Tower" construction of Israeli settlements during the Arab Revolt. "During the 1930s," writes Segev,[37]

> some 130 new settlements were established, most of them were agricultural outposts, including fifty-three new kibbutzim. Some of these settlements were constructed in the middle of the night, which gave them a clandestine, heroic aura. The settlers, nearly all of them young people with ties to the labor movement, would arrive at a site, build a fence around the land, and erect a watchtower, which is why these settlements were called *homa u-migdal*, or "stockade and tower." At first they were meant to prevent Arab farmers from continuing to work land bought by the Zionist movement. But the *homa u-migdal* system also allowed the settlers to feel patriotic and rebellious, as if they were engaged in secret military operations [although the British allowed it].

The "logic" of settler colonialism, together with Eastern European ethno-nationalism, fed into the Zionist ideology that in turn identified what had to be done to establish the settler presence. Within those guidelines, the settlers came up with practical solutions. In the first decades of the Zionist project, the settlers – who called themselves "pioneers" because they saw themselves as settling a wild frontier – struggled to cope with a harsh socioeconomic environment. The inability of few existing *moshavot* or proto-Zionist agricultural settlements established in the early years of settlement to provide employment for those arriving around the turn of the century presented a major impediment to the goal of producing a Jewish majority, especially in the rural areas where a settler workforce would be needed to hold onto acquired land. But Jewish labor could not compete with the low wages paid to Arabs. The *moshavot* could not afford to pay Jewish workers what their level of subsistence required. Faced with this dilemma, the Zionist leadership, came up with the idea of the kibbutz.

Borrowing agricultural models from Germany as it settled Slavic lands, they understood that this form of collective, cost-effective farming could replace wages with communal life. It is this innovation, funded by the Palestine Office of the World Zionist Organization (WZO), the Palestine Land Development Company and the Jewish National Fund (JNF), that gave birth to the doctrines of "conquest of labor" (*kibbush ha'avoda*) and "Hebrew labor" (*'avoda 'ivrit*). By eliminating wage labor and utilizing cooperative living – "pioneering socialist settlement" – as a vehicle of colonization, the Zionists created an exclusive Jewish workforce immune to competitive Arab wage labor. The "conquest of labor" within a collective that could be established on nationalized lands acquired by the WZO led to – and made possible – yet another Zionist principle: *kibush ha'karka*, "conquest of the land." By the start of the twentieth century, the Zionist leadership had wholly adopted these settler colonial methods.[38]

Settler projects revolve around acquiring territory. By definition, then, the ability of the settler community to seize the targeted territory depends on its ability to get the local tenants out. "Judaization" is a term used frequently since the start of Zionism. It continues to be used by the Israeli government (as in the policy of "Judaizing the Galilee"), though less contentious terms like "redeeming the Land" (*ge'ulat ha'aretz*) are preferred. In either case, the clear intention is to transform an Arab country into a Jewish one.

In practice, then, the flip side of Judaization is de-Arabization; population management folded into the management of the land and the economy. Arab peasants found themselves increasingly concentrated in impoverished urban shanty towns. By the 1920s, resentment and resistance had ignited ever-more organized resistance, leading to the Arab Revolt of 1936–39.[39] Both Judaization and de-Arabization proved violent processes, inevitable expressions of colonization. "We have forgotten," cautioned Moshe Sharett, a future Israeli prime minister as far back as 1914,

> that we have not come to an empty land to inherit it, but we have come to conquer a country from a people inhabiting it, that governs it by virtue of its language and savage culture.… Recently, there has been appearing in our newspapers the clarification about "the mutual understanding" between us and the Arabs, about "common interests" [and] about "the possibility of unity and peace" between

the two fraternal peoples.... [But] we must not allow ourselves to be deluded by such illusive hopes ... for if we seek to look upon our land, the Land of Israel, as ours alone and we allow a partner into our estate – all content and meaning will be lost to our enterprise.[40]

But this slow, piecemeal form of Judaization was insufficient for the genuine conquest of the land, for what Ben-Gurion called a "real" Jewish state. "I do not believe in the transfer of an individual," asserted Arthur Ruppin, the head of the Palestine Office of the World Zionist Organization and the official in charge of land purchases, "I believe in the transfer of entire villages."[41]

Proposals to physically transfer Palestinians out of the country have a long history in Zionism.[42] Theodor Herzl confided in his diaries: "We shall try to spirit the penniless population across the border by procuring employment for it in the transit countries, while denying it employment in our own country."[43] Israel Zangwill, the Jewish writer who coined the phrase "A land without a people," complained that Palestine is not so much occupied by the Arabs as overrun by them." Invoking the Boer's Great Trek in South Africa, he proposed that "we must greatly persuade [the Arabs] to 'trek'. After all, they have all Arabia with its million square miles – not to mention the vast new area freed from the Turk between Syria and Mesopotamia – and Israel has not a square inch." If they "fold their tents" and "silently steal away," he felt sure that the Jews would be prepared to pay their travelling expenses.[44] Ben-Gurion, the architect of the Nakba, had long advocated for "compulsory transfer." In 1937, he established a Committee on Population Transfer within the Jewish Agency.[45] And, of course, transfer, a euphemism for ethnic cleansing, was in fact carried out at a mass level in 1948 and again in 1967.[46] One of its most notorious perpetrators, Yosef Weitz, the Director of the Jewish National Fund's Land Settlement Department, wrote:

It must be clear that there is no room in the country for both peoples ... The only solution is a Land of Israel without Arabs.... There is no way but to transfer the Arabs from here to the neighbouring countries, to transfer all of them, perhaps with the exception of Bethlehem, Nazareth and the old Jerusalem. Not one village must be left, not one tribe.[47]

The physical transfer of the Indigenous population can only be contemplated and rationalized by the settlers if the Natives are first "disappeared" from their national narrative – transfer by conceptual displacement. The land must be represented as barren, waiting for the settlers to "redeem" it. Only they, those truly, worthy of possessing the land, will make it once more a fertile and populous homeland to a population that cares for it. "Disappearing the Arabs lay at the heart of the Zionist dream," writes Segev,[48] "and was also a necessary condition of its realization.... With few exceptions, none of the Zionists disputed the desirability of forced transfer – or its morality."

ECONOMIC MANAGEMENT AND CONSOLIDATION: THE PRE-STATE CYCLE

Over the four decades from the First Zionist Congress in 1897 until the outbreak of the Arab Revolt in 1936, the Zionist leadership took decisions that transformed their national movement into a typical settler colonial enterprise. Heavy investment in the purchase of land and the establishment of agricultural settlements became a mainstay, although it diversified into factories, ports and other incipient industries as well. The establishment of Tel Aviv in 1909 added a vibrant urban economy to the Yishuv.

During the Mandate period, Zionist efforts to advance the cause of political independence made the growth of a viable Jewish economy a national priority. In this the Yishuv was aided by the British authorities. Not only did they allow the Jews to bring in unlimited capital – the influx of Jewish capital in the 1920s was 41 percent greater than the Yishuv's entire economy[49] – but also to establish crucial economic franchises of their own. The Palestine Electric Company served only Jews. The Palestine Potash Company had an exclusive right to mine the minerals of the Dead Sea. The British also paid Jewish government workers higher salaries than Arabs.[50] At the same time, the crushing repression of the Arab Revolt between 1936 and 1939 left the Arab economy in shambles.

The great spur to the economic growth of the Yishuv occurred in the 1930s, when the Jewish population doubled from 185,000 in 1931 to 375,000 in just four years. This wave of settlement included middle-class Jews from Poland and Germany. Some settled in the agricultural sector, which became economically viable for the first time. Others, bringing with them enormous amounts of capital and business experience, moved to urban areas along the coast. Half of them settled in Tel Aviv and its suburbs, which tripled in size. These newcomers invested in commerce and in such industrial sectors as the metal trades, textiles and chemicals.[51] Between 1933 and 1939, $35 million ($625 million in today's currency) was transferred by German Jews to Palestine.[52] The Jewish industrial workforce grew from 19,000 to 55,000 in the decade of the 1930s.[53] Although Jews were a minority in Palestine (less than 30 percent), by the middle of the decade the Yishuv economy had surpassed the Arab one.[54] Between 1922 and 1947, the annual growth rate of the Jewish sector of the economy was 13.2 percent, mainly due to immigration and foreign capital, while that of the Arab sector was 6.5 percent.[55]

By the late 1920s, Zionism had already created a viable state-within-a-state. Among the major Zionist national institutions established in this period were: the Technion (1918); the Histadrut Labor Federation (1920); the Hagana, which became the core of the IDF (1920); the Hebrew University (1929); and the Jewish Agency (1929). Looked at from the perspective of institutions in place, 1948 is an arbitrary date. That is when political and military forces converged to make the establishment of Israel possible. The settler "state on the way," however, had come into existence effectively decades before.

THE MANAGEMENT OF LEGITIMACY: THE PRE-STATE CYCLE

Zionism's first major success in "selling" its national project came in 1917, when Zionism's first great salesman, Chaim Weizmann, shepherded through the British government the Balfour Declaration. The most influential Zionist leader between Herzl and Ben-Gurion, Weizmann, a future president of Israel, established intimate relations with the generation of British leaders who played key roles in the consolidation of Zionist settlement in Palestine. He worked closely with Arthur Balfour, the British Foreign Minister, to craft the Declaration, which proved crucial to the Zionist enterprise, marking the first time a major power recognized and legitimized Zionism.

The political effect was to legitimize the Zionist venture abroad as well as promoting it in Palestine. The contrast to other League mandates was stark. League of Nation's mandates over central and southern Africa instructed mandate holders to prepare their subjects for self-rule. They also urged local governments to rein in settler violence and to limit the alienation of Indigenous farmers from their lands. But when it came to Palestine, where 30 percent of Arab peasants were landless by 1930 and 80 percent of the rest lacked enough for subsistence, the Mandate Commission chastised British officials for failing to provide enough support to the Jewish settlers and for deploying *too little violence* in crushing Arab "rebels."[56]

THE ARAB REVOLT AND THE TRANSITION
TO STATE-LEVEL SECURITY ORGANIZATION

If 1948 marked the Zionist War of Independence, 1936 marked that of the Palestinians.[57] The Arab uprising of 1936 dispelled any ambiguity among the Zionist settlers over their ultimate goal. No one doubted anymore that a Jewish "national home" meant anything but an independent Jewish state. The Yishuv transitioned from foundational violence to more organized, institutionalized forms of control, of military, security forces and police alike. "During this period," Segev tells us,[58] "the Jewish Agency [the Zionists' *de facto* government] almost seemed like a security branch of the [British] administration, serving, as it did, as informer, subcontractor, and client."

Thousands of Jews enlisted in the British police, and a special Jewish settlement police force was established. The Hagana completely re-armed and reorganized itself as an effective military force, supported financially by Zionist organizations abroad. Charles Tegart, the British Empire's premier counterterrorism expert, trained Zionist forces and planned an elaborate system of walls and forts which proved crucial for the Jews' ability to control the countryside, and later conquer it.[59] Orde Wingate, a British intelligence officer once described as "Lawrence of the Jews," formed a private army unit within the Hagana, to fight Arab terror with Jewish terror. His Special Night Squads, integrated into British police's own counterterrorism units, brutalized the Palestinian population but has had a lasting influence on IDF combat doctrine until this day.[60] Not only did the alliance of British and Zionist forces against the Arabs during the Revolt create a feeling of common cause, but the Zionists were acutely aware that they were laying the foundations of the future Jewish army that would sooner or later engage in an existential war with the Palestinians.[61]

With the hardening of Zionist nationalist aspirations during the Revolt, no Zionist would ever refer to Palestinians as "the natives." By the same token, no Zionist would characterize Zionism as a "colonial" movement. The Iron Wall doctrine remained, but its language was totally abandoned. Henceforth the Jews were the natives and the Arabs were recent immigrants from neighboring countries. The Zionist struggle was one of national liberation, Palestinian resistance was criminalized as "terrorism." If the Arabs persisted in their resistance to what Jabotinsky called a "moral and just" colonial movement,[62] Zionism asserted both the power and moral right to enact their wholesale transfer out of the country. Vague notions about the "voluntary transfer" or "resettlement" of displaced Palestinian peasants gave way in Zionist circles to calls for outright expulsion. "I am for compulsory transfer," declared Ben-Gurion in 1938. "I don't see anything immoral in it."[63]

David Ben-Gurion, leader of the mainstream Labor Zionist movement and a future Israeli prime minister, soon adopted Jabotinsky's doctrine. Echoing "The Iron Wall," he affirmed in 1936 that

A comprehensive agreement is undoubtedly out of the question now. For only after total despair on the part of the Arabs, despair that will come not only from the failure of the disturbances and the attempt at rebellion, but also as a consequence of our growth in the country, may the Arabs possibly acquiesce to a Jewish *Eretz Israel*.[64]

Indeed, 1936 marked the shift to what Ben-Gurion called "fighting Zionism" and Menachem Begin, Jabotinsky's protégé, termed "military Zionism."

Until 1948, the Zionist's Domination Management Regime had limited authority and clout. It required the active support and intervention of the British authorities.[65] Nonetheless, the foothold the Yishuv gained in the pre-state period positioned it to conquer 78 percent of Palestine in the 1948 war. The dozens of settlements established on the land it had managed to acquire defined the future Israeli borders.[66] No less crucial, by the war's end some 720,000 Palestinians – 70 percent of the Palestinian population – had fled or were driven from the Israeli-controlled territory,[67] with up to another 150,000 becoming internally displaced persons.[68] The interworkings of the Domination Management Regime – population management, the conquest of land and the conquest of labor, all propelled by violence – set the stage for the rise of the Zionist settler state.[69]

It is telling that Palestinian scholars such as Rashid Khalidi[70] mark the Revolt of 1936–39 as a watershed event no less than the 1948 war. In the sense that it pitted Palestinian civil society against harsh British repression, with active Zionist military support, that the Palestinians emerged from the Revolt economically and politically exhausted, made it the opening round in their failed struggle for liberation. A settler colonial perspective highlights processes and turning points different from those based solely on conflict. The 1948 war, the Nakba, the event that ushered a settler state into being, was not a stand-alone event. It was not a beginning in that sense but a pivotal moment. It marked the completion of the first cycle of Zionist colonization begun in the 1880s and the entry into the next cycle, that of the Israeli state. Indeed, as we shall see in the next chapter, it is only after 1948 that the full potential of the Dominance Management Regime comes to fruition.

4

The Israeli State Cycle (1948–67)

By 1948 the settler regime was well established. It existed in a parallel universe to Palestine life under the Mandate. Because the British remained until the middle of May of that year, the Yishuv had not yet acquired the land, military sway or governmental authority necessary for asserting any meaningful level of colonial control. The 1948 war represented the major transition. The initial cycle of Zionist colonialism, that of the pre-state period (1880s–1948), had been completed. The next cycle (1948–67) was beginning in which the Israeli state would be established and consolidated.

Throughout the period of the Mandate, The Military Way had become entrenched in Yishuv society. The Zionists sought every opportunity to gain military skills and organization. They accepted training from the British, fought in British units in World War II and with the British Mandatory forces against the Palestinians. Then, after the war, they began fighting the British themselves. During the Mandate period the Zionists also gained expertise in counterinsurgency against the Arabs. Out of these experiences an effective military organization and capacity for arms production arose. By the end of World War II, the Zionists were able to muster some 30,000 trained men and women. They had at their disposal a well-organized military force, the Hagana, and an elite strike force, the Palmach, together with a number of undercover militias affiliated with the right-wing Zionism, Etzel and Lehi in particular.[1]

The Yishuv's military far outgunned the poorly armed and poorly organized Palestinian forces. By the end of 1948, as we've discussed earlier, the Zionists had conquered 78 percent of Palestine. Over 70 percent of the Palestinian population had fled or been driven from their homes, the vast majority evacuating Israeli-held territory. Supersession had become a tangible reality. The Zionists had established a state, recognized by the international community, over most of the country. It had effected the transfer out of most of the Palestinians. Most importantly, it was on the way to settler colonialism's final triumph: the normalization of the settler state of Israel and the permanent marginalization of the Arabs who remained.

The 1948 war constituted the second round of foundational violence, inaugurating the Israeli cycle of colonization. One might also argue that the Arab Revolt of the mid-1930s marked the second stage of foundational violence. It was then that the Palestinians opened a concentrated campaign for independence. And it was at this juncture that settler Zionism broke with the notion of a "national home," a phrase adopted to placate the British, and shifted explicitly to the aim of securing a Jewish state in Palestine. The year 1948 merely marked closure of the pre-state cycle of colonization.

THE MANAGEMENT OF SECURITY

After 1948, militarism, if anything, became more entrenched in Israeli culture and policy-making. Indeed, the army became the primary instrument of nation-building. Cultivating the idea that Israel's wars were forced upon it, were of "no choice" (*ein breira*), that they pitted "the few against the many," Israel's military culture kept its populace in a constant state of mobilization.[2] As IDF Chief of Staff Yigael Yadin put it: "Every [Jewish] citizen is a soldier on eleven months annual leave."[3] With the establishment of Israel, the instruments of ongoing security management evolved into the military, security and police instruments of the state. After the 1948 war, these security mechanisms blended into policies of population and land management. From 1948 to 1966, the Arab citizens of Israel live under Military Government.

The military regime that underlies Israeli democracy rested on the Defense Emergency Regulations of 1945. These had been put into place by the British in large part to manage the Jewish community during its violent campaign against them in the waning days of the Mandate. On the very first day of Israeli sovereignty, May 15, 1948, the Knesset adopted all 170 Mandatory statutes the Jews had so bitterly criticized as anti-democratic and even "Nazi-like" before statehood. All the laws, that is, except those regulations that restricted Jewish immigration and land purchase.[4] They amounted to nothing less than a regime of population management aimed at Israel's Arab citizens.

With the Military Government, the state transferred considerable sovereignty to the military. The fact that the policing of Israeli (Arab) citizens within the state of Israel had been given to the military gave the Military Government more an appearance of occupation than civilian control. The Knesset continued to add new laws, ordinances and orders to the Emergency Regulations. Law and Administration Ordinance No. 1, for example, declared the country to be in a national state of emergency, in which it remains until this day. This suspended much of due process. Cabinet ministers, together with the Military Governor (who had replaced the British High Commissioner), were empowered to issue "emergency regulations" of their own. They could suspend or amend any law for reasons of defense or public security.

Article 125 allowed local governors to declare any area of the country "a forbidden (or closed) area ... which no one can enter or leave without ... a written permit from the military commander or his deputy ... failing which he is considered to have committed a crime." In this way the Arab communities of the country were divided into small "closed areas," severely limiting movement. Article 124 empowered the military authorities to impose a curfew in any area for any length of time. Articles 122 and 126 empowered the Military Governor to prevent "the use of specific roads or roads in general." Article 109 gave the Military Government the power to banish people or hold them under house arrest for an unspecified period without legal recourse. Article 111, commonly used today in the Occupied Territory, allows Administrative Detention of any person for a year (renewable) with no charges or trial.

Articles 94 and 96 forbid the printing of newspapers or any document "containing matter of political significance" without a permit. The Defense Regulations – subsequently called the Israeli Emergency (Security Zones) Regulations of 1949 – were enforced through the Military Governor. Article 108 empowered him to do whatever necessary "for securing the public safety, the defense of Israel, the maintenance of public order, or the suppression of mutiny, rebellion, or riot." Arab citizens were tried in military courts whose decisions, in accordance with Articles 34, 46, 47, 48 and 50, could not be appealed, including sentences of life imprisonment and even death.[5]

POPULATION AND LAND MANAGEMENT: THE ISRAELI CYCLE

The 1948 war had more to do with ethnic cleansing and territorial expansion than it did with meeting existential threats.[6] Already in 1940, in preparation for the inevitable war, the Jewish National Fund (JNF), with the help of the Hagana, began a program of systematically mapping Palestinian villages, towns and urban areas. Originally conceived as a kind of data-bank that would help the JNF acquire land, the military value of these village files was quickly discovered. Using scores of collaborators, British government records and aerial photography, they recorded the precise details of

the topographic location of each village, its access roads, quality of land, water springs, main sources of income, its sociopolitical composition, religious affiliations, names of its mukhtars, its relationship with other villages, the age of individual men (sixteen to fifty) and ... an index of "hostility" (towards the Zionist project, that is), decided by the level of the village's participation in the revolt of 1936. There was a list of everyone who had been involved in the revolt and the families of those who had lost someone in the fight against the British. Particular attention was given to people who had allegedly killed Jews. [They included] the basic structure of the Arab village. This means the structure and how best to attack it.... Files in the post-1943 era included detailed descriptions of the husbandry, the cultivated land, the number of trees in plantations, the quality of each fruit grove (even of each single tree), the average amount of land per family, the number of cars, shop owners, members of workshops and the names of the artisans in each village and their skills.... [M]eticulous detail was added about each clan and its political affiliation, the social stratification between notables and common peasants, and the names of the civil servants in the Mandatory government.... [O]ne finds additional details popping up around 1945, such as descriptions of village mosques and the names of their imams, together with such characterisations as "he is an ordinary man", and even precise accounts of the living rooms inside the homes of these dignitaries. Towards the end of the Mandatory period the information becomes more explicitly military orientated: the number of guards (most villages had none) and the quantity and quality of the arms at the villagers' disposal (generally antiquated or even non-existent).... The final update of the village files took place in 1947. It focused on creating lists of "wanted" persons in each village.[7]

Use of the files, claims Pappe in his book *The Ethnic Cleansing of Palestine*,[8] "fueled the worst atrocities in the villages, leading to mass executions and torture," both before and after 1948, and, indeed, into the 1967 occupation. In 1948, he goes on,[9] the village files helped the Hagana

> identify the thousands of Palestinians who were later executed on the spot or imprisoned for long periods once the ethnic cleansing had started.... Jewish troops used these lists for the search-and-arrest operations they carried out as soon as they had occupied a village. That is, the men in the village would be lined up and those appearing on the lists would then be identified, often by the same person who had informed on them in the first place but who would now be wearing a cloth sack over his head with two holes cut out for his eyes so as not to be recognised. The men who were picked out were often shot on the spot. Criteria for inclusion in these lists were involvement in the Palestinian national movement, having close ties to the leader of the movement, the Mufti al-Hajj Amin al-Husayni, and, as mentioned, having participated in actions against the British and the Zionists.

The results are well known. At the conclusion of the 1948 War of Independence/Nakba, the remaining Palestinian population, having lost most of their lands and properties, now numbered 11–13 percent of the population, down from 67 percent just a year earlier.[10] Placing them under a Military Government addressed only part of the problem of population and land management, however. Now that Israel had relieved itself of 75–80 percent of the Palestinian population, how could they be prevented from returning and reclaiming their properties?

Israel's strategy, which would later be applied to the Occupied Territories, was to create "facts on the ground." Expropriating the refugees' land would prevent their return. From June 16, 1948, when the Israeli

Cabinet took the decision to bar their return, a host of Israeli actors – the army, the JNF and even those Jews of the kibbutzim and moshavs who had been the refugees' former neighbors – all began razing the villages from where the refugees originated and taking over their land.[11] Presaging the use they would later make of law, administration and planning as mechanisms of territorial expansion and land management after 1967, Israeli leaders prepared a Kafkaesque legal mechanism by which Palestinian property could be "legally" appropriated – a system it continues to apply within Israel and in the Occupied Territories until this day.[12] The four stages are described in the following.

Stage 1. Israel Claims Sovereignty

The Abandoned Areas Ordinance Section 1(A) defines "abandoned territory" as "any area captured by the armed forces or surrendered to them or land abandoned by all or some of its inhabitants." This definition allows land to be declared "abandoned" whether or not its residents have left it.

Stage 2. Freezing the "Lack of Ownership"

The Provisional Council of the State (1948) created a Custodian for the "abandoned areas." The Absentees' Property Law – 1950 defines an "absentee" as an owner of a property in 1947–48 who was: (a) a national or a citizen of Lebanon, Syria, Transjordan, Iraq, Egypt, Saudi Arabia or Yemen; (b) who was in any of these places or in parts of Palestine outside of Israel (West Bank/Gaza and East Jerusalem) during 1947–48; or (c) was a Palestinian citizen who left his ordinary place of residence in Palestine for somewhere else before September 1948, or for "a place in Palestine held at the time by forces which sought to prevent the establishment of the State of Israel or which fought against it after its establishment." This definition includes almost all Palestinians, including Israeli citizens, who left their homes, as most did, even to go to a neighboring village. Thus the category "internal refugees" or "present absentees" was created.

73

At the heart of the government's conviction that it needed to rule over (rather than with) the Palestinians who remained after 1948 was its zealous territoriality ...; from the day the Yishuv declared independence, its single greatest fear was that refugees both within and outside its lines would try to return and resettle on their property ... [T]he attainment of sovereignty thus inaugurated only the next phase in the Zionist enterprise of "coloniz[ing] the frontiers and the filling of blank spaces"

– a "project of colonization [in Ben-Gurion's words] far greater than all of the last seventy years."[13]

Palestinians were also removed from their land by other means. The Emergency Defense Regulations empower military commanders to declare certain areas as "closed areas," prohibiting both entrance or exit. Thirteen Palestinian villages and their lands were isolated. A curfew imposed on the Arab community from 1948 to 1966 restricted access of Palestinians to their land. Regulation 8(A) reads: "An authorized source may command a permanent resident of a security area to leave the area." Consequently, most of the upper and eastern Galilee, as well as a 10 km strip along the border with Jordan, were declared "security areas," as were sections of the Negev. This allowed widespread extra-legal expulsion of entire communities, known as "voluntary evacuation." The residents of Mag'dal, now Ashkelon, were deported to Gaza in 1950. The residents of Ikrit and Baram in the Galilee were forbidden to return to their homes. Many Bedouin communities found themselves expelled, some to Jordan, or contained within small areas of their former habitat. Thousands of individuals were moved around or expelled from the country. The "Law of Land Acquisition in Time of Emergency," moreover, empowered the authorities to issue expropriate lands deemed "necessary for the defense of the state and public security."

Stage 3. Israelification: From "Lack of Ownership" to Israeli Ownership

Legal means were instituted in the early years of the state to expropriate Palestinian lands and hand them over to Israeli owners. The Emergency Regulations for the Cultivation of Fallow Lands, 1948, empowered the Ministry of Agriculture to seize lands not (or "under-")

cultivated to "ensure" their cultivation. When used in conjunction with the "Security Areas Regulations" and the Regulations on Closed Areas, which prevented Palestinians from reaching their fields, these regulations proved an effective means of confiscation.

In 1950 a Development Authority was created, later becoming the Israel Lands Authority, with the intent of acquiring "abandoned" Arab territories and lands and "developing" them. This was in line with the policy of not accepting back Palestinian refugees or present absentees. Although compensation was offered for lands (at well below later market prices), most Palestinian owners refused it. Accepting compensation would only validate the loss of their lands and signal that they had voluntarily relinquished them. Many owners also had no authority to "sell" what were collectively owned lands, or could not agree to do so without other family members. No problem. Regulations issued in 1953 allowed the state to expropriate the lands of 250 "abandoned" Arab villages and individual parcels of land belonging to "absentees," equaling 1500 square kilometers or 586 square miles.

Stage 4. De-Arabization

In general, Israel viewed Palestinian ownership of land or even their presence as a threat to its sovereignty and the "Jewish character" of the state. The land had to be "nationalized." Israel emerged after the 1948 war in control of 78 percent of Palestine, but the JNF owned only about 6 percent of the land. Wholly 25 percent still remained in Palestinian hands, mainly in the Galilee. Through the Law of Absentee Property (1950) the JNF acquired millions of acres more. By 1962, 92.6 percent of the land "belonged" to either the state or to the JNF. Palestinians were left with 7.3 percent.[14]

Three-quarters of the Palestinians were now refugees beyond Israel's borders, and of those that remained about a third (46,000) were classified as "internally displaced" or "present absentees." They were prohibited from returning to their homes and lands. In the meantime, the Israeli government settled nearly 200,000 Jewish immigrants in the "abandoned" Arab villages, both because of the availability of housing and in order to prevent the refugees' return.[15]

Yet Israeli governments still felt their hold over the country to be tenuous. The process of displacement, then, continued by other means.

As in the pre-state period, settlements were constructed to "constitute a human wall against the dangers of invasion." "Our territorial conquests and redemptions," declared Ben-Gurion, "will not be assured if we do not succeed in erecting a great and closely linked chain of settlements, especially settlements of soldiers, on the borders, in the Negev, on the coast, in the Jerusalem corridor, around Safed, and in all other areas of strategic importance."[16] Of the 370 new Jewish settlements established in Israel – and not necessarily from Arabs who had fled or been expelled from the country – 60,000 acres of land taken for the new Jewish settlements belonged to Arabs who still lived in the country, often adjacent to their fields that now became Jewish agricultural settlements or towns. In the Galilee, where by the early 1960s only 8 percent of the population were Jews (10,000 of 120,000 people), a vigorous policy of Judaization was adopted. Thousands of acres of Palestinian-owned land were expropriated for the building of Carmiel, Upper Nazareth and other Jewish "development towns." When the Jewish population in the Galilee still did not reach a critical mass, the government established dozens of "outposts" (or "community settlements") on hilltops to ensure territorial control. Identical policies of displacement and Judaization were carried out in the center of the country and in the Negev. By 1954, more than a third of Israel's Jewish population lived either in "abandoned" Arab neighborhoods, towns or villages, or on expropriated Arab lands.[17] The model for what would occur later in the Occupied Territories was clearly emerging.

New legislation was constantly being enacted to prevent the sale, lease or rent to Arab citizens of lands or houses built on either State Lands or lands controlled by the Jewish national institutions. In the critical areas of immigration, settlement and land development, writes Uri Davis in *Apartheid Israel*,

> the Israeli sovereign, the Knesset, which is formally accountable to all its citizens, Jews and non-Jews alike, has formulated and passed legislation ceding state sovereignty (including taxation) and entered into Covenants vesting its responsibilities with organizations such as the WZO, the JA and the JNF, which are constitutionally committed to serving and promoting the interests of Jews and Jews only. It is through this procedure of legal duplicity ... that legal apartheid is regulated in Israel. And it is through this mechanism of legal

duplicity that the State of Israel has successfully veiled the reality of Zionist apartheid in the guise of legal democracy since the establishment of the State of Israel to date.[18]

Security may have been a motivating factor behind the Military Government in the early years of the state. As time went by, however, and the Arab community proved cooperative and even "quiescent,"[19] it became apparent that other forces were at play. Most immediate were fears that the internal refugees, the present absentees, would attempt to return to their lands and their homes. "Consider what would happen if we abolished the restrictions," said the Advisor to the Prime Minister.

> The Arabs who used to live in the empty villages, egged on and organized by the communists, would go back and squat on their ruins, demanding their lands back. What good would that do? Their lands are in use. And then, when they have made as much trouble as possible about their own lands, they will start clamoring for the return of the refugees. They will form organizations, parties, fronts, anything to make trouble.[20]

Segregation and internal fragmentation were also effective ways of preventing political organization. Lustick notes:

> The pattern of structured segmentation – including the Arab community's lack of large urban centers, its division along sectarian lines among Moslem, Druze and several Christian sects, and the fragmentation of Arab villages into antagonistic kinship groups – made the task of the Military Administration considerably easier, for these structural conditions all mitigated against the formation of united independent Arab political groups.[21]

In many ways, Zionist settler colonialism had "triumphed" by 1967. A stable Israeli state and civil society had rooted itself firmly on 78 percent of historic Palestine. The Arab citizens, now a small minority living in contained enclaves, had been pacified over the 18 years of military rule (1948–66) and were now quiescent. The plight of the Palestinian refugees had been largely forgotten. The Israeli military proved capable of defending the state in the wars of 1967 and 1973.

True, the Palestine Liberation Organization (PLO) had emerged and begun engaging in attacks, mainly from outside the country, but it posed no security threat. On the contrary, Israel skillfully used the image of Jews as victims and growing international concern with terrorism to turn Palestinian attacks into fodder for Israeli *hasbara*, arguably strengthening its image.

One could argue that Israel had approached the goal of every settler society: normalization. The state of Israel had been internationally recognized (the Palestinians themselves were to recognize it in 1988), and Israeli Jews saw themselves and were seen by the international community as having superseded the Arabs as natives. The Zionist project had become the only twentieth-century settler movement to attain majority status and international recognition.[22] Had the 1967 war not happened, throwing open again the Palestinian issue and ultimately Israel's legitimacy as a settler state, Israel might well have joined the US, Canada, Australia, New Zealand and other settler states in achieving normalization (despite localized Indigenous protest that erupts from time to time).

THE MANAGEMENT OF LEGITIMACY:
THE ISRAELI STATE CYCLE

Zionism asserted Jewish indigeneity and entitlement to Palestine by appropriating Jewish religious narratives, myths, memories and symbols. These they transformed into a compelling story of national return.[23] For the basic elements of Zionism's foundational narrative, the basis of *hasbara*, we can turn to Israel's Declaration of Independence.

Territory: A Land Without a People

Key to displacing the Palestinians from their land was the need to displace them from their very indigeneity, to present them as a mere "presence" without deep roots in the country. If they could be defined merely as "Arabs," part of the wider Arab world, transferring them out of the country would carry with it no trauma or difficulty. Again, this proposition rested on the Jews becoming an indigenous population "returning" to their country, while the presence of Arabs in the Land of Israel lacked the *national* qualities of Zionism. Israel's Declaration of Independence begins with that narrative. *"The Land of Israel was the birthplace of the Jewish people ... In recent decades, [Jews] returned in their masses. They reclaimed a wilderness, ... They brought blessings of progress to all inhabitants of the country."* Missing, of course, is any reference to the Palestinian Arab people of the country, their national rights and the fact that the "wilderness" was already a people's homeland, consisting of cities, towns and more than a thousand agricultural villages.[24]

Zionism's claim to entitlement over Palestine revolves, then, around an inversion: we, the settlers, are in fact the Indigenous population. The case for Jewish indigeneity rests on three key claims. First, Zionist settlers are in fact Jewish "returnees" coming back to reclaim their native country. This is the basis of settler entitlement, to which the Declaration of Independence devotes most of its text. It rests in turn on three ideological assertions:

(1) *"The Land of Israel was the birthplace of the Jewish people. Here their spiritual, religious and national identity was formed. Here they achieved independence and created a culture of national and universal significance. Here they wrote and gave the Bible to the world"*;

(2) *"Exiled from Palestine, the Jewish people remained faithful to it in all the countries of their dispersion, never ceasing to pray and hope for their return and restoration of their national freedom"*;

(3) *"Impelled by this historic association, Jews strove throughout the centuries to go back to the land of their fathers and regain statehood."*

All three of these assertions have been debunked by historians.[25] So how can the narrative be lifted out of history so that it appears self-evident and is immune from critical analysis – or an alternative Palestinian narrative? Zionist ideologues accomplished this feat by wrapping their national assertions in eternal "rights" ranging from mythical "ties to the Land" and "historical association" to "natural rights," "historic rights," "national rights" and ultimately Divine Promise. The narrative's claim to validity is a "self-evident right of the Jewish people to be a nation, as all other nations."[26] The primordial national claim was then given academic weight by several generations of Zionist historians. Their task was to build a case for unbroken "historical affinity" or a "national bond" between the Jewish people and the land, stretching from Abraham until today.[27] To render it unassailable by historic argument, the Zionist narrative asserted that "God gave us this land." It was a somewhat cynical claim from militantly secular Zionists, but effective. Israel's Declaration of Independence ends with the phrase: *"With trust in Almighty God."*

A second claim to entitlement has to do with the persecution Jews have suffered, the Holocaust in particular, and their understandable need for refuge.[28] Jews, like other asylum seekers and refugees, do have a right to refuge as individuals in Palestine or elsewhere. But to extend that individual right to a collective one and then use it as a pretext to take over someone else's country and displace them is unsupportable in international law. On the contrary, colonialism in all its forms is condemned by the Declaration on the Granting of Independence to Colonial Countries and Peoples, adopted by the UN General Assembly in 1960. Its first Article reads: "The subjection of peoples to alien subjugation, domination and exploitation constitutes a denial of fundamental human rights, is contrary to the Charter of the United Nations and is an impediment to the promotion of world peace and co-operation."

The UN Declaration goes on to state: "All peoples have the right to self-determination." How and if this applies to Jews is an open question. The vast majority of Jews abroad do not consider themselves part of a Jewish *nation* (versus a vaguer notion of a *people*). Nor do many Jews in Israel, especially the ultra-orthodox, accept this national status.[29] Then comes the question, can the self-determination of one people come at the expense of others? This was precisely the question – what do the people of Palestine want? – that moved President Wilson to dispatch the King-Crane Commission to Palestine.

The Declaration on the Granting of Independence to Colonial Countries and Peoples goes on to state: "[Article] 4. All armed action or repressive measures of all kinds directed against dependent peoples shall cease in order to enable them to exercise peacefully and freely their right to complete independence, and the integrity of their national territory shall be respected"; and "6. Any attempt aimed at the partial or total disruption of the national unity and the territorial integrity of a country is incompatible with the purposes and principles of the Charter of the United Nations."

It is clear that settler colonialism cannot be a remedy for Jewish claims to self-determination, especially when it conflicts both with the rights of other peoples and with the principle of majority rule. The plan later advocated in this book explores what appears to be the only substantially just and workable resolution of a settler colonial situation: decolonization, followed by the establishment of a single constitutional democracy.

Finally, settler Zionism claims entitlement and legitimacy from the international recognition it has received. The Declaration of Independence cites three sources of political legitimacy: the Balfour Declaration and its incorporation into the British Mandate, and the UN resolution of 1947 calling for the establishment of a Jewish and an Arab state. International recognition alone does not confer legitimacy under international law (ask the Armenians or Kurds after World War I, or present-day Taiwan). Even though the British government issued the Balfour Declaration as a diplomatic position paper, it carried with it no legal or political authority. In fact, it was only one of three diplomatic documents that Britain negotiated, each with a different promise to the local populations. In the Hussein-McMahon correspondence during World War I, the British agreed to recognize Arab independence after the war if the Sharif of Mecca would launch an Arab revolt against the Ottoman Empire, which he did. At the same time (1916), the British signed the secret Sykes-Picot Agreement with France in which they agreed to divide the Ottoman territories between them after the war.[30] By supporting the establishment of a "national Jewish home" in Palestine, the Balfour Declaration contradicted the other two. Such a position certainly violated the spirit and the letter of British commitments to the Arabs in general and to the people of Palestine in particular, as the King-Crane Commission made clear.

The same could be said for the 1947 UN partition of Palestine into a Jewish and an Arab state. Given the outspoken opposition of the indigenous Palestinians, two-thirds of the country's inhabitants, partition lacked both moral and legal authority. It lacked moral authority because the UN *knew* that ethnic cleansing would be the outcome of its decision. The UN knowingly entrusted the fate of an entire people to a settler movement declaring its exclusive entitlement to the country, and its readiness to employ violent conquest and transfer.[31] Legally the partition plan contained a fundamental contradiction. If it required a Palestinian state to arise alongside a Jewish one, then Zionism's declared policy of Judaizing by force the entire country – which in fact happened – nullifies it. The international community has continued to legitimize the Zionist settler project even though it has known full well for seven decades and more that its agenda is to eliminate a national Palestinian presence in the country.

Zionism's attempt to reduce the Arab presence to a merely cultural one – always careful to avoid the national term "Palestinian" – also played a prime role in disappearing the natives. This is most graphically illustrated in the foundational Zionist slogan: "A land without a people for a people without a land." The Zionists saw and interacted with Palestinian Arabs, of course, but did not grant them any national rights. The Declaration of Independence refers only to "the Arab inhabitants of the state of Israel."

Ben-Zion Dinur was the most foundational and ideological of Israel's historians. Israel's first Minister of Education, he was the main authority that introduced the Zionist narrative into the nation's schools.[32] In his teachings, the Arabs enter the picture only in 634 CE, when the Muslim army conquered Palestine. They have remained foreign occupiers ever since, decreed Dinur. By contrast, the Jews had always held on to the Land of Israel as their only homeland. As the Declaration of Independence says, they "remained faithful to it in all the countries of their dispersion, never ceasing to pray and hope for their return and restoration of their national freedom." By marking the entrance of the native Arabs into the geographic space coveted by the Zionists only at some later historical stage – 634 CE, according to Dinur – Jews win the race for indigeneity.[33] Unlike in the US, Canada or Australia, Palestinians were never accorded the status of "First Nations." Transfer is preferred by settler societies to subjugation, and "transfer by conceptual displacement" enables that physical expulsion.[34]

The claim that the Indigenous are less than a people with national rights is reflected in Zionism's portrayal of the Arab population. They are presented in Zionist discourse as semi-visible, unnamed individuals living in unnamed localities, elusive, insubstantial, apathetic, aimless, disorganized, impermanent, primitive, irrational – and above all violent and intractable. This Veracini calls "narrative transfer."[35] Yet another form of transfer is "Indigenous criminalization,"[36] the reducing of a people and their resistance to violent displacement and disenfranchisement to "terrorism" and, in the words of Israel's Declaration of Independence, "wanton aggression."

Normalizing Colonialism

The ultimate goal of a settler colonial project is to extinguish itself. Veracini labels as "supersession" the supplanting of a colonial situation with one of normalization, the disappearing of the colonial past.[37] This entails glossing over the violence inherent in the settlers achieving independence, or casting it as heroic self-defense. The settlers cast themselves as the peace-seeking ones. As Israel's Declaration of Independence says, "[Jews] sought peace, yet were ever prepared to defend themselves." By abdicating all responsibility and laying the blame for "wanton violence" on the colonized, the Zionists effectively delegitimized both Palestinian resistance and the very cause of Palestinian nationalism itself. Moreover, according to the narrative of the Declaration of Independence, the Zionists *"brought blessings of progress to all inhabitants of the country."* It is therefore up to the *Arabs "to return to the ways of peace"* by submitting to the settlers and normalizing life under their rule. We, the Zionists, are innocent.

Disregarding the violent process of Judaizing Palestine, we are left with a magnanimous and *civilized* Israel whose values are *"based on precepts of liberty, justice and peace taught by the Hebrew prophets."* It is that benevolent and forgiving settler movement that now calls on the remnants of the Palestinian inhabitants of a country now renamed "Israel" ("transfer by name confiscation")[38] *"to co-operate with the independent Jewish nation for the common good of all ...."* (This, as they were about to begin 18 years of military rule.) Progress in solidifying Israel's legitimacy and "making peace" is measured by the degree of Indigenous displacement and submission.

Normalization of the settler condition is settler colonialism's ultimate aim. It goes beyond the claim to indigeneity. "We came first" is only part of the equation. That we are actually products of the land, "the land made us," we *are* the land. Now that's the ultimate belonging.[39] "We came to this land to build and be rebuilt by it" – this is a classic Zionist slogan. The outcome is nothing less than the New Hebrew Man, the antithesis of the weakly ghetto Jew. He (do with the gender what you will) represents the ultimate native, the product of the soil, a reconstituted human being physically as well as mentally. The *sabra*. Even the coopting of this most Palestinian symbol makes its point: the land, even the archetypal Arab landscape, is actually Hebrew, of the Jewish nation.[40] There is nothing Arab that is indigenous.

It was after the outbreak of the Arab Revolt in 1936 that the idea of Jewish statehood crystallized as a declared political program. It became the official program of Zionism when the Zionist leadership announced the Biltmore Program, calling for a Jewish Commonwealth, in 1942. Vague notions of a "national home" were replaced by concrete military and political goals. Ben-Gurion, who assumed the leadership of the Jewish Agency, the Zionist government-in-the-making, declared: "[This is a] decision based on force, a Jewish military decision.... We want the Land of Israel in its entirety. That was the original intention."[41]

Hasbara

During the pre-state and state cycles of colonialism, *hasbara* was a straightforward form of public diplomacy. It was conducted by the Israeli government, its official Zionist bodies and Jewish lobbyists.[42] Until the rise of Menachem Begin's government in 1977, Zionism had largely succeeded in "disappearing" the Palestinian issue within the broader Arab-Israel Conflict.

Israel also had powerful sources of *hasbara* besides its political case. We cannot ignore, of course, the influence the Holocaust had in the establishment of Israel. Sympathy for the Jews formed a public backdrop to the political intrigues, as did guilt over the Holocaust. On a more practical note, Europe and the allies were faced with the dilemma of where to resettle a quarter of a million displaced Jewish persons (DPs) who refused to return to their countries of origin that had persecuted them. More than half of the DPs found their way to Palestine despite British attempts to stop them. This placed Britain in an extremely unfavorable light and generated public support for a Jewish state. In the end, circumstances forced the hand of the international community. The rising intensity of Arab-Jewish fighting in Palestine, the seeming impossibility of arriving at any effective plan other than partition, the British insistence on cutting their losses and departing Palestine, and *hasbara* focused on the Jews' fight for freedom in the wake of the Holocaust – all these factors forced the UN vote for establishing a Jewish and an Arab state.[43]

Perhaps the most influential piece of Zionist propaganda was not the product of a state agency at all, but sprang from the pen of the American-Jewish writer Leon Uris. His book *Exodus*, published in 1958, was translated into 50 languages and made into a major motion picture starring Paul Newman. Ben-Gurion proclaimed: "as a piece of propaganda, it's the greatest thing ever written about Israel."[44] And, indeed, the book and film popularized Zionism's founding narrative at the expense of the Palestinians. They were displaced once again by the emblematic figure of the heroic (and European) sabra fighting for his/her biblical/modern homeland against a dark, fanatical enemy.[45]

Since Israel virtually "sold itself" in the years before the 1967 war, Prime Minister Ben-Gurion did not find much need to pursue an orchestrated campaign of *hasbara*. That would come after the war, when Israel's occupation of the West Bank, East Jerusalem and Gaza became more contentious issues. And even more so after the rise of Menachem Begin to power in 1977, as we will see in the next chapter.

The "logic" of Zionism's settler project over the past half-century was clear. True, decisions were made, plans shelved and rethought, timelines adjusted, successes and failure registered. The very acceptance of the Partition Plan of 1947 by the Zionists is an indication of different voices and different strategies at work. So was Israel's willingness to compromise over land with Jordan at the start of the 1948 war.[46] Alternative outcomes were certainly possible at this time, as the struggle over control of the army and of national policy heightened.[47] Still, Israel's conquest of the rest of Palestine just 19 years later, its annexation of East Jerusalem and its immediate embarking on settlement construction in the Occupied Territory points to a political trajectory that cannot be denied.[48]

5

The Occupation Cycle (1967–Present): Completing the Settler Colonial Project

Zionism's colonial project took a leap forward in June 1967, when Israel conquered the remaining parts of historic Palestine, the West Bank, including "east" Jerusalem, and Gaza. During the course of the war, 350,000 Palestinians, most of them refugees from the 1948 war, once again left their homes and refugee camps. Most fled to Jordan. After the fighting subsided, 120,000 of them applied to the Israeli authorities to return to their homes, their absolute right under international law. Only 14,000 were allowed to do so.[1] Over the next two or three years, the Israeli authorities demolished some 8000 Palestinian homes and imprisoned, deported or forced the emigration of thousands of residents of the OPT in a campaign of de-Arabization that continues until today.[2]

Extending the Dominance Management Regime over the Occupied Territory was easy. The Regime had already been constructed over the past seven decades, in the form of the Military Government imposed on the Palestinian citizens of Israel in 1948. By 1966, when it was lifted, it was in fine working order. With the occupation of the West Bank and Gaza only seven months later, all that needed to be done was to transfer the institutions, policies and personnel of the Military Government into the West Bank and Gaza. Whether the West Bank and Gaza were occupied, as the international community saw it, or whether Judea and Samaria had been liberated, Israel's view, didn't really matter. The occupation regime could last indefinitely or, like the Military Government, be easily dismantled when and if the occupation ended. Since Zionism claimed the entire country, with Judea and Samaria being the heart of the Land of Israel, annexation, *de facto* or *de jure*, appeared the only options.

The fundamental difference between the occupation of 1967 and the incorporation of the lands it conquered in 1948 into Israel was the issue of citizenship. The massive displacement of Palestinians in what became Israel had left so few that they could be given citizenship without endangering Jewish demographic domination – especially with the importation of 700,000 Jews from post-Holocaust Europe and the Muslim world between 1948 and 1953. That could not happen with the territory taken in 1967, whose Palestinian population numbered more than a million. Whereas the 150,000 Palestinians who remained within what became Israel were brought into Israel's political system, albeit under a military government, Israel had to invent a new kind of governance for the Palestinians of the Occupied Territory. How could they be placed under effective, perhaps permanent, Israeli control, yet without extending to them citizenship? That, and continuing to present the settler state of Israel as "the only democracy in the Middle East," a normal, peace-seeking country.

To accomplish this feat, Israeli governance would have to fall somewhere between hegemony – "soft power" exercised from afar – and direct political and military control. The Dominance Management Regime, so effective during the first two cycles of settlement, was up to the task. Let's look at how it has been adapted to Israel's need to govern Palestinians in the Occupied Palestinian Territory.

FOUNDATIONAL VIOLENCE/MANAGEMENT OF SECURITY: THE OCCUPATION CYCLE

The 1967 war opened yet another cycle of foundational violence, this time by conquering the rest of historic Palestine/the Land of Israel. Strong as the "logic" of settler colonialism might have been, the question of what to do with the Occupied Palestinian Territory (OPT), the West Bank (though not East Jerusalem, which was immediately annexed) and Gaza generated great debate, hesitation, alternative plans, contradictory policies and ad hoc actions during the first decade of occupation. No long-term decisions were made.[3] One thing was clear, though. The Israeli government would not negotiate with the Palestinians nor even entertain the possibility of a Palestinian state.

As it was, the combination of the settler "logic," supporting ideologies, religious fervor and political opportunities propelled the colonial project onward. Instead of leveraging a resolution of "the conflict," the 1967 war inaugurated the third and final cycle of foundational violence, the occupation. The conquest of the rest of Palestine confirmed in the eyes of many Israelis the necessity and efficacy of militarism in determining political realities.[4] The Israeli political scientist Ze'ev Maoz[5] points to an Israeli "proclivity to amass and use excessive military force despite diminishing threats." For Israelis, he says,

> security has consistently dominated foreign policy. In virtually every major decision process, security considerations supersede diplomatic considerations…. The dominance of the security establishment in Israeli political affairs [derives from] the excessive involvement of former military personnel in almost every aspect of Israel political, social, and economic life. An "old boys' network" was formed within the Israeli political elite, composed of former generals who have entered political life across the entire left-right continuum…. [T]his network is characterized by a shared set of basic political and military beliefs – which largely follow Ben-Gurion's strategic philosophy.[6]

The denial of Palestinian national rights and the tautology of security gives rise to the seemingly "professional" views of military experts in Zionism. Presenting their "security challenges" as objective reality, couching their "analysis" in the politically neutral language of security, they construct a logic that "objectively" rules out any possibility of decolonization, peace, reconciliation and, ironically, genuine security.

A collection of essays by some of Israel's top military strategists, *Israel's Critical Security Requirements for Defensible Borders: The Foundation for a Viable Peace*,[7] illustrates the tautology guiding Israeli military and political doctrines. While they make sense in purely military terms, when applied to the colonial reality that Zionism has created they become what the sociologist C. Wright Mills[8] called "crackpot realism" – views, strategies, policies and actions that defeat any attempt to break out of the circular military/security logic towards an actual resolution. What are the military principles guiding Israeli security and political policies?

- *The Palestinians are Israel's permanent enemies; the Middle East is irrevocably hostile to Israel.*

[S]ince the beginning of the conflict, even before the founding of the state and all the way through the Oslo Accords, the readiness of the Zionist leadership to reach an historic compromise has failed to convince the Palestinians to forgo their commitment to "armed struggle" and other forms of opposition to the right of the Jewish people to live peacefully in a nation-state of their own in their historic home, the Land of Israel…. The lessons learned … is that the Palestinians have adhered to their historical narrative of armed struggle that denies Israel's right to exist as a Jewish nation-state, regardless of signed agreements or unilateral Israeli withdrawals.[9]

"The lessons learned" by Moshe Yaalon, a former IDF Chief of Staff and Defense Minister, that the Palestinians' historical narrative "denies Israel right to exist as a Jewish nation-state," is both wrong and justifiably right. Wrong in that the Palestinians under Arafat and the PLO did in fact recognize Israel *as a legitimate state* in 1988. (Albeit, whether Israel should be a "Jewish" state or not they left for the Israelis to decide.) Yaalon is right that the Palestinians will never recognize the "right to exist" of the Jewish colonial nation-state that dispossessed them, but, again, why should they? Does the Israeli military establishment really believe that the Palestinians can, even should, recognize the settler regime that seeks to displace and replace them? Arising from the logic of colonialism, Yaalon's views fall into the realm of the "shared set of basic political and military beliefs" Maoz refers to, not of professional military analysis.

- *Security-based diplomacy.*

Israel's vital security requirements and a conditional endorsement of a Palestinian state were laid out by Prime Minister Benjamin Netanyahu in his first major policy speech at Bar-Ilan University … in April 2009. [The] ideas he endorsed represent a restoration of Israel's traditional security-based approach to achieving a lasting peace.[10]

The "security-based" approach is doublespeak. It appears to present a logical and reasonable demand, that Israel's security come first in any negotiations. But it actually means that the Palestinians must accept Israel's legitimacy as a *Jewish* state. "Security-based diplomacy" negates Palestinian sovereignty. It requires the Palestinians' admitting the legitimacy of Zionism and its settler project in Palestine, its annexation of East Jerusalem and its continued military control over the entire country. "Peace," for Israel, means Palestinian submission to their own elimination as a people.

- *Active and constant military presence.*

Today, the relative calm on Israel's borders and in Judea and Samaria should not be misinterpreted.... [The] IDF has been working around the clock to uproot the terror infrastructure in many Palestinian areas.... The recent decline in Palestinian violence [represents]... a growing realization that Palestinian terror doesn't pay.[11]

Every colonial regime employs the same language. Palestinian resistance to colonialism, occupation, apartheid and oppression is reduced to "terrorism." This, of course, removes entirely the political context of colonialization, as it is intended to do. In this way Israel comes across as a normal country defending itself against terrorism as all normal countries would, while Palestinian resistance is criminalized, depoliticized and delegitimized. This is the hidden subtext of "security-based diplomacy."

- *No return to 1949 armistice line/1967 borders.*

Israeli withdrawal to the perilous 1949 armistice lines ... would not achieve peace – they would weaken Israel and invite war by denying the Jewish state strategic depth and topographical protection against Palestinian rocket and other attacks.[12]

From here, Yaalon's logic becomes clear. Now that we have established "objectively" and professionally that Israel's security demands military control over all of Palestine, he does not even have to argue the details anymore. The need for Israeli domination becomes self-evident.

- *Maintaining control over strategic parts of the West Bank and of a "greater" Jerusalem; Use of settlements for land and population management.*

Israel's security depends on … maintaining control over key areas of Judea and Samaria and certainly over an undivided Jerusalem…. In the event that the Palestinians obtain full sovereignty in Judea and Samaria, those areas – as Gaza before them – may be quickly taken over by Hamas and become staging grounds for attacks on Israel.[13]

[T]he mere discussion of removing Israeli settlements encourages jihadists across the globe…. We have learned from bitter experience that territorial withdrawals do not alleviate grievances; they indicate weakness and convince Israel's enemies that victory is possible.[14]

Now that Yaalon has established "security" as the primary condition for determining Israeli policy and has raised the bar so high that he knows the Palestinians can never reach it, inconvenient political issues can be removed from the agenda. The disposal of the Occupied Territory, settlements, Palestinian claims, human rights and international law, the need for regional peace, UN resolutions and negotiations – all these subsumed to Israel's indisputable, self-evident security needs. The securitization of the conflict effectively depoliticizes it.

- *Palestinian state will not have territorial contiguity.*

Palestinians might construe American references to contiguity as including a Palestinian-controlled connection from the West Bank to the Gaza Strip, like the "safe passage" mentioned in the Oslo Accords. But this would entail bifurcating Israel in two.[15]

The Israeli settlement blocs occupy 30 percent of the West Bank (plus East Jerusalem), but they also destroy any territorial contiguity a Palestinian state may have on the remaining 70 percent. Israel proposes "transportational contiguity": the ability of Palestinians to drive from one West Bank city to another, but under Israeli supervision. Nor would the West Bank be connected to Gaza. Again, having established an unreachable baseline of security, it justifies *any* Israeli concession to the Palestinians. The tautology is complete.

- *No Palestinian state, merely autonomy.*

Israeli policy immediately following the Six- Day War in 1967, and up to the Oslo Accords in 1993, centered on finding a formula that would enable Israel to avoid ruling over the Palestinians, without returning to the unstable pre-war '67 lines.... [T]he Netanyahu government is readopting the notion [of] ... defensible borders, a demilitarized Palestinian entity, control of a unified airspace with Judea and Samaria, electromagnetic communications frequency security, and other guarantees.[16]

Security defines the political parameters. Since any political settlement with the Palestinians must conform to Israeli security conceptions, which by nature preclude any political outcome, we are left at best with autonomy. Relieving itself of almost 5 million Palestinians under its control while confining them to truncated enclaves on 10 percent of their homeland is *of course* the only political option a settler regime like Israel could adopt, since it alone makes possible a successionist Jewish state. The beauty of the security paradigm is that it *requires* apartheid. No need exists to justify its political or moral terms. This closed circle of political/security thinking is evident in the security "requirements" set out by Israel's crackpot realists.

- *Validating Settler Colonialism: The Palestinians not only recognize the State of Israel but recognize it as a "Jewish state."*

Perhaps the most important element of a viable security frame-work is the requirement that the Palestinians at all levels of society inculcate in their people a culture of peace that forswears indoctrination and incitement to violence and terror, and accepts the Jewish people's 3,300-year connection to the Land of Israel and its right to live in Israel – the Jewish nation-state – in peace and security.[17]

Finally, Yaalon swings back to the original security "requirement" that defines and justifies Israel's apartheid while placing the blame for the conflict squarely at the feet of the Palestinians. Once the Palestinians "forswear indoctrination and incitement to violence and terror" and "accept the Jewish nation-state" – that is, give up their aspirations for national self-determination in their homeland and end their anti-colonial struggle – all will be fine. After all, once we achieve Palestinian acquiescence and "peace and security" for Israelis in an Israeli-controlled country, what more is there to negotiate?

POPULATION AND LAND MANAGEMENT:
THE OCCUPATION CYCLE

The third and final phase of the Zionist settler project began even before the 1967 war ended. On the fifth day of the Six Day War, the first act of occupation occurred, unrelated to any necessary military action. The Israeli authorities demolished the Moroccan Quarter in the Old City of Jerusalem in order to make room for the thousands of Israelis who were expected to come and pray at the Western Wall – 135 homes were hastily demolished in the dead of night, 650 residents were displaced; one elderly woman, too slow to get out her house, was killed.[18]

In short order Israel had conquered the rest of historic Palestine and instituted a military regime over the OPT. Yet Israel has never accepted the legal fact of occupation since it contradicts Zionism's claim of entitlement to the whole of the Land of Israel. It also denies the very notion of occupation, which denotes a territory outside of one's own, potentially detachable and subject to negotiations. Since 1967, Israel has considered its conquest of "Judea and Samaria" to be nothing less than the final stage of "redeeming" the Land of Israel. (Though it might accept, even welcome, the detachment of Gaza from Greater Israel for demographic reasons.) Israeli rule extends today from the River and the Sea, with almost 700,000 settlers now living in massive settlement "blocs" on land that will never be de-occupied. (Again, it is noteworthy that Israelis routinely use the term "settler" (*mitnakhel*), although the government is acutely aware of the subversiveness of this term to its claim of entitlement, and so it enforces the "politically correct" term of "resident" (*mityashev*) in the media when referring to Israelis living in the Occupied Territory.)

For Israel, then, the problem was more than just establishing military rule over an occupied territory, or countering the very notion of occupation. It was how to complete the colonial project and normalize it. Yigal Allon, the commander of the military operations responsible for the expulsion of the greatest number of Arab refugees in the 1948 war and a government minister during the Six Day War, wrote just before the outbreak of fighting in 1967: "In case of a new war, we must avoid the historic mistake of the War of Independence and, ... must not cease fighting until we achieve total victory, the territorial fulfillment of the Land of Israel."[19] Yitzhak Rabin, then Chief of Staff, exhorted his troops on the Jordanian front to "complete what we were unable to finish" in 1948.[20]

The mechanism for completing the task of colonization was the Dominance Management Regime, augmented by a repressive security apparatus. In the pre-state cycle of colonization the Zionists enjoyed the support and cooperation of the British, who vacillated between active intervention on behalf of the Yishuv and a turning of the head, but who, overall, put their Mandate regime at the Zionists' disposal. During the Israeli state cycle, the Military Government carried the burden of security, population control and the grabbing of land from the Palestinians. Almost immediately from the ending of the Military Government in 1966 to its reincarnation in the OPT just seven months later, the Dominance Management Regime began to take on the form of apartheid. Indeed, the occupation cycle sees the rise of a hybrid regime over Palestine, a deadly combination of settler colonialism, occupation and apartheid.

The Matrix of Control

Enter the Matrix of Control, a maze of laws, military orders, planning procedures, limitations on movement, kafkaesque bureaucracy, settlements and infrastructure intended to complete the Zionist colonization of Palestine and marginalize the Palestinians – all enforced by constant low-intensity warfare. It is by no means an invention of the occupation cycle. As a strategy of domination, expansion and control, its roots, as the previous chapters show, go back to the start of Zionism. Significant parts of the Matrix also retain elements of the British Mandate. In particular, the British Emergency Regulations of 1945 gave form to the Military Government imposed on the Palestinian citizens of Israel between 1948 and 1966, which was transferred wholly into the OPT in 1967. Hiding behind a facade of "security and "proper administration," the Matrix plays a key role in finalizing Zionist colonialism over the 22 percent of Palestine whose incorporation into the Land of Israel has yet to be completed. It creates colonial "facts on the ground," appropriating the land and securing the population (both settler and Palestinian). By allowing the military to operate in an unhurried manner over decades, the Matrix provides that time span needed to normalize the Israeli presence in the West Bank, a strategy that has shown its effectiveness. The international community has long abandoned the two-state solution as anything more than a mechanism of conflict management; the Trump Plan has actually accepted the annexation of the settlement blocs; and many Arab governments have normalized relations with Israel despite its ongoing occupation. The occupation has not been "normalized" by the Palestinians, of course, or by much of the Arab population of the region, but it represents for Israel "sufficient normalization" and annexation.[21]

I have written at length about the Matrix of Control in a previous book.[22] Let's focus here on what the Matrix contributes to our foremost concern, settler colonialism. How does it manage demographic dominance, control of the land and control of the population?

Demographic Domination and Control of the Land

The Matrix enables the establishment of demographic and physical "facts on the ground" that are so massive and irreversible they foreclose any threat to their eventual incorporation into Israel, to Judaization. More than 250 settlements that have been constructed in the OPT, home to around 750,000 Israeli settlers, have moved across the 1967 boundaries (400,000 in the West Bank and 350,000 in East Jerusalem).[23] Israel is today consolidating these discrete settlements into seven major settlement "blocs" so as to create contiguous areas of Israeli control.[24] To do so, it has expropriated about 24 percent of the West Bank for settlements, highways, "bypass roads," military installations, nature reserves and infrastructure. It refuses to recognize Ottoman or British-era Palestinian deeds, meaning that 72 percent of the West Bank is considered Israeli "state lands" and may be confiscated at any time.[25] A Regularization Law, passed by the Knesset in 2017, allows Israel to retroactively expropriate private Palestinian land on which settlements have been illegally built.[26] In this way it confines Palestinians to small and disconnected enclaves (de-Arabization) while expanding its settlements (Judaization). With the signing of Oslo

II in 1995, the West Bank was fragmented into Areas A, B and C, locking 95 percent of the Palestinian population into 64 tiny enclaves. Almost all of Palestinian East Jerusalem is "open green space," prohibiting Palestinian construction. Palestinians constitute 38 percent of Jerusalem's population yet have access to only 7 percent of the urban land for residential and community purposes.[27] Gaza, one of the most densely packed places on earth, has been under Israeli lockdown, siege and military attack since the late 1980s.

The fragmentation of the West Bank is most graphically illustrated by the 26 major Israeli highways that crisscross its length and breadth. Lined on both sides with "sanitary" margins three to four football fields wide, they eliminate all Palestinian homes, fields and orchards in their path. Some are "apartheid roads" in that they have walls down the middle separating Israeli and Palestinian drivers. On others, Palestinians cannot drive.[28] These highways incorporate the West Bank into Israel's national infrastructure, making it impossible to detach the Palestinian territories from Israel proper.[29] In the meantime, Israeli settlers enjoy a safe space in which to live and travel, never having to encounter an Arab.

Add to all this the "Separation Barrier" running through the entire length of the West Bank, 712 kilometers (460 miles) of concrete walls, in the rural areas turning to electronic fences fortified by watchtowers, sniper posts, mine fields, a ditch 4 meters deep, barbed wire, security perimeters, surveillance cameras, electronic warning devices and patrols of killer dogs. The barrier annexes *de facto* 25–45 percent of the West Bank, including some of its richest agricultural and olive-growing land. Designed, as its name indicates, to separate Jewish from Palestinian populations., the physical expression of apartheid leaves 80 percent of the settlers on the "Israeli side."[30]

The Matrix of Control employs industrial parks, located in settlements throughout the West Bank and on the border of Gaza, as a means of exploiting cheap Palestinian labor while preventing workers from entering Israel. By allowing some of its First World economy to trickle into the Palestinian areas, Israel robs Palestinian areas of their economic vitality, ensuring their continued dependence on Israel. Because of lax environmental standards in the Occupied Territories – the industrial parks house Israel's most polluting industries, aluminum factories, metalworks, plastic and chemical concerns and slaughter-houses – they turn the OPT into a dump for Israeli industrial wastes.[31]

The Israeli architect Eyal Weizman[32] describes Israel's Matrix of Control as a "vertical occupation," extending beneath the ground and into the sky. In spite of international law that forbids an Occupying Power to loot the resources of an occupied territory, Israel takes about 30 percent of its water from the West Bank and Gazan aquifers located under its settlements. Fully 87 percent of the water coming from the West Bank is channeled to Israel and its settlements, only 17 percent to its 2.7 million Palestinians.[33] Massive rock quarries, whose materials are used in Israeli settlement and road construction, scar the historic and fragile landscape. And Israel controls the West Bank and Gazan airspace, including its electromagnetic communications fields, enabling it to control and attack by means of an all-seeing and precise "aerial occupation."

Population Control by Legal and Administrative Means; the Use of Military Orders

The Matrix also employs bureaucracy, planning and law as tools of occupation and control, mainly through Israel's Civil Administration, established in 1981 in order to lower the military profile of the occupation. Despite its name, the Civil Administration is headed by a high-ranking IDF officer under the auspices of the Ministry of Defense, although it does employ some (settler) civilian workers. The Civil Administration is charged with the administration of life in the OPT. In fact, it controls the Palestinian population by entangling them in a tight web of restrictions and penalties that also lessen the need to deploy the military. Its only genuine development projects involve settlement construction and providing the infrastructure they require.

The legal and bureaucratic control mechanisms employed for population control and land expropriation are embodied in a corpus of almost 1400 military orders. Israel is forbidden by the Fourth Geneva Convention from extending its legal system onto the Occupied Territory. So it has turned to the use of military orders that, in fact, constitute a legal regime but avoid the prohibitions. They grow out of the British Emergency Regulations of 1945 and those of the Military

97

Government imposed on Palestinian citizens of Israel between 1948 and 1966. Together, they control the tiniest details of Palestinian life.

Military Order 59, for example, grants the Israeli Custodian of Abandoned Properties the authority to declare uncultivated land as Israeli "state land." Order 270 designates a further million dunams (250,000 acres) of West Bank land as closed "combat zones," which are then handed over to settlers or Israeli infrastructure. Order 363 imposes severe restrictions on construction and land use in yet other areas zoned as "nature reserves." Order 393 grants any military commander in Judea and Samaria the authority to prohibit Palestinian construction to ensure the security of the Israeli army or "public order." Hundreds of other military orders effectively curb the development of Arab communities, alienate land from its Palestinian owners and impose a draconian system of control and punishment. And more. Military Order 107 bans publications, including works on Arabic grammar, histories of the Crusades and studies of Arab nationalism. Military Order 998 requires Palestinians to get Israeli military permission to make a withdrawal from their bank account.[34]

The Civil Administration also employs administrative measures which severely restrict Palestinian freedom of movement, and which induce emigration. The Civil Administration has divided the West Bank into "security zones" between which Palestinians need permits to travel, and many roads on the West Bank are closed to private Palestinian vehicles. A system of magnetic cards issued to each Palestinian worker enables Israel to monitor Palestinian movement. Thousands of spouses live apart because they cannot get permits for "family reunification."

Among the most debilitating of administrative measures are the discriminatory zoning and planning policies. Hiding Israel's political agenda behind a facade of technical maps, "neutral" professional jargon and seemingly innocuous administrative procedures, they obstruct the development of Palestinian towns and villages and keep Area C, 62 percent of the West Bank, "free" for Israeli settlement. Israel uses two planning documents from the days of the British Mandate – the Jerusalem Regional Planning Scheme (RJ5) of 1942 and the Samaria Regional Planning Scheme (RS15) of 1945) – to freeze Palestinian development in Jerusalem and the West Bank as it was in the 1940s. RS15, for example, zones the entire West Bank as "agricultural land."

Since Israel routinely denies Palestinians building permits, it has induced a severe housing shortage, which contributes to outmigration. Israel has demolished about 55,000 "structures," many of them homes and multistory apartment blocks containing dozens of housing units, since 1967.[35]

Military Controls and Military Strikes

For all the administrative elements of the Matrix of Control, force continues to underlie Israeli control of the OPT and its ongoing settler project. Outright military attacks on resistance groups (invariably labeled "terrorist"), on civilian population centers and on Palestinian infrastructure are daily occurrences. They are not, however, Israel's preferred means of control. Military operations are too visible, too liable to rouse international as well as internal Palestinian opposition, as happened during the Intifadas or the repeated attacks on Gaza. More effective are low-intensity, ceaseless "counterterrorism operations."[36]

The extensive use of collaborators is especially effective – and debilitating – to Palestinian society. Taking a leaf from pre-state and pre-1967 tactics,[37] thousands of Palestinians have been turned unwillingly into collaborators. It was once estimated that between 120,000 and 150,000 individuals, or 5 percent of the Palestinian population under occupation, have been "recruited" through threats, extortion and "incentives."[38] Simple acts like obtaining a driver's or business license, a work permit, a permit to build a house, a travel document or permission to receive hospital care can be conditioned on supplying information to the security services. Collaborators come in many varieties. Some arrange land transfers to settlers, others intermediate between the military administration and the Palestinian population or inform on their neighbors. Still others infiltrate into political organizations, or even assist in interrogations.[39]

Mass arrests and administrative detention are other direct means of military control out of the public eye. According to Addameer, the Palestinian Prisoners' Support and Human Rights Association, over 800,000 Palestinians have been detained by Israel in the Occupied Territories between 1967 and 2014 – approximately 40 percent of the total male population.[40]

A sophisticated system for Judaizing, pacifying and achieving "sufficient normalization," the Matrix of Control represents the most operationally effective expression yet of the Iron Wall.

ECONOMIC MANAGEMENT: THE OCCUPATION CYCLE

The political decision-making regarding the OPT has taken time to consolidate. The economic management of East Jerusalem, the West Bank and Gaza began immediately upon occupation. Early on, Israel adopted a policy of controlling the Palestinian population – perhaps even coopting its business leaders – by fostering a functioning economy. Thus, in the early years of occupation, it adopted a more light-handed policy of economic management in keeping with its notion of an "enlightened occupation." Israel allowed Palestinians to continue to trade with Jordan and the Arab world through its "open bridges" policy. It sent experts to develop agriculture and modernize the Palestinian economy. It encouraged tourism. And it imported thousands of (cheap) Palestinian workers into Israeli workplaces. All this brought a wave of relative prosperity to the OPT that lasted for two decades.[41]

Israel's intentions, as we noted, were not altruistic. Bringing the Palestinian economy under its control and regulating it closely created a dependency on Israel that it could manipulate. And over time Israel's economic policy became one of de-development. Palestinian industries and banks were restricted in their activities so as not to compete with Israeli ones. A third of the Palestinian workforce become casual laborers in Israel or in the growing Israeli settlements, their work permits dependent on "good behavior." Many Palestinians had to find work abroad. Remittances from the Gulf States became a primary source of OPT income. Land was progressively lost to settlements, settlement infrastructure and military bases, constricting agriculture. The ban on new construction and Israel's policy of demolishing Palestinian homes worsened housing conditions. By the outbreak of the first Intifada in 1987, economic prosperity had shriveled and the Palestinians found themselves living under an increasingly repressive regime.[42]

Even a certain rise in economic standards could not offset the political repression that led to the first Intifada in 1987. From that uprising emerged the Oslo peace process. Although placing emphasis on economic development as a key to peace, Israel imposed an economic closure over the OPT at the very start of the Oslo negotiations. The dilemma it inherited in 1967 – how to rule over a population and take its land without granting it civil rights – only intensified by the early 1990s. By that time the Palestinian population of the OPT had doubled from 1 million in 1967 to 2 million (today it numbers 5 million). Over the two decades that had passed, Israel had made the decision to permanently incorporate the West Bank (if not Gaza) into Israel. It was moving into the West Bank a large settler population, which today numbers 430,000 (650,000 including East Jerusalem).[43] All this required the implementation of a formally apartheid regime, since Israel could not extend citizenship to the Palestinians and remain a Jewish state.

Economic management thus became a key tool of Israeli rule during the Oslo period. As we've seen, Israel increased the economic dependency of the OPT on Israel even as it isolated its economy and intensified its de-development. The economist Adam Hanieh likens the OPT to a South African bantustan. "The utilization of spatial ones like South African bantustans, which provide a veneer of autonomy but can easily be controlled from the outside, has been a feature common to most colonial projects.... They have involved the creation of isolated spaces in which limited autonomy is permitted but movement between them is dependent upon Israeli authorities."[44]

Having found a cheaper source of labor than Palestinians in foreign workers, Israel in 1993 imposed a closure on the OPT. Where up to 116,000 Palestinian workers had entered Israel daily until then, the numbers soon dwindled to less than 36,000.[45] Per capital income fell by 17 percent between 1994 and 1996. By 1998, 37 percent of the people of Gaza and 15.4 percent of those in the West Bank were living under the poverty line of $2.10 per day. Unemployment rose from about 5 percent before the closure to 28.4 percent in 1996. Given the youthfulness of the Palestinian population and its high fertility rates, each unemployed person represented a six-person family.[46] Whereas before Oslo 90 percent of exports from the West Bank and Gaza came to Israel, by 1998 the figure had risen to 96 percent.[47] Through this direct authority over the Palestinian economy Israel is able to manip-ulate it according to its own needs. Controlling exports and imports, it can dump its surplus produce on the Palestinian market to stifle competition. It can also raise or lower the number of Palestinians permitted to work in Israel or the settlements. The fluctuating numbers demonstrate the daily insecurity of one's job. Over the years, Palestinians employed in Israel have risen to 125,000 and fallen to less than 20,000. Today, some 70,000 Palestinians work in Israel and another 30,000 in the settlements, though without benefits, job security or protections from exploitation.[48]

In a much more subtle strategy of control, Israel and its allies, international and Palestinian alike, have inserted neoliberalism into the Palestinian economy, an effective if "soft" form of economic management and governance.[49] Neoliberalism replaces collective units of solidarity upon which struggle for national liberation is based with individualized preoccupations with consumerism. It undermines collective identity and ideologies, unions, political organizations, activist groups and marketing collectives. The isolation of Palestinians in the bantustans of Areas A, B, C of the West Bank and Gaza, says Hanieh,[50] "tends to foster a dynamic of cultural and national disintegration as identities come to be centered around the local."

The foundation of neoliberal control – the economic equivalent of foundational violence – was the Paris Protocol of 1994, still in effect. Signed as an annex to the Oslo II agreement, the Protocol give Israel control over Palestinian customs and trade, two-thirds of the Palestinian Authority's (PA) revenue and the source of 40 percent of its spending.[51] Since Israel controlled all the points of entry into the Palestinian territory, it also gave it veto power over imports to and exports from the OPT, thus stifling competition from Palestinian firms and keeping Palestine's economy in a depressed state. Israel's ability to withhold millions in value added tax (VAT) and fees owed to the PA has all but destroyed Palestinian commerce. The Paris Protocol also gives Israel control over the licensing of both industrial and commercial Palestinian enterprises, together with the authority to issue import/export permits, and stipulate which Israeli import agents, clearing/shipping agents and insurance agents that Palestinian businesspeople must use. All this generates high transportation, storage, insurance and clearance costs. As a result, manufacturing has declined to only 10 percent of the Palestinian economy; nearly 90 percent of industrial enterprises in the Occupied Territories employ less than five workers; 70 percent of Palestinian firms have either closed or have severely reduced production. Restrictions and trade barriers have also reduced agricultural productivity by 34–45 percent.[52]

The degree to which the international community fully supported Israel's strategy of using neoliberalism as a mode of governmentality became evident in 2005 when it forced Salam Fayyad on the PA as an unelected Prime Minister in 2005, a post he held until 2013. Fayyad was an economist with the World Bank. Immediately before becoming the PA's Finance Minister in 2002, he was the International Monetary Fund (IMF) representative in Palestine and the Director of the Arab Bank in Palestine. In 2007 he introduced the Reform and Development Plan of 2008–2010 and subsequently the National Development Plan of 2011–2013. Both were written in close coordination with the World Bank, Israel and other international donor agencies and governments. "Fayyadism," as it was called, has three fundamental pillars: public sector fiscal reform, private sector-led development and, of course, the responsibility for maintaining security.[53]

Public sector fiscal reform means austerity and cutbacks in public spending. These were popular policies in the World Bank and the IMF in those days, and they were applied to the PA more harshly than to any other state in the region. Public services were cut or privatized. The PA installed 300,000 *pre-paid* electricity meters in the West Bank, including rural areas and refugee camps, thus cutting off many impoverished families from electricity. Subsidies for water and other basic goods were eliminated, the number of public sector employees was reduced and their salaries frozen or cut. All this caused the Palestinian per capita income to fall by two-thirds in the wake of the second Intifada.

Private sector-led development was cynically renamed by Fayyad "liberation-via-reform." Fayyad's reforms prioritized West Bank development over that of Gaza, under attempts of the PA, Israel and the international community to isolate Hamas. They emphasized "state-building" and "development" while accepting the constraints of occupation. Fayyad's plans worked partly through Israeli-controlled "industrial zones" attached to settlements or at the crossings into Palestinian areas, where cheap Palestinian labor serve Israeli firms. He grounded his economic "reforms" explicitly on free-market principles. Tellingly, Article 21 of Palestinian Basic Law states: "The economic system in Palestine shall be based on the principles of a free market economy." Two of Fayyad's innovations were the establishment of a Palestinian stock market[54] and the introduction of credit cards, credit servicing now preoccupying many Palestinians more than political issues.[55]

Needless to say, it was security that won the lion's share of international funding. Fayyad placed a premium on building an effective *domestic* security force to ensure industrial quiet. The project was overseen by American General Keith Dayton from a headquarters in Tel Aviv. Fayyad's forces worked closely with Israel and the US to disband any remaining sources of Palestinian resistance – despite the fact that negotiations with Israel has largely ceased and it was clear the occupation was not about to end.[56]

By coopting the OPT into Israel's free-market economy and channeling international financing into "development" projects and security, the Zionist settler project managed to impose neoliberal governmentality over all of Palestine. As a strategy of pacification, "economic development" functions as a form of counterinsurgency. It depoliticizes – and demotes – the struggle against occupation in favor of "projects." Infrastructure construction, job training, educating women, fostering businesses, alleviating poverty – all these are good things in and of themselves, but they are incapable of generating or sustaining genuine economic and social development in the absence of sovereignty and fundamental political freedoms. In Palestine, for example, only 1 percent of development funds are invested in agriculture. This is because most Palestinian agricultural land is in Area C, outside of PA reach. Israel, with its interests in controlling a Palestinian population living under occupation, sets the agenda of the Ad Hoc Liaison Committee (AHLC), the most powerful body in development planning and implementation in the West Bank, together with major donor countries and international financial institutions. The PA is not even represented in the two major development coordinating agencies – the Joint Liaison Committee and the Task Force on Project Implementation – which nonetheless liaise with the Israeli government.[57]

The "developmental" approach has led to the NGO-ification of Palestinian public life and the domestication of Palestinian society by the international donor community.[58] It is also of no little coincidence that Fayyad tied development so closely to security, even if that meant dismantling the Palestinians' very forces of resistance to occupation. Mahmoud Abbas once called the PA's close security cooperation with the IDF "sacred."[59] In the OPT as well as in the rest of the "developing world," writes Duffield,

> the security of the West has been increasingly predicated on establishing an effective developmental trusteeship over the surplus population of the developing world.... [W]hile conflict was a defining motif of the 1990s, it is now being replaced by "instability" as the main threat to global security.... Because of the persistence or threat of instability, however, intervention [in the affairs of "crisis states"] and pacification has blurred into a new and enduring political relationship: *a post-interventionary terrain of international occupation*.... All of those interconnecting UN, donor, military and NGO endeavours that mobilized [in Iraq, Afghanistan and elsewhere] to intervene, save lives and end conflict now increasingly appear as assemblages of occupation defining a new post-interventionary society. That is, they constitute the enduring multi-agency apparatus of *Empire Lite*.[60]

The economic situation of the Occupied Territory has reached emergency proportions under this combination of Israeli economic controls and Fayyad's reforms. By 2018, unemployment in the West Bank was 31 percent. In Gaza, which suffered from the highest rate of unemployment in the world, it had reached 52 percent.[61] Real wages, labor productivity, and labor participation rates all declined. Food insecurity also reached historically high levels, with one in three households in the OPT struggling to put food on the table. Seventy percent of Palestinians, including two-thirds of the children, live on less than $2 a day, defined by the UN as "deep poverty." More than 100,000 Palestinians out of the 125,000 who used to work in Israel, in Israeli settlements, or in joint industrial zones have lost their jobs. In the meantime, welfare payments, dependent on tax monies illegally withheld by Israel under the Paris Protocol, have fallen by $180 million.[62]

Projected back over the past five and a half decades, the picture is one of deliberate de-development. Sixty percent of Palestinian imports are from Israel and 81 percent of its exports go to Israel. Not only is the Palestinian economy prevented from developing, but it is unprotected from an Israeli economy 60 times its size. Today, the OPT occupies third place on a list of the 13 most urgent targets of international aid, all the rest being in Africa.[63]

HASBARA: THE MANAGEMENT OF LEGITIMACY

Ben-Gurion tended to think that Zionism sold itself, and so he never invested much in *hasbara*. After he left office in 1963, appreciation for the value of public diplomacy as an expression of "soft power" began to grow.[64] A focused *hasbara* campaign began in earnest, however, with the election of Menachem Begin in 1977. Begin represented a break from the familiar Labor Zionist leadership, narrative and policies that had guided the Zionist movement over the past six decades. *Etzel* (the Irgun), the pre-state militia headed by Begin, had engaged in outright terrorism against British and Arab targets. Ben-Gurion referred to Begin and his comrades as "Jewish Nazis."[65] Begin felt both his government and his policies in need of a vigorous campaign of *hasbara*.

After 1967, Begin's Herut Party (soon to become the Likud) began advocating for a Greater Israel. That meant annexing the West Bank, now referred to by its biblical name "Judea and Samaria." To be sure, Israel had already begun settling the OPT immediately after the 1967 war. East Jerusalem had been formally annexed, and by the time Begin came to power, there were already 10,000 settlers in the West Bank and Gaza.[66] So while he did not radically change the trajectory of Zionism's colonial project, his brazen unwillingness to conceal the settler project behind a "national conflict" with the Arabs presented a challenge. Israel had managed to cast itself as a peace-seeking David threatened by an intractable Arab Goliath. Now Begin was parading before the world an aggressive Israel bent on settling the Occupied Territory. The two-state solution was crucial to the international community as a vehicle for conflict management. This Begin now threatened.

Thus a ramped-up campaign of *hasbara* was urgent and necessary. Hasbara returned to its familiar security framing:

- The Land of Israel "belongs" exclusively to the Jewish people. There is no other "side" in terms of national rights. The Jews are the only legitimate claimants to the Land.

- In seeming contradiction to the first point, however, Israel needed to set up the Palestinians as a "side" in a "conflict," both to conceal its unilateral settler project and to have a foil upon which to cast blame for "the conflict." By presenting "the Arabs" as its permanent enemies, Israel established the false symmetry of "both sides," upon which conflict management and the illusion of negotiation depends. It is a formulation that does not confer on the Palestinians any national rights, simply designates them as "the enemy." In this way Israel shifted negotiations to what to do with an intransigent population of terrorists – a mixture of transfer, confinement, suppression and local autonomy – rather than over genuine political compromises. As Veracini notes, for settlers "progress" towards peace is measured by the degree of Indigenous displacement.[67]

- *Hasbara* carefully nurtured the image of Israel as the victim fighting for its existence, dovetailing nicely with the Jewish stereotype. Israel's fighting with Palestinians became a trope for Jews historically fighting for their existence. The most effective consequence of this argument is that Jews/Zionists/settlers/ Israelis cannot be held accountable for their actions, since they are merely victims reacting to threats to their existential security. Security-based *hasbara* effectively cast the Zionist settler regime, now the world's fourth largest nuclear power, as the victim, and the actual victims as the perpetrators.

- Israel's treatment of Palestinians is an internal matter; internationals should butt out. Indigenous people, notes Veracini,[68] "are prevented from establishing unmediated associations with external agencies. The settler polities stubbornly insist on a capacity to treat Indigenous relations as an exclusively internal matter and have collectively opposed in 2007 the UN Universal Declaration on the Rights of Indigenous Peoples."

If the Management of Legitimacy has had some success in convincing governments that a two-state illusion that leaves Israel free to colonize the OPT is the best tool for conflict management (indications are that *hasbara* has been much less effective amongst the international public), it has taken an ominous and cynical turn over the past two decades, since the collapse of the Oslo process. Finding it increasingly difficult to argue its case on its merits, especially in light of its massive settlement drive and the specter of annexation, together with more effective Palestinian advocacy, the Israeli government and its supporters have come to portray any criticism of Israeli policy as anti-Semitism. Israel and its "pro-Israel" allies have embarked on a "Brand Israel" campaign, which Pappe describes as "a campaign to recast and rebrand the country's image so as to appear relevant and modern instead of militaristic and religious."

> Rather than winning the argument with facts, information or moral viewpoints, the [Israeli foreign] ministry proposed, it would be far more useful to brand Israel and market it like a product.... What this meant in practice was that any PR campaign for Israel should avoid any association with the conflict or the Palestinian issue.... Israel would now be identified with beauty, fun and technological achievement. This was the new version of the idea of Israel.[69]

INCHING TOWARDS DECOLONIZATION

Until now, we have devoted most of our discussion to Zionism's settler project. We have traced its stages of evolution from impetus in the 1880s and 1890s to what may be described, to use a phrase of Veracini's, as its "triumph," unfolding from the PLO's recognition of Israel in 1988 through the Oslo "peace process"; Operation Defensive Shield in 2002 when Sharon's government broke Palestinian resistance in the West Bank; the Arab League's Peace Initiative of the same year offering the settler project normalization if it would relinquish the Occupied Territory (a condition that has since been dropped by most Arab governments); the irreversibility of Israel's massive settlement construction; Trump's Deal of the Century.

What does this tell us? Not that resistance is irrelevant. The Palestinians faced overwhelming odds over the past century, a pre-state society, heavily rural and dominated by a narrow urban elite, which suddenly had to confront European colonialism that tore its societies apart and an aggressive European settler movement determined to displace them and take their lands, supported after World War I by the world's greatest colonial power, the British, who became the country's ruler. Since then the Palestinians have fought a rear-guard action, even their attempts to raise pro-active diplomatic initiatives rejected time and again by the international community. Their Hundred Years' War of resistance has recently been documented by Rashid Khalidi, who highlights both its effectiveness in preventing Zionism's actual "triumph" and its ongoing role in keeping Palestinian political goals alive. "In the face of heavy odd against them," he writes,

> the Palestinians have shown a stubborn capacity to resist these efforts to eliminate them politically and scatter them to the four winds. Indeed, more than 120 years after the first Zionist congress in Basel and over seventy years after the creation of Israel, the Palestinian people ... were no longer supposed to constitute any kind of national presence.... Yet for all its might, its nuclear weapons, and its alliance with the United States, today the Jewish state is at least as contested globally as it was at any time in the past.[70]

What the apparent "triumph" of Zionism in fact tells us is what we noted in Chapter 2: resistance on its own is not sufficient, even when coupled with diplomacy and negotiations, unless it is accompanied by a political program. That is lacking today. This book addresses that by offering the broad outlines of a political program, raising fundamental issues for discussion and suggesting decolonization strategy. While critical Israeli Jews and others have come to a realization in recent years of how a settler colonial analysis fundamentally reframes the "conflict" and leads us to consider decolonization as the way out, not conflict resolution between two sides," Palestinians have known this and written about it from the start; Khalidi discusses his ancestor Yusuf Diya al-Din Pasha al-Khalidi's anti-colonial writings from the 1890s.[71] The PLO from the start defined itself as an anti-colonial liberation organization, as we will discuss in the next chapter, and it published a seminal work by Fayaz Sayigh, *Zionist Colonialism in Palestine*, already in 1965.[72] Other early Palestinian writers on settler colonialism include Edward Said,[73] George Jabbour,[74] Nahla Abdo,[75] Jamil Hillal,[76] Israeli scholars such as Nira Yuval-Davis,[77] Uri Ram,[78] Gershon Shafir[79] and Ilan Pappe,[80] not to forget the *Matzpen* people of the 1960s[81] also adopted this perspective years ago, as have others, notably Rodinson,[82] Patrick Wolfe and Lorenzo Veracini. Since then it has come to dominate much of the academic discussion, except, of course, among Zionist academics. Overall, settler colonial analysis provides us with a solid platform upon which any political program of decolonization must be based.

Much of this vital discourse, however, has been contained within academic circles. It has yet to penetrate the popular debate in a major way. One problem, I would suggest, is that the very concept "settler colonialism" is far too academic-sounding and complex for even activists to adopt and use easily. That might be overcome by integrating settler analysis into a political program, its concrete elements being far easier to "digest" and support than theory. Few if any academic works, including those dealing with settler colonialism in Palestine, have actually gone that next step from theory to political praxis. Rashid Khalidi, in his recent book quoted above, comes close, skirting the edges of where a settler analysis leads. He asserts, as I did in my earlier review of how settler colonialism ends, that Zionism's failure to "eliminate" the Palestinians frustrated its "ultimate triumph" leaving it only one way out, decolonization, "the abandonment of colonial supremacy." "If elimination of the native population is not a likely outcome in Palestine," he asks, "then what of dismantling the supremacy of the colonizer in order to make possible a true reconciliation?"[83] After discussing why this is a difficult proposition, and offering advice on how to highlight the colonial character of Zionism (compare it to other settler colonial cases; point to the imbalance of power between Palestinians and Israel; foreground inequality), he stops short of a plan of decolonization. Instead, calling out Israel on the fact that "modern Zionism is increasingly in contradiction with the ideals, particular that of equality, on which Western democracies are based," he advocates for merely a vague principle that most would agree on: "uprooting the systematic inequality inherent in Zionism.... Absolute equality of human, personal, civil, political, and national rights must be enshrined in whatever future scheme is ultimately accepted by the two societies."[84] What he leaves us with is this:

> It is now essential for all the elements in Palestinian society to adopt a considered, long-term strategy, which means rethinking much that has been done in the past, understanding how other liberation

movements succeeded in altering an unfavorable balance of forces, and cultivating all possible allies in their struggle.[85]

To be fair to Khalidi, he is one of the few academics that even mentions decolonization as a political program. The point that Khalidi makes for us is this: the necessary theory and analysis exists, as does an active worldwide movement of support for Palestinian rights, but what is missing is the end-game. Academics, for all their critical analyses, have not been active participants in "translating" their powerful theories into political forms of use to activists and decision-makers. In particular, they have not partnered with critical activists "on the ground" to formulate a political end-game, leaving the activists foundering, without a political program for which to advocate.[86] One cannot be in a political struggle without an end-game. Resistance cannot be transformed into summoning a political power without an end-game. It is to that, the linkage of theory, analysis, program and strategic action, that we now turn.

PART III

DECOLONIZING ZIONISM, LIBERATING PALESTINE

6

Decolonization: Dismantling the Dominance Management Regime

It is at this juncture in our analysis, as we turn from studying the Zionist colonial system to dismantling it, that we must evaluate the effectivity of Palestinian agency in resisting, but more in actually overthrowing, that settler regime. It leads us into a discussion of matching the most appropriate forms of agency and power to the task at hand: decolonizing a highly embedded, powerful settler colonial state.

FORMS OF PALESTINIAN RESISTANCE AND AGENCY

Palestinians have always confronted Zionist colonialism through a mix of the three forms of resistance: *sumud*, or everyday resistance; active resistance, be it reactive or organized; and summoning power. They all have their roles to play in the process of decolonization.

Sumud is the most ubiquitous form of Palestinian resistance. *Sumud* means steadfastness or "everyday resistance," doing whatever had to be done to remain in one's house, on one's land, in one's country and a determination to carry on "normal" life under conditions of cultural, demographic and physical elimination.[1] Although articulated as a practice, strategy, attitude of resistance after the 1967 war, in fact it played a central role in Palestinian resistance since the start of Zionist colonization in the 1880s. Since the primary preoccupation of settler colonialism is acquiring land, it is not surprising that the first cases of *sumud*, a refusal to leave the land, and of resistance, at this stage localized, reactive resistance to displacement, took place in those rural areas where Zionist colonization began.[2] This is reflected in Zionist writings of the time. Yitzhak Epstein, a Russian-born teacher who settled in the Upper Galilee in 1886, said in a speech in 1905 entitled "The Hidden Question":

If instead of dispossessing the Druze of Metullah, we had divided the land with them, then we would not have spent on them even half of what we spent on bribes to scoundrels, on the expulsion of poor families, on legal proceedings and lawyers and on unworkable deals, we would not be in thrall to murderers, and we would surely be living with our neighbors and working our land in peace.... Can we really rely on this way of acquiring land? Will it succeed, and does it suit our purposes?" One hundred times, no. The children of a people that first decreed the principle that "the land will never be sold"... need not and cannot themselves expropriate their land from cultivators who were innocently settled on it.[3]

As the phrase "everyday" signifies, most of this form of resistance falls "below the radar" and is registered in the daily life of people getting on with things – '*al-hayat lazim tistamirr*' (life must go on).[4] On another level, everyday resistance is deliberate, confrontational in the sense of defying the rules and expectations of the authorities, be they Ottoman, Zionist/Israeli or British. Women organizing a communal picnic in defiance of Israeli limitations on movement, breaching the Separation Barrier to find work or going to the beach or rebuilding demolished homes – these are contemporary expressions of *sumud*.[5] Then there is demonstrative resistance, still "everyday" in that it arises in response to the oppressive conditions imposed by Israel, is not organized and does not have a political aim beyond protest, lashing out or revolting in a personal way, as in the case of "lone wolf" attacks on Israeli soldiers or police.[6]

When Indigenous agency takes the form of active resistance, it causes even more profound alterations in the settler regime. One of the most visible elements of Zionism, arising directly out of Palestinian resistance, is its reliance on what has been called The Military Way, its use of organized violence to assert its control, and traceable directly to its intrinsic conflict with the Palestinians.[7] Already in 1909, faced with stiff peasant resistance to what was described by a Palestinian official in the Ottoman regime at that time as "de-Arabization," the first Zionist paramilitary unit was established. Described as more of a gang than an army, *Hashomer* (The Guard) was hired to evict the Arab tenant farmers who had long farmed those lands and protect the Jewish settlers who replaced them.[8] Taking as its battle-cry the motto

"In blood and fire Judea shall rise again!" *Hashomer* initiated reprisal raids when the Arabs tried to resist displacement.[9] So unyielding was Palestinian resistance in all its forms that conflict and war became "a self-evident and routine part of everyday life" for the Zionists, instilling a deep-seated "civilian militarism" into Israeli culture.[10]

As described in many texts,[11] resistance took a wide variety of forms. It began as localized hostility, spontaneous attacks and collective peasant resistance to (and reprisals for) dispossession from their lands in the early years of Zionist colonization.[12] As the settler enterprise grew and consolidated itself, resistance became more widespread and organized, as the guerilla war waged between 1933 and 1935 by Izz al-Din al-Qassam in northern Palestine demonstrated. Its most consequential moments were yet to come: the Revolt of 1936–39 (which, however, suffered from the limitations of resistance, "the failure of the revolt to enunciate an achievable political goal"),[13] Palestinian engagement in the 1948 war, PLO attacks in the 1970s and the two Intifadas.

"Summoning power" is a term used by Svirsky and Ben-Arie to describe the forces that challenge those that shape the dominant patterns of the present, with an eye towards a "decolonized future." Building on ideas of power coming from Gilles Deleuze, it refers in our context to a form of pro-active agency applied to an oppressive political system that strategically attacks and dismantles it. It intervenes at those points at which already existing arrangements or systems of life – like a colonial system of rule – are targeted, and can be captured and reassembled into an alternative system. "It is the aggressive and usurping character of this operation," say Svirsky and Ben-Arie, "that we emphasise as what defines power."[14]

Summoning power, as against *sumud* and resistance (though invariably in conjunction with them), has the ability to dismantle oppressive structures – which is why it always has to be applied towards a systemic goal, like decolonization. On their own, Svirsky and Ben-Arie observe, "operations of counterattack [to which I would add *sumud*] have a low liberatory theoretical status."[15] Palestinians have long integrated summoned power in their resistance and struggle for self-determination. Qumsiyeh locates the first "stirrings of Arab nationalism and resistance to Zionism" as early as 1868, with the establishment in Damascus of the Syrian Association (*Al-Jam'iya Al-Surriya*) that included Palestinians.[16] If this is the case, then "summoning power" in the form of political organizing was a form of agency that considerably preceded resistance.

Well-articulated campaigns by Palestinian political figures and newspapers in the early decades of Zionist settlement summoned power both within the Palestinian community and among Ottoman officials, though to little effect.[17] The era of the British Mandate witnessed innumerable attempts of Palestinians to summon power. One early political manifestation was the Muslim-Christian Association, founded in 1918 in Jaffa and Jerusalem, representing what Muslih calls the "older" and more conservative generation of political and religious elites. They did, however, plead Palestine's case before the King-Crane Commission sent by President Wilson to ascertain the political desires of Palestine's population. The "younger" generation of Palestinian leaders initially advocated for Palestine's inclusion as "south Syria" in an Arab Syrian government, and to that end they dispatched petitions to the Versailles Peace Conference as well as to the American government.[18]

These two generations of early Mandate Palestinian leadership established the Palestinian Arab Congress, seven sessions of which were held between 1919 and 1928 in Jerusalem, Jaffa, Nablus and Haifa, advocating both for Palestinian self-determination and against British support for the Zionists. The Third Congress, held in Haifa in 1920, after all hopes of a union with Syria had been crushed, focused on three key issues: the establishment of a national government in Palestine, governed by a parliament of native Muslims, Christians and Jews; the rejection of Zionism; and the organization of a Palestinian Arab nationalist movement. To that end, it elected an Arab Executive, headed by Musa Kazim al-Husayni, and which eventually included 48 Muslim and Christian leaders – although it was never officially recognized by the British. Successive Congresses dispatched four delegations to England while engaging in incessant lobbying amongst British Mandate officials,[19] before it was succeeded by the Arab Higher Committee in 1936. The Jaffa-based newspaper *Filastin* published in English and distributed its copies free to British parliamentarians and local decision-makers, yet another expression of summoning power.[20]

The decline of the Arab National Congress saw the rise of a number of political parties, the Istiqlal, the National Defence Party, the Arab Reform Party, the National Bloc Party and the Palestine Arab Party, all with agendas of summoning power. There were also many other organizations, both national and local. The major religious denominations provided an outlet for their communities' political, economic and communal interests; a women's conference was held in 1929. Writers, poets, intellectuals and researchers all played their roles in keeping Palestinian culture alive while articulating visions and programs of the future, both inside Palestine and abroad. At the same time, we must appreciate *sumud*, resistance and summoning power where possible in the Palestinians' daily struggle to preserve if not develop their economy, participate in the Mandate administration and remain on their lands.

SUMMONING POWER AND THE PLO:
DECOLONIZATION VERSUS CONFLICT RESOLUTION

Summoning power infused all forms of Palestinian resistance, but it, too, takes different forms, and what are the most effective forms at any particular time must be part of the liberation strategy. The founding of the PLO in 1964 was certainly a primary act of summoning power to liberate Palestine. The question, which is still very much with us, is how to summon effective power. The history of the PLO contains valuable lessons in this regard.

Muslih[21] divides the history of the PLO into three phases: (1) the "total liberation" phase (1964 through 1968); (2) the secular democratic state phase (1969 through 1973); and (3) the two-state solution phase (1974–present). Anti-colonialism formed the basis of the liberation struggle during the first two phases. The 1967 war caused a fundamental shift in the Palestinians' situation and policy. The PLO, headed now by Fatah, took over the Palestinian cause from the Arab governments who had let them down, as reflected in the decisions of the fourth meeting of the Palestinian National Council (PNC) in July of 1968. Once faced with the responsibility of having their country's fate in their own hands, and recognizing the embeddedness of the Israeli Jewish population there, the PNC, in February 1969, made the momentous shift from total liberation to establishing a "free democratic society in Palestine encompassing all Palestinians, including Muslims, Christians, and Jews." The PNC retained the anti-colonial character of their struggle – the goal was still "saving Palestine and its people from world Zionism domination" – but the emphasis began to shift from national identity to rights (what is today called "the rights-based approach").[22] Thus the eleventh PNC (January 1973) called for the establishment of a "democratic society where all citizens can live in equality, justice, and fraternity" and which would be "opposed to all forms of prejudice on the basis of race, color, and creed."[23] This phase of the Palestinian struggle, which Muslih calls the "secular democratic state" phase, corresponds in many ways to the One Democratic State Campaign (ODSC) concept of a single state that I will present in Chapter 8. What is left out of the PNC's formulation, and which has been a shortcoming in many Palestinian initiatives,[24] is a readiness to confront head-on the question of Israeli national/political rights within the single state, and by extension the place of national identity itself, be it Palestinian or Israeli. The ODSC program wrestles with the difficult issue of decolonizing a settler state of competing nationalisms.

Through the first and second phases of Palestinian political organization anything less than liberation was rejected outright, specifically the idea of partition and a two-state solution. UN Resolution 242, the Soviet Peace Plan and the Rogers Plan of 1969, the Jarring Mission of 1971, even a Jordanian plan of confederation – all were summarily rejected. But political conditions were changing. The military confrontation with Jordan in 1970–71 led to the PLO's eviction from that country and the situation in the Occupied Territory was calling for more attention, especially given the movement in the region towards some kind of settlement following the 1973 war. Thus, as Muslih shows through the records of PNC meetings, a fundamental shift towards pragmatism began manifesting itself already in mid-1974 and grew stronger over the course of the decade. The outbreak of the Lebanese civil war; the steady disappearance of Palestinian land as Israel's settlements expanded, particularly after Menachem Begin's election in 1977; Egypt's signing of a separate peace plan with Israel in 1979; the 1982 Israeli invasion of Lebanon, culminating in yet another displacement of the PLO, this time to far-off Tunisia; international isolation; the rising expectations of the residents of the West Bank and Gaza for a Palestinian state in the OPT, leading to fears of being bypassed by the first Intifada – all these drove PLO Chairman Yasser Arafat to formally accept the two-state solution on November 15, 1988, approved by the eighteenth PNC.[25]

While seemingly a turn to a pragmatism dictated by events, this third phase of the Palestinian national movement, the "two-state solution phase," in fact represented a fundamental and ultimately self-defeating shift in the Palestinian struggle from that of liberation and decolonization to conflict resolution. Gradually abandoning an anti-colonial analysis and strategy, the PLO ended up falling into the Zionist framing of a "conflict" of two nationalisms. Not only did this plunge them into futile negotiations in which they could be cast as the intractable and violent party, a quintessential colonial framing, but it lost sight of the most basic reality of settler colonialism: that it is unilateral, that it claims exclusive entitlement to the entire country, that it aspires to take (in our case Judaize) all the land, and that the Indigenous have no standing whatsoever, are certainly not an equal "side" with legitimate rights and claims that can actually be negotiated.

Did the PLO not realize the fundamental difference between colonialism and a negotiable conflict? That is hard to accept; it was precisely that distinction that had defined the first two stages of the Palestinian struggle, and that shift had created rifts, defections (the Rejection Front) and even a revolt within the PLO.[26] More likely, they knew that Israel never intended to genuinely negotiate a two-state solution – after all, they had witnessed two decades of Israeli settlement in the OPT and the rise of the right-wing Likud party to power – but were tempted and misled (though understandably so, given the desperation of their situation) by sheer pragmatism, the need to be in the political game in order to summon the power to salvage at least a mini-state in the OPT.

There was, of course, some basis for the expectation that the international community may finally be ready to broker a peace settlement. The efficacy of armed struggle had declined over the years; the Palestinian leadership finally renouncing it in 1988 in order to give diplomacy a chance.[27] The PLO's recognition of Israel in 1988 had led 55 states, including the US, to recognize and deal with the PLO.[28] It also led Jordan to relinquish its claims to the West Bank and to support the PLO's demand for a Palestinian state in the OPT. "Pressed by these external forces," Muslih concludes, "the Palestinians were galvanized to cut through their internal ambiguities and to move definitively beyond the struggle between what they believed as *just* and what they realized was *possible*."[29]

The fruits of diplomacy since 1988 failed to justify the Palestinians' turn to pragmatism; as we will see, it was an inappropriate form of summoning power given the nature and strengths of Israel. The Madrid Conference of 1989 bypassed the PLO altogether. When the PLO was finally brought into the political process in the 1993 Oslo Accords, it merely became bogged down in two decades of "negotiations" that never had a chance of success, until finally collapsing altogether during John Kerry's initiative in early 2014. Not only diplomacy had failed to resolve the "conflict," but the Zionists had even succeeded in establishing a Palestinian Authority in order to manage the conflict. While the Israelis understood that illusionary two-state "negotiations" or "security cooperation" would hold the Palestinians at bay until Judaization could be completed, Arafat and the remnants of the PLO saw in the Palestinian Authority a vehicle for summoning power through continued negotiations, international recognition and "nation-building."

Although the PLO had attempted to summon power by jettisoning armed struggle and liberation for diplomacy and conflict resolution, that form of power proved inappropriate to the type of political struggle the Palestinians faced. In fact, it worked to Israel's advantage by legitimizing the colonial project. The lesson seems to be that the colonized cannot rely on diplomacy and negotiations alone to free them from a settler colonial situation. Indeed, the Oslo process, seemingly the most serious and "hopeful," endorsed by almost the entire international community, demonstrates best how colonial powers use the rules of diplomacy to their advantage.

Non-state actors like Palestine stand in a disadvantageous position from the very start. At the outset of the Oslo negotiations, Israel insisted that the Declaration of Principles established itself as "the sole source of authority," replete with the privilege of "granting Palestinians limited powers" – or not. "Israel tried to impose on [the Palestinians] a security doctrine requiring everything Israel considered important to remain under its control," writes Israel's chief Oslo negotiator, Uri Savir. In fact, the Palestinians entered the Oslo "peace process" without Israel recognizing even their right of self-determination or the right of return. "Eventually," says Savir, "the Palestinians had little choice but to agree to all of Israel's demands, including recognition of Israel's legitimacy as a Jewish state, although they received very little, not even a pledge that a Palestinian state would emerge at the end of the peace process." Insisting on the exclusive right to draft the Declaration of Principles, the very foundation of the Oslo process, the Israelis "agreed to insert the Palestinians' objections into the draft, in parentheses."[30] At the same time, international law and human rights covenants were deliberately set aside by the US and Israel, since they may have supported Palestinian claims and acted to "level the playing field."[31] The fate of the "negotiations" was decided before they began.

But what of international law and human rights? Many Palestinians speak of a "rights-based approach" to gaining Palestinian rights.[32] Isn't that a source of power the Palestinians could summon? In principle, only. Rather than an example of how non-hegemonic actors arising out of civil society have acted through the UN system to institute laws and articulate norms that constrain the actions of hegemonic powers, the emergence of international humanitarian law (IHL) and human rights can be sees as promoting "universal" values that in themselves become a mechanism of Big Power hegemony hiding behind liberal forms of governmentality. Looking at who is tried in the International Criminal Court (to which the US and Israel refused to sign on), looking at the rulings of the International Court of Justice and even of UN resolutions, IHL appears to be imposed on the weaker by the stronger in ways that discipline the entire world-system.[33] And, of course, as Oslo and Israel's continuing violation of the Fourth Geneva Convention shows, the strong state powers can simply ignore them. In fact, Israel has launched a campaign against what it describes as "lawfare": when non-state actors – invariably characterized as "terrorists" – appeal to IHL for protection. Thus:

The enemies of the West and liberal democracies are pursuing a campaign of lawfare that complements terrorism and asymmetric warfare. Terrorists and their sympathizers understand that where they cannot win by advocating and exercising violence, they can attempt to undermine the willingness and capacity to fight them using legal means. Moreover, serious legal questions remain unanswered which must be resolved in the best interests of democracies, such as: *What legal limits should be placed on those who fight the war against terrorism and what rights should be granted to the terrorists we are fighting? Should a U.N. voting bloc comprised largely of non-democratic member states have the power to dictate international human rights norms?* The precedents set by lawfare actions threaten all liberal democracies.[34]

Indeed, international law is skewed against non-state actors in an international system of states. *In principle*, Israel's occupation is governed by the Fourth Geneva Convention. Even Palestinians of the OPT are considered Protected Persons "entitled, in all circumstances, to respect for their persons, their honour, their family rights, their religious convictions and practices, and their manners and customs" (Article 27), but the substance of the Convention is unenforceable. Israel honors neither that provision nor any other. Although mechanisms of enforcement exist – the High Contracting Parties to the Geneva Conventions can call a tribunal to impose sanction for grievous violations, and the Security Council could send peacekeepers or even force Israel to relinquish the OPT – such sanctions exist only on paper, to be enforced only when the most powerful states agree. Indeed, in 1999 a group of Palestinian NGOs succeeded in getting the High Contracting Parties to agree to convene the tribunal in Geneva. It was convened, but in the understanding that it would immediately adjourn. The High Contracting Parties issued this dismal statement:

> After consultations among High Contracting Parties, the Conference, as recommended by UN GA Resolution ES-10/6 in its tenth Emergency Special Session/1, convened in Geneva on 15 July 1999. The participating High Contracting Parties reaffirmed the applicability of the Fourth Geneva Convention to the Occupied Palestinian Territory, including East Jerusalem. Furthermore, they reiterated the need for full respect for the provisions of the said Convention in that Territory. Taking into consideration the improved atmosphere in the Middle East as a whole, the Conference was adjourned on the understanding that it will convene again in the light of consultations on the development of the humanitarian situation in the field.[35]

It is inconceivable that the US and Europe would sanction Israel in any meaningful way for its violations of the Fourth Geneva Convention or other bodies of international law, not to mention exerting the political pressure required for it to withdraw from the OPT. And Israel knows it.

What, then, of the UN's Declaration on the Granting of Independence to Colonial Countries and Peoples, passed in 1960? Well, it deliberately excluded settler colonialism. After all, many of the states having to approve this declaration *are* settler states, including the US, which abstained in the vote. That omission was addressed in 2007, when the UN passed the Declaration on the Rights of Indigenous Peoples (UNDIP). Tellingly, however, some of the world's most powerful states – settler societies all – voted against, including the US, New Zealand, Australia and Canada.[36] But UNDIP is also unenforceable in the case of the Palestinians. To begin with, Israel would have to be recognized as a settler colonial regime over all of Palestine, not merely the OPT, and there is no indication that either the UN or governments would ever do so. Then we come back to *realpolitik*. The US, Canada, Australia, New Zealand and other countries do recognize themselves as settler colonial states because they are beyond any meaningful threat of decolonization in the sense the Palestinians mean it. To avoid any legal challenge, they refuse to submit themselves to international regulations, casting their treatment of their indigenous peoples as an "internal affair." Even if the Security Council could be persuaded to intervene on behalf of the Palestinians, any major change in the status quo would be impossible given the veto of the US and Israel's other allies on the Security Council, which is charged with the enforcement of resolutions. Decolonization may have the *moral* backing of international law, but it remains an issue to be fought out just as it was in Fanon's time.

Asserting a settler colonial perspective highlights the original and underlying issue, Zionism's exclusive claim to the entire country, which should be at the center of attention.[37] This is not to say that the OPT is not occupied according to international law, or that we should stop appealing to legal remedies or ceasing our political campaigns against occupation. Only that occupation is a sub-issue that must be addressed only in the context of a wider process of decolonization.

Not only is there no legal or political pathway to decolonization, there is no blueprint for how it would look. Article 3 of the Declaration on the Rights of Indigenous Peoples proclaims that "Indigenous peoples have the right to self-determination," but it has in mind small indigenous communities living within larger states – "Fourth World" peoples. Article 4 qualifies their right to self-determination, specifying that they "have the right to autonomy or self-government in matters relating to their internal and local affairs."

The Palestinians fall between the two recognized forms of colonization and indigeneity. One the one hand, they are a nation that should enjoy the right to independence granted to Colonial Countries and Peoples in 1960. But the international community refuses to see any more of Palestine than the 22 percent occupied by Israel as the country where their self-determination would be fulfilled, even though almost 2 million Palestinians live in the territory of Israel. Even if the OPT would somehow manage to become an independent state, that does not address the national rights and claims of the Palestinians living in colonial Israel or the refugees. And on the other hand, the Palestinians are not merely an indigenous community seeking rights as a special case within a larger legitimate state, as defined in the Declaration on the Rights of Indigenous Peoples.

In the end, Bisharat[38] suggests a more modest role for international law in "conflict resolution."

[A] rigorous rights-based approach is a necessary, though not sufficient, ingredient to successful Middle East peacemaking. While not all aspects of the Palestinian-Israeli dispute are amenable to resolution along legal lines, some are … International law is not a substitute for negotiations between the two parties to the dispute, but rather establishes parameters that can help structure and guide negotiations toward resolutions that are mutually respectful of the rights of all [– particularly in] maximiz[ing] the legitimate rights, interests, and aspirations of the greatest number of Israelis and Palestinians [and realizing] the rights of Palestinian refugees to return to their homes and homeland.

BACK TO DECOLONIZATION – AND THE SEARCH FOR APPROPRIATE FORMS OF POWER

We have to go back to the first and second stages of the PLO's political program, almost half a century, to find a comprehensive and relevant vision of what form decolonization might take. The steady abandonment of the anti-colonial struggle for a two-state solution and conflict resolution in the 1970s and 1980s meant that from that time to this, no detailed program of decolonization has ever been presented, not by the Palestinian leadership or by its academics or civil society activists. Nonetheless, the rise of a new cycle of settler colonial analysis in the last two decades has revived this perspective, both theoretically and politically. Today a massive literature exists that has relocated the issue of Palestine firmly back into the colonial frame. More significant politically, settler colonialism, always the language of the Palestinian people, has become accepted as part of the mainstream political discourse. I would humbly suggest a fourth phase of Palestinian political mobilization (reflected in civil society, however, not the PLO, the PA or the political parties): the return to an anti-colonial analysis. Although the progression from the two-state solution to a one-state conception happened over time (and is still ongoing), it may be useful to mark the transition to a one-state/decolonization position roughly from the collapse of Kerry's diplomatic initiative in 2014, the subsequent completion of Israel's settlement project (i.e., Judaization) in East Jerusalem and the West Bank, and the rise of a discourse of settler colonialism, first in academic circles, slowly spilling into the popular discourse.

What seems clear from all this is that decolonization remains the only way out of Zionist settler colonialism. The Palestinians must struggle for their self-determination within a new, inclusive polity that replaces Israel and its occupation. Given their non-state status, however, they must do so by summoning sources of power outside of the formal international system of international law and diplomacy, finally forcing the international system to deal justly with their rights and claims. We will suggest in Chapter 9 that mobilizing the international civil society is key to a grassroots strategy, perhaps the only one available to a colonized people facing an internationally recognized colonial regime. Before we consider a plan of decolonization, organization and strategy, let's return to the key question before us: what is the most effective form of summoning power in the Palestine/Israel situation?

My agenda here follows that of Svirsky: "to trace the forces that cause the settler structure to fail and remain incomplete – forces that work either by compelling retreat in specific policy areas, or because of the ineffectiveness of the settler structure in territorialising its logic and imposing its discourse, codifications, and meanings in all areas of life."[39]

Surveying the vast landscape of Palestinian resistance and agency, one can only appreciate the many forms it has assumed: demonstrations and attacks, armed resistance and martyr operations, Intifadas, non-violent resistance and BDS campaigns (Boycott, Divestment, Sanctions); remaining *sumud* (steadfast) and engaging in the constant mini-resistance of daily life with all its gendered nuances; non-cooperation and anti-normalization; a poetics of Palestinian resistance (music, art, poetry, theater, film, literature, popular culture, sports, research); marking memorial dates and preserving, restoring and carrying on life activities in the demolished villages; employing new forms of digital resistance (hacking, establishing sites like the Electronic Intifada, online organizing and mobilization); engaging in diplomacy and negotiations, advocacy and lobbying; hosting conferences, publishing analyses, engaging in "dialogue" with Israelis; voting, engagement in political parties and religious institutions, running municipalities; raising funds for development projects; appealing to international courts and bodies, raising legal challenges in Israeli courts – all these forms of resistance and agency played their roles in "unsettling" Zionism, keeping the Palestinian issue on the political map and preserving the Palestinians as a national collective.

The project of decolonization now calls for a focus on a strategic and well thought-out program. The first question, of course, is: you might have a great program, but how are you going to accomplish it? The question of what power to apply to the Zionist colonial system is paramount.[40] The original strategy of the PLO called for an "exclusive reliance on armed struggle." That proved ineffective against the type of power being attacked: an entrenched colonial state able to control and defeat the Indigenous people from within or without through a highly developed and militarized Domination Management Regime, coupled with a virtual monopoly over the production of knowledge regarding Jewish claims. "Armed struggle for the liberation of Palestine has been a rallying cry of the Palestinian national movement since its emergence in the 1960s," notes Sayigh, "but its results have never been more than marginal. Instead, military groups have served a primarily political function, offering Palestinians in the diaspora organizational structures for political expression and state building."[41]

That position thus evolved, with armed struggle gradually supplemented by diplomacy, until armed struggle was jettisoned altogether in 1988 – although the PLO reaffirmed the right to resist occupation.[42] But, as we have seen, diplomacy, too, proved an ineffective type of power against the Zionist state. By recognizing Israel and forsaking "terrorism," the condition imposed by the international community for access to the diplomacy and negotiations that had been denied to the Palestinians for decades, the Palestinians not only legitimized the Zionist project, they by definition redefined a colonial project into a "conflict" between two roughly symmetrical "sides" – even though the settler colonial project had never changed form or purpose and even though it redoubled its efforts to complete its goal of Judaizing Palestine during the very process of negotiations. Diplomacy, it turns out, cannot decolonize if the targeted power continues to enjoy international support. A new form of summoning power is required, the summoning of support *for a political program* from the international civil society. Like the supplementary forms of agency such as *sumud*, resistance and diplomacy that must be retained, the mobilization of civil society is not new; in fact, a vast and vibrant movement for Palestinian rights exists the world over. The "new" element that turns a struggle against Zionism into an effective campaign for decolonization is placing civil society at the center of the liberation strategy, not merely as a diffuse form of pressure supporting diplomacy. And in order to mobilize civil society effectively, we must have a clear, focused, detailed political plan, an end-game. This, I suggest, is a form of summoning power that is most appropriate to the effort to decolonize Palestine. We will examine such a plan in Chapter 8.

The Palestinian national movement, we noted earlier, got it right the first time. Their struggle was indeed one of liberation from (settler) colonialism, so a return to a model of liberation – albeit one that must take into account Zionism's colonial legacy – is not a departure from historical Palestinian aspirations.[43]

THE PROGRESSION OF AGENCY FROM RESISTANCE TO SUMMONING POWER

Figure 6.1 depicts (in the shaded boxes) the logic, structure and evolution of Indigenous agency as it steadily summons power to confront, dismantle and replace settler colonialism.

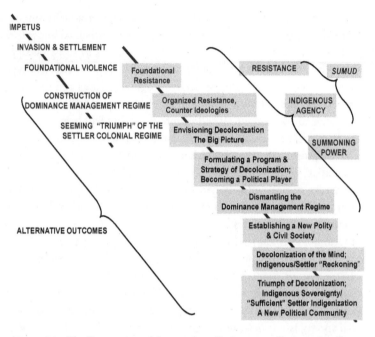

Figure 6.1   The Progression of Agency from Resistance to Summoning Power

Since the evolution of indigenous political power happens in relation to and interaction with the settler project, the progression proceeds from inchoate resistance in its foundational stage of resistance, where the settler threat is not fully perceived and organization against it is minimal, through more organized resistance and onto strategic "summonings of power."

Ultimately, as cases of decolonization of one kind or another demonstrate, the claim is that agency, if it strategically locates the vulnerable interstices of the colonial structure and applies appropriate forms of power to it, is capable of decolonizing any settler colonial enterprise. It is also capable of forging a liberatory post-colonial reality, though success in this regard has been mixed – a cautionary tale for us.[44]

Since the focus of this book is on future decolonization rather than on past or even present resistance, I want to focus on what forms of summoning power are most effective in terms of "capturing and reassembling" the colonial system. Essentially, we begin where the settler regime feels it has "triumphed," although, again, our project of decolonization is built upon past resistance and agency that has prevented the settler enterprise from genuinely triumphing and from eliminating the indigenous population and its ability to summon power. The progression presented in Figure 6.1 is, of course, drawn in broad strokes and cannot be as lineal as presented. Nonetheless, it has emerged from an attempt to eke out of the academic literature, including conferences on the topic, an analysis of settler decolonization based on other decolonization efforts (South Africa being the most relevant) and the political programs of One Democratic State organizations – much of which is set out in this book.

To help focus our analysis and present as detailed a program and a strategy of decolonization as possible, I have organized the main elements of settler colonialism targeted for dismantling and reassembling into what I call a Dominance Management Regime. All these suggest the progression of summoning power depicted in the figure. Guided by ideology and experience, decolonization requires an "envisioning" combining ideology, ideals and a concrete conception of where we would like to go. That is then translated into a political program brought forward by organization, an effective strategy and mobilization, all intended to insert the decolonizing forces into the political arena as a potent player. Armed with a detailed plan of the colonial structures to be dismantled, the decolonization effort proceeds systematically with the process of decolonization, coping with resistance to that effort and the complicated power politics involved.

Recognizing that dismantling is but half the task, we then move on to reassembling the post-colonial polity, economy, civil society and political community to which we aspire – again, without downplaying the complexities of negotiating that vision and program among the many stakeholders. As we move towards establishing a new polity, we must engage in the deeper process of establishing new relationships between the indigenous population and the (almost former) settlers. This must occur between the two communities, in part through a national project of acknowledging what has been done to the Indigenous people in the settlement process, leading to a kind of closure if not reconciliation. But this "decolonization of the mind," this dealing with the colonial legacy, must take place within the different communities themselves. Though their sovereignty has been restored – they have gained independence, freedom and the power to regain their subjectivity as empowered-selves capable of shaping their future – the indigenous community is nonetheless diverse, its various constituencies having had different experiences under more than a century of colonization and often at odds on matters of politics, religion and privileges. For their part, the Zionists (who have not stopped being Zionists) must cope with their collective responsibility of shedding the deeply ingrained assumptions and worldview inherited from the colonial paradigm that defined their national ideology and life. In return, what awaits them is integration into an inclusive political community that offers them if not indigenization, then "sufficient indigenization." After all this has been accomplished, the refugee community returned and set to the path to reintegration, and access assured to the country's lands and resources, the conditions exist for the rise of a new political community, a new state-defined "national" identity – and with it the name of the new state itself.

Let us now explore these phases in the context of a concrete program of decolonization, that formulated by the One Democratic State Campaign.

7

Constructing a Bridging Vision and Set of Acknowledgements

In order to begin the journey to decolonization, we might heed Farid Abdel-Nour,[1] citing John Rawls, as he calls for identifying *and collectively acknowledging* a preliminary set of principles on which both Palestinians and Israeli Jews can agree. Why do we need that? Am I suggesting that the Palestinians need an Israeli Jewish buy-in or agreement for decolonization to take place? No, I am merely referring back to the type of decolonization that the Palestinian/Israeli case requires, one in which two peoples (and others, such as non-Jewish Russians and a large permanent community of African asylum seekers), all of which are internally diverse, must come together in a common polity, civil society and, ultimately, a shared political community. Looking to the African National Congress (ANC) strategy of fostering a common national identity (which in our case would find expression in a new political community) as embodied in the Freedom Charter and the new South African Constitution, and in order to avoid the inter-communal conflicts that embroiled, for example, Zimbabwe or the Ukraine, we might strive to articulate and nurture a broad "overlapping consensus" that provides a common working foundation for our project of decolonization.

For the moment, a kind of "working consensus," what Rawls/Abdel-Nour call "freestanding terms of cooperation," will enable the peoples involved to accept some common terms of cooperation even if they hold conflicting and irreconcilable worldviews. "It is possible," argues Abdel-Nour,[2] "to conceive of just and stable relations between Israelis and Palestinians under which the two peoples would largely continue to uphold irreconcilable political narratives and to expect from one another an affirmation of their respective causes. For both can agree on basic acknowledgments ...."

It is admittedly unlikely that we can arrive at common acknowledgements on a wide scale among either Palestinians or Israelis. What we should strive for, then, is to create an *avant-garde*, a working political group of people from both national communities that can come together on basic principles. We need to create a core of activists at the center of what I call a Tripartite Alliance among Palestinians, critical Israelis and their international allies, a constituency we must constantly endeavor to broaden. What binds this core initially, what makes us comrades capable of working together is solidarity with the Palestinian people. Even a commitment to an (admittedly vague) "just peace" is a start. Participation in joint political activities, whether it is BDS, membership in an advocacy group, actual solidarity work in Palestine or merely staying informed, builds on those "basic acknowledgements." If we begin to add to that a vision, a program and a strategy along the lines suggested below, and make that process participatory, our solidarity begins to acquire a firmer political footing, a greater focus and direction. Over time our efforts become more strategic, enabling us to systematically recruit new populations to our Alliance.

Our immediate task is to build on that base, even if it is small – though given the global dimensions of the Palestinian issue, it may be larger than we expect. After all, how many South Africans did the ANC represent in the early struggle against apartheid? How many Jews did Zionism represent? How many Palestinians signed on to the PLO's program in the early 1960s? Not many. Activists agreeing on basic principles and "acknowledgements" is a strategic place to begin the decolonization struggle.

We begin transforming that inchoate, fragmented, relatively undirected Alliance into a community of focused activists by identifying some "basic acknowledgements," the first stage of an ongoing reframing project. We might initially consider the following:

1. *A joint struggle against colonialism enables a vision of a shared future.*
One advantage of beginning with an activist community of like-minded people is that they are predisposed to considering such essential but controversial concepts as "settler colonialism" than is the mainstream. It is easier to communicate – educate around – the fundamental idea of settler colonialism that, despite its "academic" sound, does *name* the thing we are dealing with. There is no alternative to this term as

yet, nothing more easily digestible. If we are to take aim at the logic, structure and process of the political problem facing us, if we are to formulate a solution that effectively addresses it, then we must address squarely the reality and dynamics of settler colonialism.

Again, we are dealing with a particular kind of settler colonialism, one in which the settlers and the Indigenous have arrived at a draw. Neither can defeat the other, and both have constructed compelling national narratives. Both narratives make the case for "our" side while negating the story, memories, rights, claims, grievances and national aspirations of the Other.[3] If "winning" is out of the question – and why this is so needs to be set out clearly to both publics – then deconstructing or negating the other's narrative no longer makes political sense. Focusing on a joint future, while initially jarring to both peoples, brings us all into a common collective space. It confronts us with a shared and concrete task. Grappling publicly with issues of concern to both peoples – constructing a new political polity based on universal citizenship, equal rights, democracy and pluralism, one in which both narratives and key memories and symbols can be integrated – replaces futile and abstract attempts at negating the other's experiences, narrative and aspirations. It's a worthwhile project, even if limited initially to intellectuals and already committed activists. What, indeed, would a win-win vision of the future look like? Put this way, the challenge is two-fold. What in my narrative, my bank of memories and my aspirations is essential for me to hold on to? And in what way can I reconcile them with what the other "side" feels is essential?

This was the process followed by the ANC in formulating its detailed vision document and political plan, the Freedom Charter. In 1955, following the Defiance Campaign, a broad coalition of racial and political organizations in apartheid South Africa banded together and dispatched 50,000 volunteers throughout the country to collect "freedom demands" from the public. The demands were then grouped into ten key commitments. The Congress of the People, convening in Soweto and attended by 3000 people, then adopted that document as the Freedom Charter, which guided the anti-apartheid movement for many years. Even the disagreements and splits it caused served to sharpen the issues at stake, clarify political positions and activate the masses. Many of its principles were later incorporated into the South African Constitution.

Despite the racialized polarization engendered by the apartheid regime, the Freedom Charter provided a political space in which hard truths and "radical" anti-colonial restructuring could be expressed and debated. It also laid the foundations for dialogue across racial, class and ideological barriers, articulating the only just and workable way South African settler colonialism could be ended. It began with the inclusive declaration: "South Africa belongs to all who live in it, black and white." And it adopted a conciliatory if firm language. "Our people [*all* "our" people] have been robbed of their birthright to land, liberty and peace by a form of government founded on injustice and inequality. The Freedom Charter then went on to communicate the vision of a common future upon which political negotiations could be built. "Our country will never be prosperous or free until all our people live in brotherhood, enjoying equal rights and opportunities; that only a democratic state, based on the will of all the people, can secure to all their birthright without distinction of colour, race, sex or belief."

Finally, the Freedom Charter translates its inclusive vision into a political program. The people shall govern. All national groups shall have equal rights. The people shall share in the country's wealth. The land shall be shared among all those who work it. All shall be equal before the law. All shall enjoy equal human rights. There shall be work and security. The doors of learning and of culture shall be opened. There shall be houses, security and comfort. There shall be peace and friendship. The ANC's slogan put the program succinctly: "Freedom in our lifetime."[4] While the ANC knew that this would not convince the White population as a whole that apartheid was wrong and should be replaced, the inclusiveness of the Freedom Charter laid the foundations of the peaceful negotiated transition by imparting a sense of ownership to wide segments of the population.[5]

Uri Davis, a self-described "Palestinian Hebrew" and a member of Fatah's revolutionary Council, has set forth a concrete suggestion that advances just such a project in Palestine/Israel:

It has long been my view that the progressive demise of the PLO is largely due to its moral, emotional, ideological and political failure to take a page from the book of the African National Congress (ANC) and reform itself politically and legally from the sole legitimate representative of the Palestinian Arab people (currently [in 2003] some nine million people) to the democratic alternative for all Palestinians, Arab and non-Arab (currently some five million people), and develop a political narrative that encompasses a common future, on an equal footing, for both peoples of Palestine, both the native indigenous Palestinian Arab people and the people that has its origins in the political Zionist colonial project in Palestine.[6]

This, for Davis, is an integral part of what he calls "the struggle within." How to transform protest and resistance, the negation of the Other's narrative and aspirations, into common political frameworks that facilitate concrete dialogue over a shared future.

If an anti-colonial perspective is capable of inspiring people to envision a better future, we must also recognize its drawbacks so that we may offset them. To begin with, it sounds accusatory to Israeli Jews. Viewing them as "settlers" seems to delegitimize their claims to a nationality as well as "belonging to" Palestine/the Land of Israel. But, as we discussed in Chapter 1, there is no contradiction between Jews identifying themselves as a national group motivated by a sincere connection to the Land of Israel/Palestine and their *choice*, as Zionists, to adopt settler colonialism as their strategy of transforming Palestine into Israel.

Decolonization aspires to uncouple national feeling and residence in the country from settler colonialism. It does so by offering the Zionists a "deal." If you go through a process of decolonization, then the indigenous Palestinians, now in a position of parity, will agree to integrate you into the new "national" political community. You may retain whatever identities you wish, even national, since we value cultural pluralism. But you must accept life in a new polity and civil society based on equal individual rights and common citizenship. In so doing you can surmount your settler status (and privileges); you can attain "sufficient indigeneity." Zreik describes this post-colonial "deal," or "contract," as he calls it, as follows:

One of the main tensions in establishing the category of citizenship is that it assumes a certain "we" that is not yet there and is waiting to become. This *becoming* requires some measure of solidarity between the members of the assumed community that forms the new "we" what it is – or rather, what it should be. This solidarity

– the minimal glue – presupposes certain duties by citizens towards fellow citizens ….

This means that while the Palestinians say "No" to Jewish supremacy they can say "Yes" to Jewish equality, while they say "No" to Jewish privileges they can say "Yes" to Jewish rights, "No" to Jewish superiority but "Yes" to Jewish safety. Such a "Yes" can be both the ultimate triumph and ultimate defeat of the Zionist project as a settler-colonial endeavor. It is victory, because after a hundred years the project may finally manage to fully normalize national Jewish existence in Israel/Palestine. It is defeat, because the project must give up its colonial aspects, and give up all privileges and claims to supremacy. But the Palestinian can do that only if the settler gives up his settler project, recognizes his role in Palestinian dispossession – the Nakba and its ongoing consequences – and takes responsibility for his actions; stands ready to offer reparation, gives up on his privileges and seeks partnership instead of domination.[7]

The second drawback of anti-colonialism is the issue of accountability. Unlike conflict resolution, an anti-colonial perspective rejects the false symmetry of "both sides." We cannot forfeit the truth – in this case the fact of Zionist settler colonialism – simply to render "peace-making" easier. For in so doing we lose the power of our analysis to address the underlying causes of the "conflict." Any genuine "peace-making in Palestine/Israel must take the form of decolonization, for settler colonialism is the problem. And any attempt to address settler colonialism must grapple with its central driving force: Zionism's urge to Judaize Palestine. There is no other way. Zionism must be held accountable for the unjust reality it has created in Palestine. The colonial structures of domination and control must be dismantled.

In the end, it is the vision of a shared future that must overcome the narrower, unjust and violent reality of unequal "sides." Accountability and decolonization are the only path to inclusive post-coloniality. The settlers can indeed become "sufficiently" native, Zionism can fulfill its dream of "returning to the East," but only if it decolonizes. As it is, holding the powerful party accountable is proving a formidable challenge.

*2. The notion of a single state has a hallowed tradition among the indig-
enous Jews as well as in Zionism, and may serve as a bridge to a new
political reality.*

Sephardi Jews considered themselves part of the indigenous population, as did native Mizrahi Jews and even long-time ultra-orthodox
Ashkenazi (European) Jews. "Before Zionist immigration began
making a historical impact by the third decade of the twentieth
century," note Svirsky and Ben-Arie,[8]

> the Arab majority of Palestine lived not just in reasonable harmony
> with the Jewish minority – most of them Oriental Jews. As has
> already been widely established in research, these two communities
> were socially espoused by way of a myriad of cultural, political and
> economic everyday practices. Shared life was a form of normality
> that structured the everyday of the *natives of Palestine, Arabs and
> Jews....* We use "shared life" not to stress the mere cohabitation of
> different racial subjects in the same space, but to voice the histor-
> ical implications of Arab-Jewish familiarity as it evolved during
> hundreds of years in the Arab world, and particularly in modern
> Palestine.

Prominent Sephardi figures from Chief Rabbis and businesspeople
to those serving as Zionist officials cautioned against a nationalism
that would alienate the Arabs and, before World War I, the Ottomans
as well.[9] Mizrahi immigrants like Albert Entebbe and Nissim Behar
had very different relationships to the country and its Arab population than did Eastern European Zionists. So, too, did the orthodox
Jews arriving in the Holy Cities of Palestine as religious immigrants
or, later, as refugees of Czarist pogroms. To employ Veracini's distinction,[10] they were immigrants, economic or religious, not settlers, in that
they had no desire to take over the country but were looking to merely
live there as a religious community. If we add the economic immigrants from Poland in the 1930s and refugees from Nazi Germany,
it turns out that the large majority of Jews in Palestine leading up to
1948 were not settlers at all – although from the Palestinians' point of
view, they became settlers as soon as they integrated into and came to
support the Zionist national institutions and policies, which they soon
did. Still, it was only on their arrival that they discovered they had

become part of a settler project. Their willingness to do so, suggests the critical historian Hillel Cohen, had more to do with the conflict they found themselves embroiled in with the Palestinians as part of the Zionist Yishuv. They were pushed into the settler project, although they themselves had no quarrel with the local Palestinian population.[11] What option did they have other than going along with the Zionist leadership, and eventually identify with it?

Even within the Zionist camp voices could be heard expressing reservations over Zionist views and policies towards the Arabs, and towards the idea of an exclusively Jewish state. As opposed to the "political Zionism" of the Labor mainstream, "cultural Zionists" argued that Jewish nationalism could flourish in tandem with Arab nationalism in a common land. In 1925, a group of Jewish intellectuals established Brit Shalom, the "Covenant of Peace." They represented a notable if politically marginal exception to the exclusivist logic of settler colonialism. Inspired in part by Ahad Ha'am's concept of Palestine as a cultural home for Jews, they realized that for both moral and practical reasons the domination of Jews over Arabs would not work. Instead, they focused on the part of the Balfour Declaration that promised that "nothing shall be done which may prejudice the civil and religious rights of existing non-Jewish communities in Palestine" – a half-sentence that ignored, it must be noted, Palestinian *national* rights. Nonetheless, Brit Shalom sought accommodation between Jewish and Palestinian Arab nationalities within a binational state.

Among the leading Zionist intellectuals of Brit Shalom were Ahad Ha'am, Eliezer Ben Yehuda, Martin Buber, Judah Magnes, Henrietta Szold, Haim Kalvaritsky, Ernst Simon, Hugo Bergmann, Gershom Scholem and Hans Kohn. Its chairman for a number of years was none other than Arthur Ruppin, the head of the Zionist Organization's Palestine Office and the person responsible for many of Zionism's initial land purchases. As late as 1930, when the settler project was well underway, he wrote:

> In the foundations of Brit Shalom, one of the determining factors was that the Zionist aim has no equal example in history. The aim is to bring the Jews as second nation into a country which already is settled as a nation – and fulfill this through peaceful means. History has seen such penetration by one nation into a strange land

only by conquest, but it has never occurred that a nation will freely agree that another nation should come and demand full equality of rights and national autonomy at its side. The uniqueness of this case prevents its being, in my opinion, dealt with in conventional political-legal terms. It requires special contemplation and study. Brit Shalom should be the forum in which the problem is discussed and investigated.[12]

Brit Shalom even aspired to formulate a joint Constitution for the shared country.

Cultural Zionism offered an alternative over an exclusive ethno-nationalism. Cultural Zionists argued that the Jewish people needed only a cultural space where it could develop and flourish. They understood the pluralistic nature of pre-state Palestinian society and the necessity of acknowledging the Palestinian presence. In their efforts to revive Jewish culture and place it on a par with other contemporary cultures, the Land of Israel assumed a central importance, but as a national home, not yet a political state. They questioned early on the sustainability of an ethnocracy living in permanent fear, alienation and conflict with the very people with whom it shares its country.

Cultural Zionism had little chance of prevailing against Political Zionism and The Military Way. But it demonstrated that seeds of an alternative to zero-sum colonization were to be found in the settler enterprise, illustrating Ram's contention that "actual events explain history, not some disembodied 'inexorable systemic logic.'" As it has turned out – predictably, to be sure, Political Zionism "won." But has since exhausted itself. Although Zionist colonialism succeeded beyond the dreams of the Zionist "pioneers," it has reached a dead-end. Cultural Zionism, though defeated in its time, may well resurface as a bridge between the Israeli Jewish public and the Palestinians as they move together towards decolonization and a newly constituted political community, offering a way out of zero-sum colonialism.

3. *A single state already exists over all of Palestine; our task is to transform it from an apartheid state to a single, pluralistic democracy.*
Judaization has already succeeded in creating one governing authority between the River and the Sea, the state of Israel. Israel's deliberate, systematic and forthright elimination of the two-state compromise,

which favored Israel itself, demonstrates the irreversibility of its colonial program. Given that stark political reality, our task is crystal-clear: to transform the apartheid regime that Israel has imposed on all of Palestine into a democratic state of all its citizens. The logic is compelling. It begins with the party responsible for the problem, but offers a just and practical way out.

4. *The promise of a shared political community.*
Again, an anti-colonial program could appeal to Israeli Jews with the promise of "sufficient indigenization." If "returning home" is the very purpose of Zionism, then decolonization is the way. Could concepts like *Indigenous colonist*[13] or *Native settler*[14] point to a way out of this zero-sum game? Could it hold a key to decolonization? What is the ultimate achievement for settlers, the ultimate concession to them by the Indigenous? To have their indigeneity, if not entitlement, acknowledged. That can only be granted by the Indigenous themselves at the conclusion of the process of decolonization, when a fundamentally new post-colonial relationship is forged. That, of course is unlikely. As Mahmood Mamdani points out, "So long as the distinction between settler and Native is written into the structure of the state, the settler can become a citizen, but not a native."

But there is, Mamdani suggests, a third status between citizen and native that might result in what we could call "sufficient indigenization." That is, membership in a common *political community*. Political community begins with common citizenship, a common civil society. "In the context of a former settler colony," he writes,

> a single citizenship for settlers and Natives can only be the result of an overall metamorphosis whereby erstwhile colonizers and colonized are politically reborn as equal members of a single political community. The word reconciliation cannot capture this metamorphosis. For this is not some Latin American dictatorship that can hope to return to some pre-existing political arrangement. This is about establishing, for the first time, a political order based on consent and not conquest. It is about establishing a political community of equal and consenting citizens.[15]

While Mamdani does not spell it out, he clearly envisions a potential evolution of settler in the direction of the Native when he writes that political community may eventually "transcend the political divide between settlers and natives, between civic and ethnic citizenship." There is no need in any plural society for citizens to share ethnic identities. But sharing a common civil society, especially one based on justice and consent as Mamdani envisions, does possess an affective dimension that goes beyond mere citizenship in a common state. His proposal of this "third way" between civic and ethnic citizenship prefigures Kevin Bruyneel's notion of a "third space of sovereignty."[16] "Restoring the sovereignty" of Native peoples through decolonization, Bruyneel suggests, means restoring their "sovereign" rights to their land, resources, culture and communal rights – the "justice" component of political community that Mamdani cites, which follows the dismantling of all colonial structures of domination and control, and the institution of new polity. If the creation of such a political community addresses these Palestinian expectations of decolonization (of which the return home of the refugees is central), the "third space" would also provide an arena of interaction, shared nation-building and the emergence of a shared civic identity that would go a long way towards Israeli Jews reconciling themselves to the Palestinians as "Indigenous colonists." This approximates "sufficient indigenization," a shared space of Indigenous/settler sovereignty.

5. Decolonization addresses the deeper sources of insecurity.
Settler colonialism engenders a pervasive, constant sense of insecurity among settlers and the colonized alike. Even in cases where the settler state is well established and the Indigenous have been marginalized, issues surrounding Native rights and cultures do not disappear. Indeed, those countries – Canada and New Zealand/Aotearoa are good examples – continue to face an Indigenous "resurgence."[17] Under the Zionist settler regime, the sources of insecurity remain strong. The Indigenous majority remains under military control in conditions of colonization, apartheid and occupation. Most Palestinians live as refugees or exiles. A hot conflict has been waging for a century. And the best efforts of the world's powers have been unable to broker a just resolution. Again, decolonization shows a way out.

These are some of the "acknowledgements" that might "bridge" the current antagonistic non-dialogue. These conform to Rawls' and Abdel-Nur's "overlapping consensus" around "freestanding terms of cooperation" that both peoples can accept, even if they hold conflicting and seemingly irreconcilable worldviews. Gur-Ze'ev and Pappe add other potentially effective approaches. One is to adopt a humanistic perspective that steps back from the particular claims and grievances of each narrative and stresses common, universal elements. "We want," they write, "to clarify the special link that connects Palestinians and Israelis and challenge the ethnocentrism on both sides which enables the victimization of the Other while maintaining the self-conception of victim."[18] Adding human rights and justice to such a dialogue further strengthens and broadens the consensus without being accusatory. So, too, does expressing reservations over nationalism and ethnocentrism. Yet all these elements highlight accountability and asymmetric power relations.

We may also focus strategically on the early stages of settlement colonialism: the "invasion," the foundational violence and the construction of the Domination Management Regime. Although these are "hard" issues, the passage of time has "softened" them by placing them within an historical context. This doesn't imply they are no longer of political relevance, of course, or that they can be dismissed as the fundamental causes of the "conflict." Only that focusing on them allows the polarized "sides" to address the colonial project from a distance, disconnected to some extent from the immediate political realities. This might allow some common "acknowledgements" to emerge from each narrative. Victimhood, for example, or the struggle for freedom, the need for security, the right to an identity and other universal values. That, in turn, might facilitate the reconstructing of each narrative (we're not ready for a joint narrative yet) that acknowledges fundamental elements of the other's narrative. In a sense, we're instrumentalizing universalism, humanism, anti-colonialism, anti-nationalism, justice, human rights and other more easily accepted values. In this way we bypass the mutual unwillingness to concede in direct dialogue and confrontation.

Now good faith and a certain conciliatory stance are necessary, especially as the dominant party feels accused, attacked or threatened. Still, Israeli Jews are not ready for that dialogue. On the contrary, Israeli government agencies have skillfully transformed the feeling of insecurity inherent in their colonial regime into effective security politics.[19] Israel exploits its insecurity to gain international support. And in that it has been successful, it evinces little incentive in ending "the conflict." Israeli Jews remain convinced that only The Military Way insulates them from the inevitable violence of Palestinian anti-colonialism. Convinced that Palestinians are their permanent enemies – which is true as long as colonialism exists – Israeli Jews look on the concessions necessary for a just peace as making them more vulnerable, not as ensuring their safety. They are caught in their zero-sum game.

Nonetheless, the ANC's experience demonstrates that a readiness to construct a process of negotiations that was transparent, inclusive, done in good will and was participatory went a long way towards bringing in the South African government – only, however, when accompanied by constant domestic and foreign pressures.[20] "A freedom fighter," wrote Nelson Mandela,[21] "must take every opportunity to make his case to the people." Attempting to bridge the "sides" does not mean avoiding fundamental issues or creating a false symmetry of power or responsibility. It merely suggests that reframing can ease that difficult process.

8

A Plan of Decolonization

As the Freedom Charter demonstrated, in order to mobilize the public behind a political vision, it must be translated into a concrete political program. Both the Palestinian Communist Party and the Brit Shalom movement envisioned a binational state during the Mandate period, but it had no traction at that time. The Zionists had their sights set on their own independent state, while the Palestinians were preoccupied with simply repulsing Zionist advances. Cherine Hussein[1] marks the beginning of the modern one-state discussion with a 1999 article by Edward Said in *The New York Times* entitled simply, "The One State Solution." A spate of publications burst forth after the collapse of the Oslo Process. It began with Tony Judt's influential article in 2003 in *The New York Review of Books*, "Israel, the Alternative." The same year Virginia Tilley published "The One State Solution" in *The London Review of Books*, and a book with the same title later that year.[2] Mazin Qumsiyeh's *Sharing the Land of Canaan*,[3] Ali Abunimah's *One Country*,[4] Ariela Azoulay and Adi Ophir, *The One-State Condition: Occupation and Democracy in Israel/Palestine*,[5] Hani Faris's anthology *The Failure of the Two-State Solution: The Prospects of One State in the Israeli-Palestinian Conflict*,[6] Ghada Karmi's *Married to Another Man*[7] (and many other writings on the one-state idea), and Ofra Yeshua-Lyth's *The Case for a Secular New Jerusalem*,[8] among other writings, soon followed.

The first working plan towards a one-state solution came out of the Lausanne conference on "One Democratic State in Palestine/Israel," held in 2004. A London Declaration was issued, in 2006 entitled "Challenging the Boundaries: A Single State in Palestine/Israel." In 2009, three one-state conferences were held, each producing diverse and rich position papers: *Israel/Palestine: Mapping Models of Statehood and Paths to Peace*, York University, Toronto; *Re-envisioning Palestine*, Human Science Research Council, Cape Town; and *One State for Palestine/Israel: A Country for All Its Citizens?* at the University of

Massachusetts, Boston. In 2010, yet another one-state conference took place, The Haifa Conference on the Right of Return and the Secular Democratic State in Palestine. In 2012, the Munich Declaration was issued, followed by that of the One Democratic State Campaign (ODSC) in Haifa in 2018, each program and declaration building on the previous ones. In 2019, the One Democratic State in Palestine group (ODS-Pal) issued its "Call for a Palestine Liberation Movement," a call for support of the Palestinian struggle rather than an actual program.

The one-state movement is still tiny. "No one has taken it up as a serious political program," writes Leila Farsakh.

> Palestinian parties to the left, such as the People's Party (formerly the Communist Party), the PFLP, or the Palestinian Initiative *(al-Mubadara)* under Mustafa Barghouti, have been tempted by it. They have focused on the importance of enhancing civic participation in framing the struggle and defending citizens' rights. Yet, they are mainly active in explaining why and how Israel has killed the two-state solution, rather than defining what the one-state solution is, let alone campaigning for it.... During the 6th Fatah National Convention, held in Bethlehem in August 2009, the delegates were concerned with the direction the party should take *vis-a-vis* the Oslo negotiation process, the question of armed resistance, and of relations with Hamas, not with the one-state option.... What has been noted is that the young Fatah cadres in the West Bank at least have started an internal debate on whether or not to adopt the one-state solution as a political project. While many are in favor of it and assert how Fatah has been at the lead of the one-state idea, no one has yet articulated it as a political project. Both young and old cadres cannot yet envisage a political struggle for citizenship and equal rights before first obtaining their own Palestinian state. [Hamas's] main priorities now are not the one-state solution [but] is focused mainly on asserting itself as the main Palestinian political party of resistance and in proving itself capable of controlling and managing Gaza on its own since 2007.[9]

Nor is there an agreed-upon plan – although the single state initiatives are anti-colonial – and not all the initiatives agree on details.[10]

They all flow, however, from the *logic* of decolonization rather than conflict resolution. Some envision a binational or multicultural state that recognizes both Israel and Palestinian national identities, while others insist only on equal individual rights. Key issues such as the land regime, the fate of the settlements (dismantled or integrated?), the nature of the economy (socialist? capitalist? a mixture?), the role of religion (should the new state be secular or does religion play a formal role?), even the right to one's sexual orientation – all these and more still need to be ironed out. Nonetheless, the different one-state groups have endeavored to coordinate with one another. Their different political programs share the following common elements:

- The historic land of Palestine belongs to all who live in it and to those who were expelled or exiled from it since 1948, regardless of religion, ethnicity, national origin or current citizenship status.
- The implementation of the Right of Return for Palestinian refugees and their descendants in accordance with UN Resolution 194 is a fundamental requirement for justice, and a benchmark of equality. It also signifies Palestinian national sovereignty, the ability to address one's peoples' needs with a significant measure of self-determination.
- Any system of government must be founded on the principle of equality in civil, political, social and cultural rights for all citizens. The regime of ethno-religious nationalism should be replaced by a constitutional democracy based on common citizenship, thus enabling and fostering the emergence of a shared civil society.
- The recognition of the diverse character of the society, encompassing distinct religious, linguistic and cultural traditions, and national experiences. Constitutional guarantees will protect the country's national, ethnic, religious and other communities.
- There must be just redress for the devastating effects of decades of Zionist colonization in the pre- and post-state period, including the abrogation of all laws, and ending all policies, practices and systems of military and civil control that oppress and discriminate on the basis of ethnicity, religion or national origin.

- The creation of a non-sectarian state that does not privilege the rights of one ethnic or religious group over another and that respects the separation of state from all organized religion.
- In articulating the specific contours of such a solution, those who have been historically excluded from decision-making – especially the Palestinian Diaspora and its refugees, and Palestinians inside Israel – must play a central role.
- Putting into place an inclusive economy offering economic security, sustainability, meaningful employment and just compensation.
- Acknowledging a connectedness to the wider Middle Eastern and global community that requires engagement in creating new regional and global structures of equality and sustainability upon which the success of local decolonization ultimately depends.

Let's take as a starting place in our project of decolonizing Zionism/ liberating Palestine the 10-point program of the One Democratic State Campaign. The ODSC is a Palestinian-led group of Palestinians – primarily, though certainly not exclusively, '48 Palestinians – and Israeli Jews that came together in Haifa in 2017. It makes sense that the initiative began with '48 Palestinians. "As the Palestinian state project has been transformed into an aid-dependent Palestinian Authority fragmented and constrained in its ability to defend the Palestinian cause," says Farsakh,

> it seems inevitable that the only alternative for protecting Palestinian rights and representing all of its constituents is a solution based on equal rights in all of historic Palestine. The Palestinian citizens of Israel are the best placed to articulate the Palestinian cause in those terms and to lead it by virtue of their experience with the Israelis over the past 60 years.[11]

I have been involved from its inception. Its political plan, which I'm using as a "gateway" into issues of decolonization in Palestine, was forged over two years of discussion involving a core network of some 50 activists and academics, both from within Palestine and abroad, including members of other One State groups. The ODSC plan is not intended to be the final word, of course; in fact, it is a project in its infancy which nevertheless integrates previous work and initiatives in order to move the urgent project of decolonization forward. It emerges out of a Palestinian civil society that has been left leaderless by its parties and political establishment (in the OPT, the refugee camps and the Exile/Diaspora) or that feels itself isolated and motivated to help unite the Palestinian people (in the case of '48 Palestinians) – supported by anti-colonial Israeli Jews. Underlying our efforts is an often-expressed desire to resuscitate the PLO as the Palestine vehicle of liberation, but the urgency of the political moment does not permit civil society to wait on that important development. Many of the old leadership, PLO, political party and civil society, have joined our campaign, together with young people who take their energy from more recent events (I'm refraining from naming them because I cannot coopt their voices into my analysis of our movement and program; their names are available on their endorsement of our manifesto, found at the ODSC website: https://onestatecampaign.org).

Although we are just at the beginning of a participatory process that will involve Palestinians and Israeli Jews from every community – our 10-point program is brief and will require filling out with substance as we progress – we have established a strong base for blocking out a process of decolonization and envisioning the post-colonial polity and civil community that might emerge. In particular, the ODSC has set the political logic of its program firmly in that of settler colonialism, thus returning to Palestinian analysis and political actions going back a century and a quarter, reflected as well in formative PLO documents. From there the ODSC program "thinks through" the process of decolonization from how Zionist colonial structures must be dismantled to what Palestinian sovereignty requires (beginning with the return of the refugees, return to access to land and the gaining of political power necessary to enact sovereignty) and on to the emergence of a shared political community. Significantly, the ODSC approach places the decolonization of Palestine within its wider regional and even global context. At a minimum, the ODSC program and the analysis on which it is based provides a useful and provocative basis for a much-needed and urgent discussion of where we are going as a liberation movement. In all this we address a major challenge posed by Leila Farsakh: how to frame the one-state solution in realistic, rather than utopian terms. "Developing the ability to address the difficult issues of identity, equal rights, civic responsibility, and political power is also a prerequisite for building a one-state movement that can surmount the serious domestic, regional, and international challenges it faces."[12]

Let us now turn to the political program itself. Again, my analysis of each item is grounded in years of collaboration with the program's architects, as well as in years of activism "on the ground" in Palestine and, simultaneously, significant grounding in the academic literature. I say this to make it clear (again) that this is *my* analysis that, while reflecting in good faith the views and intentions of my comrades, it by no means represents them. We are far too diverse in our views, and too many issues remain unresolved, for there to be one voice. But I believe the analysis is powerful and extremely useful in generating and focusing the political exchange we must have. It is in the spirit of moving the one-state project ahead that we enter into the following discussion.

THE ODSC PROGRAM FOR ONE DEMOCRATIC STATE BETWEEN THE MEDITERRANEAN SEA AND THE JORDAN RIVER

Preamble

In recent years, the idea of a one democratic state as the best political solution for Palestine has re-emerged and gained support in the public domain. It is not a new idea. The Palestinian liberation movement, before the Nakba of 1948 and after, had promoted this vision in the PLO's National Charter, abandoning it for the two-state solution only in 1988. It was on this basis that, in September 1993, the Palestinians entered into the Oslo negotiations. The two-state solution was also endorsed by all the Palestinian parties represented in the Israeli Knesset. But on the ground Israel strengthened its colonial control, fragmenting the West Bank, East Jerusalem and Gaza into tiny, isolated and impoverished cantons, separated from one another by settlements, massive Israeli highways, hundreds of checkpoints, the apartheid Wall, military bases and fences. After a half-century of relentless "Judaization," the two-state solution must be pronounced dead, buried under the colonial enterprise on the territory that would have become the

Palestinian state. In its place Israel has imposed a single regime of repression from the Mediterranean Sea and the Jordan River.

The only way forward to a genuine and viable political settlement is to dismantle the colonial apartheid regime that has been imposed over historic Palestine, replacing it with a new political system based on full civil equality, implementation of the Palestinian refugees' Right of Return and the building of a system that addresses the historic wrongs committed on the Palestinian people by the Zionist movement.

We, Palestinians and Israeli Jews alike, have therefore revived the one-state idea. Although differing models of such a state range from binational to a liberal, secular democracy, we are united in our commitment to the establishment of a single democratic state in all of historic Palestine.

As formulated below by the One Democratic State Campaign (ODSC), the goal of this political program is to widen the support for such a state among the local populations, Palestinian and Israeli alike, as well as amongst the international public. We call on all of you to join our struggle against apartheid and for the establishment of a democratic state free of occupation and colonialism, based on justice and equality, which alone promises us a better future.

The ODSC Program

1. *Decolonization.* The only way to resolve a settler colonial situation is through a thorough process of dismantling the colonial structures of domination and control. An inclusive and democratic polity, ruling over a shared civil society, replaces the colonial regime. Once a new political community arises offering equal rights for all, once the refugees return and once all the citizens of the new state gain equal access to the country's lands and economic resources, a process of reconciliation may begin. Israeli Jews must acknowledge both the national rights of the Palestinian people and *past colonial crimes*. In return, and based on the egalitarian democracy that has been established, the Palestinians will accept them as legitimate citizens and neighbors, thereby signaling the end of Zionist settler colonialism. Having entered into a new post-colonial relationship, the peoples and citizens of the new state – whose name will emerge

through the process of shared life – will be able to move on to the future they and their children deserve.

This first Article bridges the Preamble's presentation of the problem – Zionism as a settler colonial project – with the detailed program of decolonization offered. It lays out the entire process of decolonization. The ODSC program begins with the dismantlement of the Domination Management Regime and its replacement by a new, shared, inclusive and democratic polity and civil society. It progresses into the new post-colonial relationship between Palestinians and Israeli Jews. In this new relationship, the Palestinians regain their sovereignty,[13] their rights and their country, within the framework of a single democratic state shared equally with Israeli Jews and others. For their part, Israeli Jews, by accepting this new relationship in a political community enabled by the indigenous Palestinians, play a now-constructive role as the decolonized polity moves on towards its post-colonial future.

Only the Indigenous can declare an end to the colonial situation. Replacing the Zionist settler state with a unitary democracy entails two major challenges. How can Israeli Jews be induced – or forced – to accept the status of equal citizens in an inclusive democracy, one that dismantles their domination and control but then allows them to end their otherwise unresolvable estrangement as settlers? And how can the Palestinians be induced – though they cannot be forced – to allow "their" country to be transformed into a civil polity that includes Israeli Jews?

> 2. *A Single Constitutional Democracy.* One Democratic State shall be established between the Mediterranean Sea and the Jordan River as one country belonging to all its citizens, including Palestinian refugees who will be able to return to their homeland. All citizens will enjoy equal rights, freedom and security. The State shall be a constitutional democracy, the authority to govern and make laws emanating from the consent of the governed. All its citizens shall enjoy equal rights to vote, stand for office and contribute to the country's governance.

As befitting an anti-colonial program, the ODSC program relates to the entire country of Palestine as the object of liberation, and not merely pieces of it. The great revolution here and in other one-state programs is that after decolonization, all the country's inhabitants will enjoy equal rights as citizens. A constitutional democracy replaces the settler regime in which one's place in society is dictated by one's ethnic, religious and national identity. The state no longer "belongs" to one particular group but to its citizens. One citizenry, one parliament, one set of laws, one civil society of equals whose civil, human and national rights are guaranteed by a Constitution and a High Court that enforces it.

The role of religion in the new state is a major point of contention among single state advocates, specifically, should the state be secular? That term has different connotations to different constituencies. Although the PLO's National Charter of 1968 makes no reference to religion, Palestine National Council (PNC) Resolutions in the years Muslih characterizes as the "secular democratic state phase" (1969–73) envision a state that has been described as "secular" in the sense of being non-sectarian. They called for the establishment of a "democratic society where all citizens can live in equality, justice, and fraternity" and which would be "opposed to all forms of prejudice on the basis of race, color, and creed."[14] When a draft of the Palestinian Constitution was drawn up by the Palestinian Authority under Arafat in 2003, however, it stipulated that Islam would be the sole official religion in Palestine and the principles of Islamic *sharia* the principal source of legislation.[15]

This is a fundamental issue that will have to be decided in the future. The ODSC program adopts the PLO's position of non-sectarian government. Its vision of the new state is secular in the sense that the authority to govern and make laws emanates from the consent of the governed and not from religious law, and there is no official religion, although religious laws may still function alongside civil institutions. Since the term "secular" has so many connotations, mostly negative to religious people, and since the majority of Palestinians and Israelis alike describe themselves as "religious" or "traditional,"[16] our strategy, like that of the PNC, is to advocate a non-sectarian democracy while refraining from using the red-flag term "secular."

3. *Right of Return, of Restoration and of Reintegration into Society.* The single democratic state will fully implement the Right of

Return of all Palestinian refugees who were expelled in 1948 and thereafter, whether living in exile abroad or currently living in Israel or the Occupied Territory. The State will aid them in returning to their country and to the places from where they were expelled. It will help them rebuild their personal lives and to be fully reintegrated into the country's society, economy and polity. The State will do everything in its power to restore to the refugees their private and communal property of the refugees and/or compensate them. Normal procedures of obtaining citizenship will be extended to those choosing to immigrate to the country.

Coursing throughout the ODSC plan is a commitment to human rights. Article 2 acknowledges and prioritizes the right of Palestinian refugees and their families to return to their homeland. But the refugees do not possess only the *right* to return. Based on the political logic of our program – that of equal citizenship – refugees *should* return as part of the in-gathering of our country's citizens. Just because people flee a conflict, are driven out or merely choose voluntarily to reside elsewhere, they do not lose their citizenship unless they take steps to revoke it. The return of the refugees and their descendants represents nothing more than restoring to them a civil status they should never have lost in the first place. Indeed, UN Resolution 194, adopted in December 1948, resolved that

refugees wishing to return to their homes and live at peace with their neighbours should be permitted to do so at the earliest practicable date, and that compensation should be paid for the property of those choosing not to return and for loss of or damage to property which, under principles of international law or equity, should be made good by the Governments or authorities responsible.

The ODSC program goes further than mere return and enfranchisement of the refugee community, however. It recognizes that this population is, in large part, traumatized, impoverished, undereducated and under-skilled. It will need a generation or more, supported by a vigorous program of affirmative action and economic investment, before they truly "come home" as integrated, and productive members of society. Hence Article 2 affirms that the new state "will help them rebuild their personal lives and to be fully reintegrated into the country's society, economy and polity. The State will do everything in its power to restore to the refugees their private and communal property of the refugees and/or compensate them."

4. *Individual Rights.* No State law, institution or practices may discriminate among its citizens on the basis of national or social origin, color, gender, language, religion or political opinion, or sexual orientation. A single citizenship confers on all the State's residents the right to freedom of movement, the right to reside anywhere in the country, and equal rights in every domain.

As a liberal democracy, the post-colonial state envisioned in the ODSC plan guarantees equal rights to all citizens regardless of their national, religious or ethnic affiliations. This goes a long way towards dismantling the structures of domination and separation. It also reorients Arab-Jewish relationships around the principles of equality, shared human rights and coexistence, thus paving the way for the emergence of a shared civil society, as proponents of a "rights-based approach" envision.[17]

5. *Collective Rights.* Within the framework of a single democratic state, the Constitution will also protect collective rights and the freedom of association, whether national, ethnic, religious, class or gender. Constitutional guarantees will ensure that all languages, arts and culture can flourish and develop freely. No group or collectivity will have any privileges, nor will any group, party or collectivity have the ability to leverage any control or domination over others. Parliament will not have the authority to enact any laws that discriminate against any community under the Constitution.

Perhaps the most debated issue around one-state conceptions has to do with binationalism, defined by Bashir as recognizing "the reality of the existing national and ethnoreligious diversity and calls for democratic designs based on power-sharing, federative arrangements, or some combination thereof within which the various groups enjoy communitarian and national rights."[18] It stands in contrast to two other alternative modes of integration into a single state: the "liberal strand," which "emphasizes individual rights and promotes an inclusive and egalitarian state, which represents all of its citizens regardless of their national, religious, or ethnic affiliations" (promoted in the ODSC plan), and the "shared sovereignty," in which "the answer to the two groups' conflicting claims to self-determination ... is an arrangement that is premised on shared power and overlapping territorial jurisdiction."

To this we must add, of course, those for whom the two-state solution is still preferable, the most notable being governments, including, officially, the Israeli government. For them, it appears, the two-state solution is less useful as a plan for resolving "the conflict" than it is a mechanism of conflict management. Nonetheless, there are Palestinians who also support it, prominent among them being, besides the officials of the Palestinian Authority and the Joint Arab List, Salim Tamari. Although Tamari recognizes the serious drawbacks of the two-state solution, he argues that a state of their own would both grant the Palestinians their civil rights and protect their national identity, while dismantling the settlements and ending Israeli occupation. In addition, he fears that in a single state the weaker Palestinian economy and society would be incorporated into the stronger industrialized European Israel. In particular, Tamari is reacting against the idea of binationalism, which he sees as legitimizing Zionist colonialism, in the end, a program that is "counterproductive and escapist."[19]

While none of the single state options is acceptable to Israeli Jews, the binational one would in principle be the easiest to "sell," since it validates Israeli Jewish national identity and leaves it intact as a fundamental component of the new state, one that would find institutional expression in government. Given the deep binational reality of Palestine/Israel, Bashir prefers binationalism, "creating power-sharing mechanisms, decentralizing authority, and forming inclusive coalitions [while still granting] autonomy in policy fields" – although he recognizes that this is not decolonization and understands Palestinian resistance to "validating settler colonialism."[20] Omar Barghouti, for one, rejects the binational idea because it elevates the Israeli Jewish national identity to a valid equivalency with that of the Palestinians. "Recognizing *national* rights of Jewish settlers in Palestine or any part of it cannot but imply accepting the right of colonists to self-determination," and therefore contradicts the very notion of decolonization.[21] In this Ali Abunimah concurs.[22]

The notion of shared sovereignty occupies a kind of middle ground between binationalism and a liberal democracy. As Farsakh[23] points out, it shifts the emphasis from sovereignty to recognizing an Israeli identity and sociocultural reality, thus creating a kind of symmetry with Palestinian identity and culture – lowering the clash of "nationalisms" by sharing sovereignty. This approach appeals to Israelis, both Israeli Jews of the Left[24] and Palestinians with Israeli citizenship,[25] who already share (in a sense) a common state and can easily envision a shared sovereignty ("a state of all its citizens"). It in no way denies Palestinian nationalism, but it makes a distinction between the two kinds of sovereignty we have discussed: sovereignty that requires a state as its vehicle for self-determination, which the shared sovereignty approach is willing to subordinate to a wider state sovereignty shared with the settlers, and sovereignty expressed in more cultural terms, the more limited Indigenous sovereignty conceived by Fourth World peoples. As Azmi Bishara puts it:

> This project [of establishing a political party in Israel in the wake of the "disintegration" of ideologies, Arab nationalism, Oslo, the Palestinian national movement, and the global left] "is expressed on two levels. The first concerns the idea of a state of all its citizens and the development of our program of equality in the context of our struggle with Zionism. And the second is affirming our national identity as part of the modernization of Arab society and against concepts of tribalism, sectarianism and other such alternatives.[26]

This concept of shared sovereignty in Palestinian thought appears to be specific to the conditions of Palestinians in Israel. It is essentially a practical program, the best that can be expected by a national group forced by its colonizers into a kind of Fourth World situation. Shared sovereignty *within Israel* forms the basis of The Future Vision of the Palestinian Arabs in Israel (2006),[27] the Haifa Declaration (2007) and the Democratic Constitution (2007), all of which also call for a Palestinian state in the OPT.[28] And in fact, Balad/Tajamu', Bishara's party, like the other parties in the Joint Arab List, have long been centered on dealing with their lives in Israel rather than on wider issues such as establishing a single state. At the same time, shared sovereignty seems to have very limited if any appeal outside the Green Line, however, where a "real" and robust anti-colonial struggle carries political possibilities foreclosed by life within Israel.

The "Two States, One Homeland" initiative of Israeli Jews with minor Palestinian support (since renamed "One State for All") represents the idea of shared sovereignty today. It retains strong two-state elements – separate Israeli and Palestinian citizenships and government institutions, for example, and refugee return – but envisions itself being carried out in a single territory primarily because the two-state solution was no longer possible, or perhaps because a genuinely binational state could never be sold to the Israeli public. Thus

> the two countries will determine an agreed number of citizens of the other country who will live in their territory and receive permanent resident status, with all entailed rights. Such agreement will allow Israelis, including those who currently live in the territories where Palestine will be established, to live as permanent residents of Palestine [thereby retaining the settlements]. The IDF will also continue under the Israeli state.[29]

The notion of shared sovereignty has given rise to a number of confederation proposals (tellingly, few by Palestinians). Aryeh Eliav,[30] David Elazar,[31] Matthias Mossberg and Mark LeVine,[32] and Lev Grinberg[33] have all written on the subject, and several initiatives have been launched, among them: the Federation of Hebrew and Palestinian Nations, based on the Jewish Bundist idea of National/Cultural Autonomy,[34] the Israel/Palestine Confederation,[35] The Israeli-Palestine Federation,[36] and is reflected in the pages of the *Palestine/Israel Journal*.

Primarily because of stiff Palestinian resistance to binationalism and because the logic of our settler colonial analysis leads us to a project of genuine decolonization, the ODSC has adopted what Bashir calls the "liberal" approach, although our subordination of ethno/religious national identity to a state nationalism, citizenship and political community borrows from the notion of shared sovereignty, without the confederation aspect. It must be said, however, that the doors have not closed on altering our concept, particularly in order to accommodate strong supporters of binationalism, including Palestinians who consider it the most practical considering absolute Israeli refusal to consider other options.

The ODSC program recognizes the binational character of the country, of course, but understands that reinforcing ethno-national segregation through binationalism not only contradicts the goals and processes of decolonization, it makes the emergence of a political community impossible. Its "liberal" approach, based on individual rights, the nurturing of a shared civil society and, ultimately, the emergence of a new, affective "national" (state-based) identity and political community, proposes to handle nationalism (as an expression of a people's collective identity) in two ways. first, by acknowledging its presence and centrality, and second, through a policy of cultural pluralism.

Article 5 of the ODSC program on "collective rights" thus states: "Within the framework of a single democratic state, the Constitution will also protect collective rights and the freedom of association, whether national, ethnic, religious, class or gender." In our experience, most Palestinians (except, perhaps, the refugee community living in the neighboring Arab countries, whose contact with Palestine/Israel and Israeli Jews has been limited or non-existent) understand that Israeli Jews will remain in the country after decolonization. That is not the problem. The problem is Palestinians being forced to legitimize – and in a binational state or one with shared sovereignty, even institutionalize – Zionist national rights. Israeli Jews, like Palestinians, may retain their national, ethnic and other collective identities, institutions and practices as a community (or linked communities), as in any multicultural state, of course. But institutionalizing governmental systems based on proportional representation, formal power-sharing mechanisms and communal autonomy in making policy that affects the entire populace, preserves and legitimizes settler colonial identities and structures. Competition over resources of the state may even strengthen rather than ameliorate international differences. Only the "liberal strand" is capable of genuine decolonization and the creation of a new political community.

Still, the ODSC plan recognizes that the process by which a shared political community will emerge will take time, perhaps several generations. It also realizes that national identity can be harnessed for purposes of integration, its centrality being a necessary ingredient of the earlier stages of nation-building but which may be ameliorated over time as shared life becomes more routinized. This process is described by Zreik, who asks: "What comes after the native and the settler? What and where they can meet and on what middle ground?" The answer, he offers, "is the old, boring category of citizenship."

> For the Palestinians, injustices of the past cannot be overlooked, and the way the colonial past has shaped the relationship between the two communities must be tackled and unpacked. The formal abstractness of citizenship must thus be supplemented by a certain visibility and relevance of history; of the past.... I think those parts of the past that leave their traces and shape fragments of the peoples' life, wealth, conditions of existence and material well-being should be allowed to figure in any arrangement and need to be taken into account, at least for some considerable time. The settler cannot simply one day stop being a settler as if there is no past: the past injustices and dispossessions must be settled and addressed.
>
> The collective communal and national aspect must also be taken into account for the Israeli Jews. Any forward-looking solution must take the collective Israeli-Jewish identity into account and give an answer to people's need and interest in their culture, religion, nationality, and history. In this sense, the category of citizenship does not aim to comprehensively replace these interests, but rather to create a space where a conversation based on an equal footing can take place. Citizenship, in this regard, stands for the new "we," based on equal terms of engagement. It does not abolish identity but puts it in its place and tames it.[37]

The need to undergo a process of civilization while retaining meaningful collective identities and community is most graphically illustrated in the case of the Palestinian refugees and their descendants. After more than 70 years in difficult, often brutal exile, many want to come home to Palestine, as Palestinians. They have had little experience with a civil society comprised of equal individuals, however. Many will even reject – understandably – sharing a new "national" identity with Israeli Jews. For some time after their return they will need a collective space within which to reorient themselves, overcome the traumas of exile and acquire the skills needed for a modern economy and inclusive polity. These are processes that will take a generation or more.

Refugees cannot simply be pushed into a civil society not entirely their own.

In response to the continued saliency of communal identities, the ODSC plan balances the nurturing of a new polity based on equal citizenship with robust cultural pluralism. Indeed, Palestine/Israel is full of national, ethnic, religious and gendered communities that need collective support as they move from poor or lower-class status, or from oppression and pariah status, to equality. They include Palestinian residents of the OPT and Israeli alike; Mizrahi and Ethiopian Jews; non-Jewish Russian citizens; African asylum seekers and foreign workers who have become permanent residents; smaller ethnic minorities such as Armenians, Circassians, Druze and Bedouins; and others. Collective spaces provided by religious schools, institutions and museums, vehicles of language such as newspapers and literature, and even the celebrating of ethnic foods, music, theater, holidays and customs will, in the end, promote a shared civil society, yet one that is multicultural and supportive of its pluralism.

Creating these cultural spaces, together with the dismantling of colonial structures and the establishment of a liberal democratic state, also addresses the issues of the imbalance Barghouti perceives between the inalienable rights of the indigenous Palestinian people to self-determination and the *acquired* rights of the indigenized former colonial settlers. Under the rubric of "ethical decolonization," he accepts the possibility of the birth of a common, post-oppression identity where "the indigenous Palestinians and the indigenized settlers" can live in equality, peace and security, individually and collectively.[38] It still leaves unresolved, however, the national element of Israeli Jewish identity. In the ODSC proposal it is up to the collective in question to define the nature of its own identity; if Israeli Jews seek to maintain a national identity within the framework of a democratic state, that is their right. This does not seem to be acceptable to Barghouti and Abunimah, who reject the legitimacy of any Israeli national element.

Any program for a single state will also have to deal with the fears the two peoples harbor of the other's communal identity, understandable on the background of more than a century of colonialism, resistance and suffering.[39] Besides their refusal to recognize the legitimacy of Zionist national identity, many Palestinians simply do not believe that Israelis will actually relinquish power. They fear that the one-state solution may be merely a guise for continued Israeli domination, especially if the Israeli ethno-nation is allowed to survive. They need to be convinced that the Domination Management Regime will be genuinely dismantled. They must *see* how this would happen.

For their part, the large majority of Israeli Jews also resist inclusiveness in a democratic, citizen-based civil society with "Arabs," their permanent enemies and contestants for ownership of the land. (Whether Mizrahi Jews, who shared common language, history and cultural experience with Palestinian Arabs, will play a role in arbitrating a new civil society remains to be seen.) The fears of Israeli Jews are understandable. If the Palestinians are the majority population in the single state, as they will be, what will prevent them from doing to us what we today do to them? What will prevent the tyranny of the majority? And in fact, the danger of majoritarianism cannot be dismissed, especially in our era of nativistic populism.

Article 5 attempts to address the fears of the two national communities. "No group or collectivity will have any privileges, nor will any group, party or collectivity have the ability to leverage any control or domination over others," it affirms. "Parliament will not have the authority to enact any laws that discriminate against any community under the Constitution." There is no "quick cure" for all these issues. The dynamics that Article 5 deals with cannot be seen in isolation. Taken as a whole, the ODSC plan offers a comprehensive and practical vision for what is possible in the future.

Figure 8.1 depicts the shift from the Israeli ethno-national "ethnocracy" of today into a shared post-colonial state and society of equal rights for all its citizens that the ODSC plan envisions.

The very process of engaging in this dual process of decolonization and nation-building may well help forge a new civil society and shared national identity. That project is likely to initially attract the more secular, more educated middle classes, and the young. But over time, as civil life assumes a normalcy and routine, it will expand until it eventually encompasses, to one degree or another, all sections of the population. Todorova proposes "an inclusive politics of belonging" rather than the stress on identity as the basis of legitimization. "What I mean by this," she writes,[40]

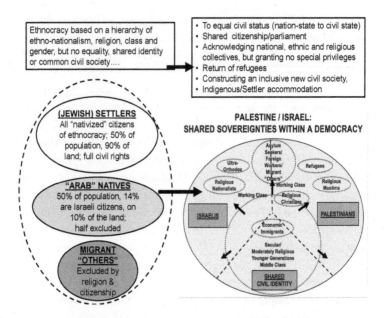

Figure 8.1   The Shift from a Settler Colonial Structure to One of Post-coloniality

is that there is a need to consider established Jewish Israeli settlers as belonging in Palestine-Israel by virtue of their sense of emotional attachment to the place, and therefore as having the right to actualise themselves as individuals and as a cultural collectivity in a decolonial and non-dominating way…. In this sense, "Jewish Israel" or even "Israeli", as a potentially secular category, could function in much the same way as the "Afrikaner" identity functions in post-Apartheid South Africa. Thus, although at present "Israeli" carries the connotation of violence and dispossession by association with belonging to the Israeli settler-colonial state, in a post-apartheid situation it has the potential of becoming a *cultural* and not a *political* signifier. Over time, Israeli Jewishness has the potential of being re-articulated as a civic identity, allowing for Jewishness to be reclaimed as an ethno-religious and/or cultural self-identification rather than the racialised category it signifies in the current settler-colonial state of Israel. It also helps to avert the rather problematic attempt by some to reduce Jewishness to religion and religious practice.

One example might illustrate how this process of nation-building might work. In the 2019 international FIFA football standings, Israel was ranked 93 and Palestine 103 (out of 211 national teams). Neither team has managed to break into the World Cup. Imagine if, by combining them, a strong enough team would emerge that would be a World Cup competitor. That alone would go a long way towards creating a common national identity and acceptability of the Other. Examples of immigrants or minorities becoming stars of international teams demonstrate the dynamic power of sports, entertainment, the media and other sectors of civil society towards integration.

6. *Economy and Economic Justice.* Our vision seeks to achieve justice, and this includes social and economic justice. Economic policy must address the decades of exploitation and discrimination which have sown deep socioeconomic gaps among the people living in the land. The income distribution in Israel/Palestine is more unequal than any country in the world. A State seeking justice must develop a creative and long-term redistributive economic policy to ensure that all citizens have equal opportunity to attain education, productive employment, economic security and a dignified standard of living.

We begin by deracializing the economy. In an ethno-nationalist state like Israel, access to land, natural resources and economic opportunities and the right to social benefits all depend on what national, ethnic and religious group you "belong to." Decolonization must first of all ensure equal access and equitable redistribution of resources to all the country's citizens. But it must go deeper than that. A neoliberal economy is incapable of offering equitable access to resources or providing social and economic security, regardless of how democratic it is, since neoliberalism replaces society with a collection of competing individuals. The vast majority of these units of human capital (which is how neoliberalism defines individuals)[41] will belong to the "precariate" working people and middle-class professionals alike whose employment is precarious and does not provide a living wage.[42] While Palestinians and Israeli Jews alike desire a modern economy, and many are enraptured of capitalism's promises of a good life as consumers, our role in establishing a new polity is not merely to replace one set of political and economic elites with another.

Article 6 sets out briefly the fundamental expectations that the new economy must fulfill. Much work remains to be done in the sphere of land reform, economics and social policy. A proper balance must be found between a market-based economy – which, after all, is still the global norm – and a kind of eco-socialism that is egalitarian and sustainable.[43] It must offer equal access to all forms of employment, a safety net of job protections and benefits, and shelter for non-commodifiable social and cultural resources.

> 7. *Constructing a Shared Civil Society.* The State shall nurture a vital civil society comprised of common civil institutions, in particular educational, cultural and economic. Alongside religious marriage the State will provide civil marriage.

Article 7 turns to the next phase of decolonization: the processes of constructing a post-colonial polity and shared civil society. The goal of a single state is to normalize relations among its citizens. That requires a shared civil society. Settlers can only be "sufficiently indigenized|" if a civil space is opened to them, conditional on their readiness to engage in the decolonization process. Indeed, only when citizenship is deracialized can a level civil "playing field" emerge.

Once participation in a democratic polity and a civil society of equals becomes normalized, the conditions arise for the forging of a new post-colonial *relationship* between Palestinians and Israeli Jews that transcends the legal formalities of common citizenship. In this new relationship, which, following Mamdani, we are calling a *political community*, the Palestinians regain their sovereignty, their rights and their country within the framework of a single democratic state shared equally with Israeli Jews and others. For their part, Israeli Jews, by accepting this new relationship enabled by the indigenous Palestinians, are now able to join in fully as the country moves on towards its post-colonial future. Only at this point does the name of the country emerge (whatever it will be), the expression of a new state-generated "national" identity.

> 8. *Commitment to Human Rights, Justice and Peace.* The State shall uphold international law and seek the peaceful resolution of conflicts through negotiation and collective security in accordance with

the United Nations Charter. The State will sign and ratify all international treaties on human rights and its people shall reject racism and promote social, cultural and political rights as set out in relevant United Nations covenants.

If I have expressed reservations about the potency of a "rights-based" approach to liberation given the weakness of international law and human rights as actual political instruments, they do play a key role in structuring the parameters of equal rights so as to ensure the rights of all, collective as well as individual. This means that the new state will commit itself to the UN Charter, international humanitarian law, human rights covenants and international conventions, especially those that have continuing meaning in the decolonization process, such as the Declaration on the Granting of Independence to Colonial Countries and Peoples and the Declaration on the Rights of Indigenous Peoples.

9. *Our Role in the Region.* The ODS Campaign will join with all progressive forces in the Arab world struggling for democracy, social justice and egalitarian societies free from tyranny and foreign domination. The State shall seek democracy and freedom in a Middle East that respects its many communities, religions, traditions and ideologies, yet strives for equality, freedom of thought and innovation. Achieving a just political settlement in Palestine, followed by a thorough process of decolonization, will contribute measurably to these efforts.

Article 9 turns to decolonization in its regional context. It does not take place in isolation, disconnected either from its region or, globally, from international politics or racialized capitalism.[44] Indeed, the Palestinian themselves have moved beyond the national frame.[45] Although few would give up on the project of reconstituting their national presence in their homeland, in fact a significant proportion of the Palestinians live in a mix of Diaspora and Exile. Many will undoubtedly choose to remain where they are, having established lives there (Jordan in particular), while others may choose to relocate to other countries. This does not mean that Palestine ceases to hold a central place in their identities and communal life, only that diaspora arises as an added and voluntary dimension to Palestinian life. No less significant, these out-of-state communities – refugees, exiled and displaced, that is, those centrally imbricated in, but benefitting little from, the current hegemonic national project – "challenge its central logics and/or break free of its fallacies? ... In this sense [write Salih and Richter-Devroe], we feel the urge to go beyond understandably defensive nationalist stances by making visible the multiple ways in which Palestinians think, become subjects, act, or mobilize through visions and political practices outside of – but not necessarily oppositional to – national frames."[46] A vibrant Palestinian life exists and will continue to exist beyond the borders of Palestine itself.

The Palestinians of the ODSC consider themselves as both situated in the wider region and in solidarity with its progressive elements. Indeed, the history of Palestine is a microcosm of the range of issues the Arab and Muslim world has had to deal with until today. Palestine has experienced classic colonialism (British rule, even under the technical auspices of the League of Nations) and settler colonialism (Zionism). The Great Powers have interfered in regional affairs from the Capitulation Agreements of the nineteenth century through Sykes-Picot, the division of Syrian/Palestinian between the British and French, to embroilment in US and European intrigues and military ventures. It has suffered regime change (Arafat and the PA), and has even been forced into neo-colonialism, based on Israel's role as an American surrogate in the region. The decolonization of Palestine has important lessons for the wider struggles for liberation still raging in the region, whether against neo-colonial powers or local elites.

In their struggle against Zionist colonialism, Palestinians have long sought to align their efforts with broader anti-colonial struggles.[47] "Such an alignment" of Palestinians with broader liberation struggles, argue Salamanca, Qato, Rabie and Samour,[48]

> would expand the tools available to Palestinians and their solidarity movement and reconnect the struggle to its own history of anti-colonial internationalism. At its core, this internationalist approach asserts that the Palestinian struggle against Zionist settler colonialism can only be won when it is embedded within, and empowered by, broader struggles – all anti-imperial, all anti-racist, and all struggling to make another world possible.

While participating in regional liberation, Palestinians will continue to make the entire region (and beyond) their diasporic "home." Whether they aspire to return or expect to find social justice and full rights in their places of exile, Palestinians present a model of a "political society" pushing forward a claim for radical regional democracy rather than only a nationalist project.[49]

Their ability to imagine their national community in regional and international dimensions may well contribute to the loosening of the nation-state as a central organizing principle and return the region to other forms of political and communal life that characterized it for millennia. Just to "throw out" that kind of imagining of new political communities, Figure 8.2 presents one fanciful model of a "Middle East Confederation of Cultures" that takes into account different interlocking identities, state, national, ethnic, religious, gender, age and political orientation.

Such a Confederation may be "fanciful" today, but as we begin to search for new, more representative and more egalitarian ways to structure our political lives, we need to be playing with new

MIDDLE EAST CONFEDERATION OF CULTURES

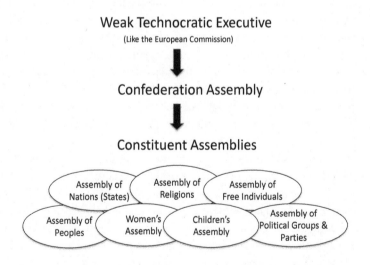

Figure 8.2   A Middle East Confederation of Cultures

possibilities that reflect our analysis of what has to be changed – especially ways of broadening the "third space" of not only indigenous but other forms of sovereignty Indeed, the Confederation of Cultures resembles (if extends) the Kurdish leader Abdullah Öclan's notion of Democratic Confederalism,[50] as well as other forms of re-existence, from bio-regionalism[51] and social ecology,[52] to liberation geographies[53] and other conceptions.[54] On a global scale, the Zapatisa uprising in Chiapas, Mexico, inspired the "movement of movements" against neoliberal globalization throughout the world.[55]

10. *International responsibility.* On a global level, the ODS Campaign views itself as part of the progressive forces striving for an alternative global order that is just, equitable and free of any oppression, racism, imperialism and colonialism.

As Linda Tabar and Chandni Desai[56] note: "Decolonization is a global project [whose operations transcend] the seeming bounded logics of settler sovereignties, territorialities, capitalist accumulation and the gendered and racist violence." Adom Getachew describes the views of the African liberation thinkers in the 1950s and 1960s as "worldmaking." Beyond the colonial relations specific to any particular struggle, they understood that their dependency and inability to truly develop economically and politically was due no less to "alien rule within international structures of unequal integration and racial hierarchy." Accordingly, liberation "required a global anticolonial counterpoint that would undo the hierarchies that facilitated domination." They therefore conceived of liberation as three interrelated projects: obtaining the right of self-determination for their own peoples, forming regional federations, and working towards a New International Economic Order.[57]

Edward Said certainly shared that "worldmaking" perspective, and it is something to which anti-colonial, anti-neo-colonial and anti-globalization forces must return. John Collins,[58] Bichler and Nitzan[59] and I[60] have written extensively on Global Palestine, on how the struggle for decolonization is but a microcosm of larger global struggles to decolonize from an oppressive world system enforced by the world's hegemons, amongst whom Israel plays a key role.

9

Towards Post-coloniality

Now that we have a fairly detailed picture of what the problem is (decolonizing settler colonialism) and where we are going (the outlines of a single democratic state end-game), we need to mobilize the political will necessary to achieve it. We need to summon power in new and effective ways. Without a political program and a strategy for effecting it, we have no political direction. We are reduced to small, localized activist groups capable of protesting and analyzing but little else. How can the diverse elements of an activist movement be brought together into an effective, broad-based anti-colonial campaign? It is to the issue of strategy that we now turn.

STRATEGY: HOW DO WE GET THERE?

The good news is that the campaign to decolonize Palestine is further along than we realize. Grassroots resistance among Palestinians has succeeded in mobilizing major segments of the international civil society – trade unions, religious denominations, intellectuals, academics and students, political and human rights organizations, activist groups, alternative media outlets and social media, general public opinion, and even some government officials and parliamentarians. The Palestinian cause has attained a global prominence equal to that of the anti-apartheid movement. Palestinians have become emblematic of oppressed peoples everywhere. A wide range of activities advance the Palestinian cause. Protest actions in the OPT, grassroots campaigns, lobbying, hosting international conferences, producing a wealth of books, articles, films, social media presentations and advocacy materials. Israel's panic over the BDS campaign demonstrates that it has already lost in the Court of Public Opinion. Only the shallow support of governments, Christian evangelicals and a diminishing Jewish Establishment remain.

What is lacking, of course, is a political end-game. The illusionary two-state solution collapsed with the Oslo "peace process" in 2000, leaving us all floundering. It is that crucial piece, a political program together with a strategy for summoning power in its pursuit, that the ODSC, alongside others, is attempting to insert. So armed with an analysis, a shared vision of the future and the outlines of a political program, let's now turn now to strategy. How do we get there?

Surveying the history of settler colonial regimes, the anti-apartheid movement in South Africa offers a useful model for the decolonization of Palestine/Israel. Despite some major differences, the fundamentals of South Africa and Israel/Palestine are similar enough to suggest to us a working strategy. Indeed, as far back as 1961, Hendrik Verwoerd, the South African prime minister and architect of the "grand apartheid" vision of the bantustans, saw the parallels. "The Jews took Israel from the Arabs after the Arabs had lived there for a thousand years. Israel, like South Africa, is an apartheid state." Added Ronnie Kasrils, then a Jewish South African cabinet minister and former ANC guerrilla on a visit to Jerusalem, "Apartheid was an extension of the colonial project to dispossess people of their land. That is exactly what has happened in Israel and the occupied territories; the use of force and the law to take the land. That is what apartheid and Israel have in common."[1] For us the most relevant similarity is that Israel is an established and strong settler state just as South Africa was, yet neither was able to defeat or marginalize an Indigenous population with state-national aspirations.

Here, in fact, the Palestinians enjoy an advantage over the resistance movement of South Africa. While the anti-apartheid movement benefited from its moral dimensions and the quality of its leadership, apartheid itself ranked low in geopolitical importance. South Africa hardly had the strategic importance that Israel has, nor did it play as central a role in international politics that Israel does. Yet the ANC managed to summon a source of power that finally defeated apartheid: mobilizing the international civil society and through it, governments who would otherwise have continued their normal political and economic relationship with the apartheid regime. The fact that the Palestinian issue has achieved the global proportions of the anti-apartheid movement *despite* its poor national leadership bespeaks two realities. First, the moral significance of occupation and repression has managed to break through, if not supersede, Israel's ability to harness Jewish suffering to its side, a testament to the moral if not political authority of international law and human rights. And second, the Israeli/Palestinian issue has been viewed as a major source of disruption throughout the Middle East, and thus of key interest to the global powers to resolve. It is in this ability to harness the international civil society to its side – to mobilize and focus this as-yet underutilized source of power – that Palestinian political strength lies.

The strategy of political organization proposed here builds on the international support the Palestinian cause has generated. It seeks to offset Israel's strength as a recognized state and its military and economic superiority with civil society organization. That approach may be illustrated as shown in Figure 9.1.

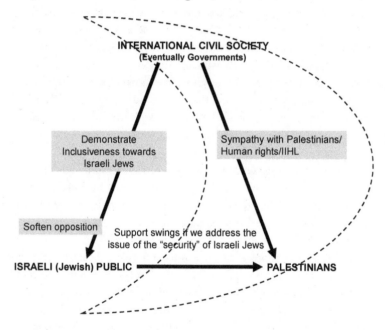

Figure 9.1 The Tripartite Alliance

This model sets out a strategic "tripartite alliance" among three main political actors: the Palestinians at home, in exile and abroad; the Israeli Jewish public; and the international community, both civil society and governments.

The Palestinians. The struggle for decolonization must be led, of course, by the Palestinians themselves. It is their struggle. No other party can define for them what decolonization entails, what will replace it. No one else can represent their collective voice. On the surface it appears that the Palestinians have little power or leverage. Yet as strong as Israel is, it is not winning in the Court of Public Opinion. True, it has the support of many governments, but that does not translate into widespread support among the world's peoples. Indeed, a worldwide Palestine solidarity movement already exists. For all its seeming clout, Israel has not been able to bring its colonial venture to completion. It has not been able to normalize itself as the replacement of Palestine. Nor has it succeeded in removing Palestine from the international agenda.

Needless to say, any anti-colonial movement must be led by those seeking their liberation. The Palestinians had a broadly representative organization in the PLO. It was effectively neutralized, if not dismantled, however, when the Palestinian Authority was established, even though the PA represents only the Palestinians of the OPT. Even before then, however, we saw that by the early 1970s the PLO had shifted from an anti-colonial liberation struggle to an attempt to resolve the Israel-Palestine "conflict" through negotiations over a Palestinian mini-state. Now, at this stage of the struggle, when anti-colonialism has become once again the only option, can a moribund PLO be revived? Can it become, as Uri Davis proposes, a liberation organization like the ANC that incorporates all voices, Israel Jewish and Palestinian Arab alike?[2] And what do we do about the collaborationist PA? Must we invent a new political vehicle entirely?

In terms of a strategic alliance with anti-colonial Israelis, can the Palestinian grassroots – academics at the head – overcome their crippling stance of "anti-normalization"? While justified overall (no one wants to normalize before decolonization), how can we engage in a joint struggle for liberation, the only effective strategy? These, indeed, are the urgent questions of the day facing the Palestinian people.

The international community. The international civil society represents the Palestinians' strongest potential ally. It represents the source of summoning effective power that we have spoken of in previous chapters. Although the struggle for freedom in Palestine has become a global issue, neither the PA nor Palestinian grassroots leadership has taken advantage of this wellspring of support to support a political plan. Even when the international public has been tapped, support remains limited and unfocused by the lack of a political end-game. The BDS campaign supports a "rights-based" approach but its three demands – ending the occupation, enacting the Right of Return and ensuring equal rights for Palestinian citizens of Israel – do not comprise a political program; on the contrary, having been formulated in the 2000 Call of Palestinian Civil Society, they reflect a two-state approach. The recent Gazan March of Return, from March 30, 2018–December 2019, highlighted the Palestinians' plight, but with a demand for Return that cannot stand alone. Palestinian human rights organizations appeal to the UN or governments to intervene, but realize full-well that human rights and international law have no political teeth. (Indeed, the NGO-ization of Palestinian civil society has served only to depoliticize and domesticate it.)[3] Joint resistance activities with such Israeli organizations as ICAHD, Breaking the Silence, Ta'ayush and Rabbis for Human Rights, together with campaigns of lobbying and public information conducted by international support groups, express solidarity with the Palestinian cause, but with no end-game articulated by the stakeholders themselves, they have no real political effect, and in effect have no concrete political program for which to advocate.

Armed, however, with an end-game, the international civil society is eminently mobilizable. Activist groups, trade unions, religious denominations and institutions, university students and faculty, allies from other ethnic and class struggles, NGOs, think tanks and even parliamentary members – all are primed to act if given a direction and leadership. Within that coordinated, focused and Palestinian-led international campaign, the moral and legal authority of international laws and treaties, together with such mechanisms at the Palestinians' disposal as international courts and tribunals, can be called upon. "The lesson from … African struggles for independence," observes Tignor,[4]

is that while nationalists can make life violent, often unbearable, for settler populations, by themselves they cannot succeed. An imperial power, if there is one, must make the critical decisions to curb the ambitions of colonial or external settlers, such as the Israelis, and assist the indigenous population, in this case the Palestinians, to realize statehood. Where the outside power departs, as the British did in Southern Rhodesia and South Africa, and in 1948 when the state of Israel came into being, international pressure on the successor state is vital.

In the end, governments, with their power to support popular struggles for decolonization, as in the South African case, must and can be mobilized by their constituencies, if they are directed by a political program, strategy and effective organization.

Israeli Jews. There is a large literature on the importance of engaging settlers in the process of decolonization. How to first "unsettle" their narratives, their views of the colonized. How to unsettle their very "settler common sense" of themselves and the world they built. All on the way to unsettling and ultimately decolonizing the country altogether.[5] This is not an easy undertaking, even among liberal settlers predisposed to "peace." As we witnessed during the Oslo peace process, dialogue groups had virtually no effect on changing the views even of those participating in them, or of "unsettling" Zionism. Nor did joint Israeli-Palestinian activities attract more than a few of the already committed.

Although the international community poured millions of dollars into "joint" activities of dialogue and NGO cooperation, their programs were so unsuccessful that Palestinians came to see them as little more than exercises in "normalization." Because they endeavored *not* to unsettle Israelis, they avoided tough political issues.[6] So strong were feelings against these misguided "encounters," so much did they strengthen "anti-normalization" attitudes amongst Palestinians, virtually all Palestinian-Israeli cooperation was paralyzed, even with anti-colonial Israeli organizations.[7]

While strategic outreach to wider Israeli Jewish populations should continue, the lesson of Oslo suggests that that may be futile. Engagement, unsettling, decolonization, the construction of a new, shared political community and, ultimately, reconciliation in a post-colonial reality – these are not processes that interest settlers. Dominant populations do not voluntarily give up their privileges or compromise their security vis-à-vis those they consider their permanent enemies. If South Africa is an example, decolonization must be imposed on Israeli society, after the Palestinians have been empowered to a point where

Israeli Jews *must* engage with them. That means that the Israeli Jewish public must be largely written off as a partner in the run-up to decolonization. Trapped in an ethno-national paradigm, having internalized the zero-sum logic of "either us or them," Israeli Jews are satisfied with what they have achieved: "substantial pacification," "substantial colonization," "substantial national and personal security," the "substantial normalization" of their settler state in the international community.

This does not mean that Israeli Jews are irrelevant. Particularly relevant is that (small) segment of the population who, in Ben-Eliezer's terms, have largely left "ethno-militaristic" nationalism for a more open civil or "liberal nationalism" that could entertain a pluralistic democracy.[8] As in South Africa, the presence of Israeli co-resistors, "colonists who refuse," lends credibility to the struggle. Their involvement also demonstrates the possibility of coexistence. Indeed, it offers an opportunity for members of the settler society to "earn" their "sufficient indigeneity." The academic literature affirms the possibility of settlers being transformed through anti-colonial resistance.[9] Extending that possibility into the decolonization process suggests that shared resistance may, over time, broaden as the post-colonial society and polity begin to emerge. That is the promise in decolonization that carries us beyond expected settler resistance.

While it is clear that the vast majority of Israeli Jews will not support any process of decolonization, we also understand that their inclusion in an expanded civil society is essential to its success. This is why the ODSC program insists on the *transformation* from an apartheid regime to a democratic state. A political process of decolonization might have to be inaugurated without the active participation of the vast majority of Israeli Jews. They cannot, however, be excluded. The inclusive nature of the decolonization process and the dynamics of everyday life will over time lead to the rise of a new civil society. Limited at first as people begin to reconcile their collective political, cultural, religious and communal identities with their new civil reality, over time (one, two generations?) a shared civil society will expand to embrace all citizens to different degrees.

The Tripartite Alliance that thus emerges among Palestinian Arabs, their Israeli Jewish allies and the international civil society has one primary objective. Given the inability to overcome settler colonialism from the inside, it seeks to marshal those forces, especially of international public opinion, that can cause its collapse. Israeli settler colonialism, like that of South Africa, is only sustainable as long as it has international support. The main task of the Triple Alliance must be to mobilize public opinion abroad so that governments change their policies towards Israel and the issue of decolonization.

Here is where the BDS movement of boycotts, divestment and sanctions can have its greatest effect – *if* it is linked to a political program. Adam and Moodley[10] confirm this view:

> In the case of South Africa, economic sanctions have often been overestimated as causal factors of compromise.... Boycotts of South African goods were easily circumvented.... It was in the psychological realm, rather than through unbearable cost increases, that sanctions contributed to a readiness to entertain negotiated solutions to escalating unrest. Paradoxically, the moral sanctions of ostracism by supposedly anti-Communist Western allies bothered the Afrikaner politicians more than the economic losses....

The infrastructure already exists to render Israeli apartheid unsustainable. Armed with an end-game, the journey to a post-colonial future can be said to have begun. Still, massive amounts of organization and consensus-building around a program of decolonization remain to be done. The range of actors engaged in the decolonization of Palestine is vast. Simply a rough survey of the terrain turns up seven major target populations, as illustrated in Figure 9.2.

Figure 9.2 The Seven Major Target Populations

Each of those populations, of course, divide up into a wide range of sub-groups based on religion, class, locale, political affiliation, gender and other parameters. *But together they define the base of our Tripartite Alliance.* Ways must be found and structures created to reach out and bring them all into active engagement in the struggle for decolonization. Yet even among those who agree with the vision and general direction, fundamental differences exist. Whether led by a rejuvenated

PLO or by a coalition of Palestinian and Israeli grassroots organizations, the liberation struggle must be as participatory and inclusive as possible.

As we move into political mobilization around a strategy of decolonization, we must constantly evaluate where we are in the process of decolonization and what yet needs to be done. We need to get into specifics. What in the Domination Management Regime are we exactly dismantling? And what do we suggest in terms of reconstruction? Let's begin with population management.

DISMANTLING THE REGIME OF POPULATION CONTROL

Expanding on Mamdani's seminal question: When does a settler become a native? Let's ask: How does settler colonialism actually end? The answer is when a new, inclusive political community arises. Decolonization means *replacing the colonial regime and its unequal structure of settler/indigenous relations with a new polity, economy (including access to land and resources) and civil society which is genuinely inclusive and democratic, yet also accepting of cultural pluralism.* Replacing an ethnocratic colonial state that "belongs" to one particular group with a democracy based on universal citizenship removes significant control from the settlers. This, then, enables a new political community to emerge. It will incorporate the cultural identities, traditions and communal institutions of the new state's diverse population, of course. The new state we envision will protect and value pluralism. In the end, however, these "old" cultural and political identities, reflective of times before decolonization, must be transcended by new, shared civic identities, symbols, holidays, norms and institutions. Something new and shared must emerge, says Mamdani, if we are to fashion a future different from the past, a new political community.

> We need to recognize that the past and the future overlap, as do culture and politics, but they are not the same thing. Cultural communities rooted in a common past do not necessarily have a common future. Some may have a diasporic future. Similarly, political communities may include immigrants, and thus be characterized by cultural diversities, even if there is a dominant culture signifying a history shared by the majority. *The point is that political communities are defined, in the final analysis, not by a common past but by a*

*resolve to forge a common future under a single political roof, regardless
of how different or similar their pasts may be. Our challenge is to define
political identities as distinct from cultural identities, without denying
that there may be a significant overlap between the two.* One way of
doing so is to accent common residence over common descent –
indigeneity – as the basis of rights.[11]

Only a new political community, a democratic polity accompanied
by an inclusive civil society, will engender the new settler/indigenous
relationship upon which decolonization can build. "In the context of
a former settler colony," writes Mamdani,[12] "a single citizenship for
settlers and natives can only be the result of an overall metamorpho-
sis whereby erstwhile colonizers and colonized are politically reborn
as equal." This opens the possibility for what Mignolo and Walsh,[13]
quoting Adolo Albán Achinte, call "re-existence." Redefining and
re-signifying collective life in conditions of dignity underlies any possibility of resetting settler/indigenous relations.

Bruyneel[14] adds that the post-colonial condition should not be
simply a kind of compromise between the former colonizers and the
colonized. The issue is not merely granting the colonized access to the
political, legal, economic and social resources formerly controlled by
the settlers.[15] Instead, a "third space of sovereignty" must emerge. The
colonized must be empowered to control the conditions that determine their lives free of any post-colonial domination or constraints.
The Indigenous must regain their sovereignty, their ability to say "no."
Their rights to their land, resources, culture and community must
also be reinstated.[16] Over time the third space of sovereignty could
give rise to other forms of re-existence, such as bio-regionalism,[17]
social ecology,[18] the Kurdish experiment with democratic confederalism in Rojava[19] or other conceptions.[20] The very localized Zapatisa
uprising in Chiapas, Mexico, focused on access to land, inspired a
"movement of movements" against neoliberal globalization throughout the world.[21]

It should come as no surprise that the Indigenous throughout
the world might prefer to return to a pre-colonial state of being.
They realize, however, that an "institutional legacy of colonial rule"
will remain to be dealt with. The settler presence is a major part of
that colonial legacy. Even in those few cases where the settlers have

actually left, as in Algeria, Angola, Mozambique, Kenya and Ireland, their presence remains. As ever the danger, a neo-colonial relationship often replaces the colonial one. How much more difficult it must be for the Indigenous to carve out a meaningful degree of sovereignty in places where, despite the formal end of settler colonialism, like in South Africa, they continue to be marginalized? Fanon warned of the resilience of the alliance between the former colonists and a new native "national bourgeoisie."[22] "Now, Comrades, now is the time to change sides" wrote Fanon in an incipient, more innocent (and less gender-sensitive) phase of the anti-colonization struggle.[23]

> Let us leave this Europe which never stops talking of man yet massacres him at every one of its street corners, at every corner of the world.... So, my brothers, how could we fail to understand that we have better things to do than follow in that Europe's footsteps? ... Let us decide not to imitate Europe and let us tense our muscles and our brains in a new direction. Let us endeavor to invent man in full.... No, we do not want to catch up with anyone.... The Third World must start over....
>
> *So, comrades, let us not pay tribute to Europe by creating states, institutions, and societies that draw their inspirations from it.* If we want to transform Africa into a new Europe, [Latin] America into a new Europe, then let us entrust the destinies of our countries to the Europeans. They will do a better job than the best of us.... If we want to respond to the expectations of our peoples, we must look elsewhere besides Europe.... We must make a new start, develop a new way of thinking, and endeavor to create a new man.[24]

Fanon is arguing here precisely for a "third space of sovereignty." Indigenous peoples must jockey for space with a Europe (Fanon might have referred instead to the G-7 in today's terms) that has "taken over leadership of the world with fervor, cynicism, and violence," but is unwilling to cede the space and authority the indigenous masses have struggled to liberate.[25] In the 60 years since Fanon wrote *The Wretched of the Earth*, the transition from a colonial to post-colonial reality has proven elusive. Fanon's warnings over the devastation of the unholy alliance between the neo-colonial metropolitan bourgeoisie and the national bourgeoisie would bring upon the newly independent peoples have come to pass. The old Third World, the Global South in which we all had such faith, has sunk into a poor and repressive shadow of its colonizers.[26]

This has certainly been the experience of the Arab peoples of our region. While the Palestinians have their fair share of liberationist thinkers, crowned by Edward Said, the politicians, religious sects and national bourgeoisie currently running Palestinian affairs seem lifted from Fanon's caricatures of oppressive, corrupt and limited elites. Add to that the effects of Israeli colonization and apartheid, and the Palestinian people have their work cut out for them. The very process of struggle, however, against the backdrop of a century of colonization, might well impart to them that critical liberationist perspective enabling them to carve out their space of sovereignty. They are not left alone in this endeavor. Algeria and South Africa aside, few anti-colonial struggles have enjoyed the international support and active intervention of the Palestinian cause. They at least have a shot at meaningful decolonization.

What about the Israeli Jews? Presumably the political space opened by decolonization must address them as well, or we fall back to a reverse ethnocracy. Here is where the post-colonial pact comes into play. As we mentioned earlier, the Indigenous have the power, after decolonization, to grant the (former) settlers what they covet the most in a post-colonial reality: *sufficient* indigeneity and membership in a shared political community, both of which signify political closure on the settler colonial project, if not reconciliation and certainly not the need to remember. If you Zionists will accept your place in our political community, the Palestinians might say when their sovereignty and rights have been restored in their post-coloniality, then we will accept you as equal citizens, possibly as partners in a future political community. Thus, writes Omar Barghouti,

is the most magnanimous – rational – offer any oppressed indigenous population can present to its oppressors. Only by shedding their colonial privileges, dismantling their structures of oppression, and accepting the restoration of the rights of the indigenous people of the land, especially the right of Palestinian refugees to return and to reparations and the right of all Palestinians to unmitigated equality, can settlers be indigenized and integrated into the emerging nation and therefore become entitled to participating in determining the future of the common state.

For their part, he goes on,

> The indigenous population ... must be ready, after justice had been reached and rights had been restored, to forgive and to accept the former settlers as equal citizens, enjoying normal lives – neither masters nor slaves. The above explained process of de-dichotomization at the identity and conceptual level, not just in the concrete reality, that must proceed in parallel to the realization of rights is the most important guarantor of minimizing the possibility of lingering hostility or, worse, a reversal of roles between oppressor and oppressed once justice and equal rights have prevailed. The ultimate goal should be justice, equality and ethical coexistence, not revenge.[27]

This post-settler compact can be tricky, Veracini[28] warns. Settler societies attempt to avoid "apologizing" for past crimes. They may make certain material concessions without fundamentally recasting the settler/indigenous relationship, or offer symbolic concessions like restoring parts of Indigenous lands. "Good faith" is difficult to gauge, as is the point when decolonization and reassembly is achieved. Zreik says that settlers stop being settlers when they end their settlement expansion and "give up all privileges, individual or collective. Practically, this means giving up his supremacy and accepting full equality with the native. This way, the settler stays but colonization goes, and when colonization goes he stops being a settler because the situation is no longer one of settlers and natives."[29] But that place where colonialism ends can be evasive. That is what makes concepts like the Dominance Management Regime so useful. They give us clear and measurable benchmarks for dismantling a colonial regime. And that is why it is so important to have a political end-game that provides a clear blueprint for decolonization, and not only a vision.

DISMANTLING THE REGIME OF LAND CONTROL

For Palestinians, like other colonized peoples, land is perhaps *the* major issue. It stands as the measure by which any plan of decolonization is deemed genuine and acceptable. As we saw in Chapter 3, the legal mechanisms by which Palestinian land has been taken is well documented. Seldom, though, have proposals for land redistribution under a process of decolonization been put forward.

The manifesto of the One Democratic State Campaign bookmarks the land issue as of prime importance. Still, it does not go beyond the broad declaration that "public land of the State shall belong to the nation as a whole and all of its citizens shall have equal access to its use." It is clear that the new state cannot go back to the Ottoman land regime that remained in effect until 1948. That has been altered beyond recognition over the past century. But should it institute a land regime based on private ownership, as a neoliberal economy would propose? The Israeli system actually offers a model that might be retained. The land of the country is held in custodianship by the state, which allocates it for public purposes as the need arises. It is a system that balances national conservation policies with such priorities as making land and housing accessible to the entire population. The problem with the Israeli land regime is not its conception – state ownership of land – but the state's policy of making land available for Jewish use only. Under a land regime opening the country's resources to all its citizens, such a system might prove sustainable and equitable. Such a regime would dismantle a key element of the Domination Management Regime.

No matter what the plan, it is clear that land redistribution is a crucial piece of decolonization. Zionism's land laws and regulations, as we've seen, alienated over 93 percent of land within the "Green Line" from "non-Jewish" ownership and use, while 75 percent of the West Bank has been brought under Israeli control. Tremendous disparities in housing and infrastructure separate Israeli Jews from Palestinians. Merely ending the policy of allocating land and segregating communities on ethno-national and religious grounds will eliminate much of this abuse.

It is the return of the refugees, however, that poses the main challenge to the equitable distribution of land. Here there is some good news. According to the Palestinian geographer Salman Abu Sitta,[30] some 85 percent of the land taken from the Palestinians in 1948 is still available for settlement. It is either Israeli agricultural land or has been converted into national parks. Returning refugees may not be able to reclaim their ancestral homes or resettle their destroyed villages and towns. But they can be resettled in the part of the country from whence they hail. Two right-of-return organizations, Zochrot and Badil, have already drafted Palestinian planners and architects to plan new communities with modern infrastructure for the returning residents.[31]

DISMANTLING THE REGIME OF ECONOMIC CONTROL

The establishment of a single state will effectively end Israeli colonial dictates to and control over the Palestinian economy, although putting the two economies together and achieving Palestinian parity will take time. It might take less time than expected. Although the Israeli economy is 250 percent larger than the Palestinians' (GDP of $370 billion and growing versus $16 billion and shrinking),[32] and despite the debilitations of displacement, impoverishment, occupation, economic discrimination and inadequate services, the Palestinians are nevertheless in a strong position to achieve parity with Israelis in a relatively short period. While education under occupation or in refugee camps presents great challenges, Palestinians enjoy one of the highest literacy rates in the world (91 percent) and significant rates of higher education. During the Oslo period, the Palestinian economy was one of the world's fastest growing, showing its potential if unleashed. Agriculture, tourism and business, including a thriving hi-tech sector, all possess great economic potential, particularly as they enter into the wider economy of the region. Palestinians, then, are poised to enter into an advanced economy. They also possess one other great economic resource, the highly educated and affluent Palestinian Diaspora. Their readiness to invest in the Palestinian economy during the early stages of the Oslo process can be repeated, if they are convinced that the economy – both the Palestinian sector and the larger national economy of which it will become a part – is genuinely open and free. Like the Jewish Diaspora was for Israel, the Palestinian Diaspora must be considered when we are speaking of economic viability (and, if fact, one could envision them joining forces in supporting, and profiting from, the joint economy).

For the ODSC, however, a neoliberal economy does not equate with liberation. Although Palestinians and Israeli Jews alike aspire to economic prosperity, the ODSC asks: if we are creating a new polity and civil society based on progressive values of democracy, human rights and liberation, why would we envision the future state as merely another neoliberal entity with all the inequities, income differentials and environmental unsustainability that that entails? Now there are aspects of the economy not determined locally. To the degree that the new state's economy has to be integrated into the capitalist world-system, there are structures, policies and trading realities it must adhere to. But not totally. In fact, the struggle for economic justice may well be one that cross-cuts working-class Palestinian and Israeli societies, just as joint economic projects will bring the two business communities together (again, as happened briefly in early Oslo). And just as the new state may want to retain elements of the Israeli system – the state control of lands, for example, or, ironically, its highly developed military and police forces – so, too, it may borrow from the elements of Israel's socialist past: its well-organized national health service, its welfare structures, state financing of essential institutions and services.

The ODSC model, while it needs considerable refinement, envisions a mixed eco-socialist/regulated capitalist economy, which as much as possible avoids the inequities of unregulated neoliberalism. It does so not only for reasons of sustainable economy and social equality, but because, as we discussed in the last chapter, neoliberalism becomes a form of governmentality, of control, antithetical to our liberation struggle. As the ODSC program makes clear in Articles 9 and 10, decolonization must be regional and global in scope; it is not viable in one country alone. This is true in the economic realm as well as the political. While the new state will have to find ways of dealing with a world-system of predatory capitalism, and in so doing will support a regulated capitalist sector, the thrust of our economic and social vision is towards a sustainable, equitable eco-socialism.

REFRAMING: DISMANTLING THE MANAGEMENT OF LEGITIMACY

In the last chapter, we discussed the importance of (re)framing the "conflict" as a settler colonial enterprise. This was not only an academic exercise. Without a reframing we cannot accurately analyze the problem and reach a resolution. We have witnessed the failure of poor analysis, bundled into misguided schemes of conflict resolution over the past many decades. Reframing also helps us block out some common understandings – "acknowledgements"; it keeps us on the same page. It is a key to decolonization, since the process is one of forging a common future, not merely finding unsavory, short-lived compromises.

Abdel-Nour[33] concurs that in the final analysis, arriving at a post-conflict situation requires a "bridging narrative," a "fusion of horizons" between the two peoples. It must "denationalize" the discourse between the contestants, while helping to fashion a new, shared "re-national" identity.[34] He argues, however, that that cannot be achieved too early in the process. First the basic "acknowledgements" we laid out in Chapter 7 have to be accepted by a critical mass of both peoples – beginning, we suggest, with the activist community. Sooner or later, a *largely shared* but not uniform narrative and set of common national symbols must emerge in a common civil society and polity.

We may be further along in this process than we think. Pappe describes how a "harsher," more fundamentalist, more religious, even more cynical neo-Zionism arose after the collapse of the Oslo peace process and the outbreak of the Second Intifada, eclipsing a more critical post-Zionism of the 1990s.[35] That may be true in Israel, but as he and the neo-Zionists both recognize, the post-Zionist critique still informs much of the discussion abroad.[36] The fundamental "acknowledgements" we set out – that a joint struggle against Zionist colonialism will enable us to articulate a compelling vision of a shared future; that a single apartheid state already exists *de facto* over all of Palestine, and it must be transformed into a pluralistic democracy; and that the promise of indigenization addresses the deepest sources of settler insecurity, plus other critical perspectives – have been generally accepted by large swathes of the international public. Young people, including young Jews, have shifted to that view.[37] Or more. In 2019 the American Jewish Voice for Peace issued an explicitly anti-Zionist position paper. It opens by declaring: "Jewish Voice for Peace is guided by a vision of justice, equality and freedom for all people. We unequivocally oppose Zionism because it is counter to those ideals."[38]

Abroad and in the activist Left circles in Israel, post-Zionism is alive and well. It is playing its role in laying the foundations for a bridging narrative that Jews can live with. Not yet the vast majority of Israeli Jews, to be sure, but we should not measure the progress of our reframing by the degree to which it is accepted by Israeli society. We know that for good reasons, Israeli Jews will be the last party to fall into place as decolonization becomes a fact of life. At this stage we should be encouraged that the Tripartite Alliance has such a narrative on which to build as it seeks to broaden its base of support.

Key to the new narrative is "writing the Indigenous back in."[39] More precisely, rewriting a shared narrative, as post-Zionism has begun to do. With that, of course, other non-settler immigrants (such as Russians and Christians), peoples imported into Israel (foreign workers who stay) and others who find themselves there (African asylum seekers) must be "written in" as well, in addition to Arab Jews, women and marginalized others. Reframing will not be confined to and completed in the decolonizing project, of course. The new narrative will continue to evolve through the very dynamics of shared daily life. Narrative-building is a part of nation-building.

Reframing is a process that helps reconcile, or bridge, seemingly irreconcilable narratives, ideologies and views. But it also provides a mechanism for collectively "thinking through" what the daunting prospect of decolonization entails and promises. This visioning is not easy for the colonized. For Palestinians, the anti-colonial struggle still goes on in all its intensity and violence, with no resolution in sight. But as Mamdani[40] cautions, the colonized should not replicate in reverse colonialism's invidious politicization of indigeneity. In order for a post-colonial society to emerge, identities, like the rest of the colonial system, need to be deracialized, denationalized – yet not denationalized to the point of denying one's national identity. Anti-colonial struggle is a struggle for national identity and rights. "Denationalization" means lowering one's national boundaries so that an additional layer of common pan-national civil identity may emerge. Our reframing must challenge the idea that we must define political identity, political rights and political justice solely in terms of indigeneity.

Barghouti[41] frames the future settler/indigenous reconciliation as "ethical coexistence." Decolonization for him is restoring

> the inalienable rights of the indigenous Palestinian people, particularly the right to self-determination, and the *acquired* rights of the

indigenized former colonial settlers to live in peace and security, individually and collectively, after ridding them of their colonial privileges.... In parallel with the process of ending injustice and restoring basic Palestinian rights, and while oppressive relationships are being dismantled and colonial privileges done away with, a conscious and genuine process of challenging the dichotomy between the identity of the oppressed and that of the oppressor must *simultaneously* be nourished to build the conceptual foundations for ethical coexistence in the decolonized future state. Only then can the end of oppression give birth to a common, post-oppression identity that can truly make the equality between the indigenous Palestinians and the indigenized settlers as just, sustainable and peaceful as possible.

This state of ethical coexistence has also been described as "shared life," harkening back to a time of (idealized?) pre-Zionist harmony, extending all the way back to Canaanite times.[42] Other formulations speak of Indigenous/settler reconciliation,[43] settler/indigenous de-dichotomization;[44] a post-colonial compact and the creation of a "third space" of sovereignty,[45] a new political community[46] or a state of re-existence, defined as "the redefining and re-signifying of life in conditions of dignity."[47]

Reframing is an ongoing process of dismantling the mental infrastructure of colonization. At root, it liberates the subordinate identities and categories of exclusion into which the Indigenous have been confined by the settler narrative.[48] But it also liberates the colonizers by enabling them to see beyond their own exclusive, self-serving narrative, to imagine a radically new post-coloniality.

Decolonization, we must understand, is a threatening prospect for those who have ruled for so long. They are forced to confront not only challenges to their racialized ideology and society, but their very "common sense." Settlers internalize seeming self-evident notions of gender, race, religion. Stories of their own hegemony and their rationalization of the crimes they have committed against the Indigenous become undeniable "fact." Even their privileged lifestyles appear natural, normal and deserved. Decolonization, which "unsettles" all of this, to say the least, is undoubtedly threatening. Add to this the fact that those challenging them are the people whom they have ruled over and dismissed for so long. And they are being called upon to give up deeply held beliefs, narratives, claims and sense of security – for what? An unclear future that places them in a vulnerable situation dictated by their permanent enemies? The very fact that, yes, the native population and other marginalized groups are asserting their own agency, cultures and agendas only confirms and magnifies that fear and anxiety.[49]

Paradigm shifts are always threatening. Reframing, if it is transparent, participatory and done in good faith, softens the transition by giving people somewhere to go. "If you give up this," it suggests, "you will get this, which is much better for everyone. Now let's think it over and talk about it." If conceived and presented as an inclusive win-win package, if the focus is on the vision *and* practicalities of the future rather than on the past (whose day of reckoning will come), then reframing makes the process of decolonization less threatening and more inclusive.

Reframing, the dismantling of the "mental" infrastructure of colonization, is also crucial for carrying forth the project of fostering a new sense of political community, so crucial for achieving post-coloniality.[50] A genuinely new and emancipatory national life restored to the Palestinians by their decolonization struggle will be extended to Israeli Jews as well. It is their entrance into this new space of sovereignty that will largely define the form and depth of their integrating into the new polity. This does not mean, of course, that the Jews and other communities cannot contribute out of their own cultures and experiences to expanding this shared "third space." Indeed, a myriad of ethnic, religious, cultural, class, gender, political, geographical sub-groups and communities that comprise the broad categories of "Palestinians," "Israeli Jews" and other sectors of the society all have their contributions to make to the emerging pluralistic society, influenced as well by regional and global cultures.

When, at last, we reach the stage where decolonization shades into post-coloniality, we also enter into the final phase of reframing, best described by the Kenyan writer Ngũgĩ wa Thiong'o as the "decolonization of the mind."[51] After all, colonial perspectives, narratives, culture, language and even psychological hegemony that have been internalized over generations by the colonized as well as by the colonizers must be unlearned. New epistemologies need to emerge.

DISMANTLING — OR REFRAMING — SECURITY

The final element of the Dominance Management Regime requiring dismantlement is that of security. "Security" was always the element upon which the settler project rested. Decolonization poses the issue of security in a new form. Instead of how can we ensure our security in a situation of built-in conflict, they now ask worriedly: What sources of security can we rely on if, in a process of decolonization, we relinquish our military, policing and other forms of control, including political and economic? What, they may ask, will prevent the Palestinian majority from doing to us what we, in our "only democracy in the Middle East," currently do to them?

We must supply answers to these questions. No political system, even one sincerely dedicated to equal rights, equal access to political power and economic resources, and meaningful channels for expressing communal identities can offer iron-clad guarantees of absolute security. The best that can be done is to construct a win-win system in which the security and well-being of every community depends on that of the others. Mechanisms can be devised to address the inter-communal conflicts that inevitably arise. In particular, four steps can be taken that maximize the likelihood of a stable polity able to control social tensions and grievances.

First, the polity will extend constitutional guarantees protecting the civil rights and rights of association to all citizens. Additionally, the Constitution will deny parliament the authority to pass laws that discriminate against citizens or collectives in any way, as set out in Article 1 of the ODSC plan. Article 8 also incorporates human rights covenants and international humanitarian law into the corpus of the new state's laws. Laws and policies providing for proper representation in national institutions based on gender, communal and religious backgrounds could be enacted as well.

Second, the military, security services, police, the judicial system and other agencies of social order will be staffed on the basis of individual merit (supplemented by an affirmative action program in the early years). Again, while policies may be enacted that ensure diversity, no group or collectivity will have any privileges, nor will any group, party or collectivity have the ability to leverage any control or domination over others (Article 4 of the ODSC plan).

Third, over time (perhaps as short as a half-generation), a new civil society will emerge based on shared daily experiences, especially among the youth. In a society where people live and work together and essential services are integrated, a new national identity will emerge, and with it a new name for the country that embodies its inclusive character. As Mamdani notes, "the process of state formation generates political identities that are distinct not only from market-based identities but also from cultural identities."[52] Removing the sources of conflict in a democratic polity, removing the ability of any collective to dominate others and nurturing integrated institutions, associations and identities – all these go a long way towards creating a sense of social security.

And fourth, a process of settler/indigenous reconciliation must be initiated. The (former) settler population must acknowledge the crimes committed by them on the colonized. Addressing them permits a healing process to work.

10

Addressing the Fears and Concerns of a Single Democratic State

The vision of a single democratic state is clear: to enable the country's peoples, communities and citizens to create a shared life based on political equality, justice and inclusiveness. But after decades of colonization, conflict and oppression, fears and doubts abound over whether Palestinians and Israeli Jews can coexist in peace and security. Reframing cannot be confined to the realms of vision, broad acknowledgements, hopes or assumptions alone. It must contend with concrete facts, perceptions, fears, ideologies and arguments that pervade the thoughts of the affected people themselves. Over time I have collected many of these concerns and questions. The responses I provide here, while by no means authoritative or complete, help us reframe from conflict resolution to decolonization, find common ground without sacrificing the restoration of Indigenous sovereignty or the need for the settler population to redefine itself as part of a new political community and identify those "acknowledgements" upon which a shared struggle for a just post-coloniality must be based.

✓ *What is the ultimate aim of the one-state solution?*

Decolonization. The dismantling of all structures of domination and control in the present system of colonization, occupation and apartheid, replacing them with a single democratic polity and an inclusive civil society. Rooted in the equal rights of all the country's citizens, the goal is to achieve a shared life that protects and nurtures the national, ethnic, religious and cultural identities and heritage in a pluralistic society.

✓ *Why do we need a particular political solution? Isn't it enough that the Palestinians demand justice and equal rights, to fight against colonialism and occupation?*

Human rights and international law are important guidelines to the resolution of any conflict, but they do not add up to a political program. Restoring Palestinian national and civil rights is imperative. But how can they be protected and promoted? In a single state, two states or some kind of confederation? A democracy or some kind of bi-national arrangement (like Lebanon)? What will be the role of religion? How will the rights of minorities be protected? Do the refugees return? What protections will minorities have? What about economic justice? Will the economy be neoliberal, socialist, or some kind of a mix? Who can immigrate to the country? Who controls the military and police forces?

These issues and many more call for a *political* program, not merely the assertion of rights, important as that is. No one will "give" Palestinians their rights. That's not how the world works. They must win their rights through struggle, but pro-active struggle in which they promote political programs that meet their needs, in which they formulate effective strategies and build strategic coalitions. We – but especially the Palestinian stakeholders – must think *politically*.

✓ *Doesn't characterizing the early Zionists and Israeli Jews of today as "settlers" delegitimize their claims to the country and Israel as well?*

No. Even though Zionism represented a tiny fraction of the Jewish people, it did express a deeply felt Jewish sense of connection to the Land of Israel/Palestine. That did not confer on them ownership, however. Had the Zionists come to Palestine with the intent of pursuing a Jewish religious, cultural or even national life in tandem with the native Palestinian population, existential conflict may have been avoided. Instead, Zionism knowingly *chose* settler colonialism as its strategy of transforming Palestine into Israel. By denying the rights and even the national existence of the Native population, the Zionist settler project invariably generated resistance. Yet conquest, displacement, violence and military domination cannot bring peace or security. Only decolonization can create the conditions for the mutual well-being of Israeli Jews and Palestinian Arabs. It is the only way out, the only way Israeli Jews can find a normalized existence within a shared political community.

✓ *The two-state solution works and has been accepted by the international community. Why abandon it now?*

Had it been implemented, the two-state solution *might have* worked, even if it wasn't fair. Palestinians would have had a viable, sovereign (if small) state on 22 percent of historic Palestine. Refugees could have come back (albeit into a small state). The Palestinian state would have had borders with both Israel and two Arab countries (Jordan and Egypt), as well as a seaport and airport in Gaza. The international community, of course, accepted the two-state solution already in 1967. The PLO officially accepted it in 1988 (before the Oslo peace process). And in 2002 the Arab League did so as well.

But Israel rejected it. Israel governments going back to 1967 have rejected the notion of a viable, sovereign Palestinian state alongside Israel. They even reject the very fact of occupation. Instead, Israel annexed East Jerusalem and moved 700,000 settlers into the territory that would have been a Palestinian state. It confined 95 percent of the Palestinians to the tiny islands of Areas A and B in the West Bank, and a besieged Gaza. In January 2020, Prime Minister Netanyahu announced that Israel would annex the Jordan Valley "and all the settlements," in accord with Trump's "Deal of the Century" – without even offering the "annexed" Palestinians Israeli citizenship. Nor is there any will on the part of the international community to sanction Israel or force it to withdraw from the Occupied Territory.

So, true, while the two-state solution may have worked, it was never accepted by Israel. Regardless, it is now dead and gone, buried under massive settlement blocs. We must move on.

✓ *The two-state solution is easier to implement than the one-state option.*

Maybe it was, four or five decades ago. Today the one-state solution is the only option. Its great advantage is that it already exists. Israel's conquest of the West Bank and its imposing of its rule over the entire country from the River to the Sea – not reinforced by its annexation of large swathes of the West Bank – amounts *de facto* to a single state. All that remains is to transform that one-state reality *Israel* has created into a democratic state of all its citizens.

✓ *Jews and Arabs hate each other and can never live together in peace.*

Such sweeping, a-historical assertions are never useful or accurate. Let's break this down a bit:

- Palestine, like the rest of the Middle East, had long been multicultural, multiethnic and multi-religious.[1] Despite occasional (*very* occasional) exceptions, Jews have lived in Arab and Muslim countries far more securely than in Europe. The very basis for the persecution of Jews, anti-Semitism based on the enmity of Christianity to Judaism, is missing in the Arab/Muslim world. Jews and Muslims lived shared if communally separate lives. When the Inquisition forced Sephardi Jews to flee the Iberian Peninsula, they found refuge in the Muslim world. Indeed, Jews (and Christians) were formally recognized religious communities there. Nowhere in the Muslim world were Jews submitted to the type of discrimination, exclusion and persecution found in Europe.
- Jews shared in the fate of the Muslim countries they live in. True, as European colonialism penetrated the Middle East it created tension between the Jewish (and Christian) communities and the Muslims. Being more engaged in international trade and often educated in European-supported schools, Jews and Christians often became identified with the colonizing powers. But the social breakdown and violence induced by colonialism over the past two centuries cannot be taken as representative of long-standing shared Muslim-Jewish life. Nor of any fundamental hostility between the communities.
- In Palestine, Sephardic, Mizrahi and orthodox Ashkenazi Jews were integral parts of the indigenous population. Native Palestinian Jews shared not only the Arabic language with the Arab Palestinians but also memories, cultural traditions, customs and sense of belonging and relations to the land. From the Palestinian perspective, Jews living in the region were merely another

religious community. Having no experience with European nationalism, they could not understand, or accept, the idea that Jews were a national group which claimed exclusive "ownership" over their own country – particularly Jews living in Russia, Poland, Britain and the US. The enmity that has existed for the past 125 years between European Jewish settlers and the Arabs of Palestine does not arise from some historic or religious enmity between the two peoples. Rather, it stems from the colonial practices of Zionism and the resistance to Zionist displacement on the part of the Palestinians. A single state resolves that colonial situation. Once the political "conflict" is resolved, there is no reason why Jews and Arabs can't live together like citizens of other pluralistic societies. Mizrahi Jews in particular could play a key bridging role in this.

• Finally, let's remember that Israeli Jews and Palestinian Arabs already live together in a single state – Israel. Palestinians represent 21 percent of Israeli citizens and participate (if under substantial limitations) in the country's political and economic life. Indeed, despite displacement, occupation and repression, the vast majority of Palestinians in the Occupied Territory also seek an inclusive political solution.

✓ *What about Palestinian terrorism?*

"The battle against Palestinian terrorism" is the lynchpin of Israel's security framing. But "terrorism" is a quintessentially colonial term. By necessity colonialism and occupation generate resistance among the indigenous population. Colonial regimes delegitimize the resistance of the oppressed by criminalizing it, pretending that the "law and order" of the strong is in fact just and good.

What is terrorism? Amnesty International avoids the term altogether, finding it far too loaded to be useful. After all, one person's terrorist is another person's freedom fighter. Instead, they employ the terminology of human rights and international law. *All* attacks against innocent civilians are illegal and must be condemned. This avoids the false symmetry between attacks by states with powerful militaries on civilian populations, such as that deployed by Israel in the Occupied

Territory, and legitimate resistance, both armed and peaceful, by its Palestinian victims.

The term "terrorism," we must note, is applied only to non-state actors. But what of *state* terrorism? Benjamin Netanyahu's own definition of terrorism – "the deliberate and systematic murder, maiming, and menacing of the innocent to inspire fear for political ends" – defines state terrorism "from above" as well as non-state terror "from below." Indeed, state terrorism is far more deadly. Non-state terrorists have claimed less than a thousand victims per year worldwide; states kill hundreds of thousands.

Oppressed peoples cannot be expected to abrogate their own human rights, indeed their very lives, without resistance. International law gives people suffering from oppression the right to resist, even to armed resistance – although they, like state armies, cannot harm civilians. Since only states claim the right to have armed forces, resistance on the part of oppressed people is by nature deemed "illegitimate" and criminal, *including non-violent resistance*. Casting them as "terrorists" effectively nullifies any struggle for national rights. We must insist on the right of the oppressed to resist – which is their only hope of liberating themselves – while condemning all forms of terrorism, state and non-state alike.

✓ *Israel must remain a Jewish state.*

As this book has endeavored to show, this proposition that any country with a diverse population can "belong" exclusively to one particular group is inadmissible. Can a state of different nationalities, religions, ethnic groups and political views be "Jewish"? Or "greater" Israel, in which the Jews are a minority? Isn't the idea of a "Jewish democracy" an oxymoron, particularly if it hinges on expelling and excluding the vast majority of that country's indigenous population, the Palestinians? And by what right does it claim to represent *all* Jews? Or for that matter, *all* Israeli citizens, only about 72 percent being Jews?

Decolonization aims to bring all the inhabitants of the country under the same democratic tent, including Palestinian refugees and their descendants. It is the only workable alternative to settler colonialism, occupation and apartheid, especially given Israel's refusal to even entertain a two-state solution. Jews in a democracy can continue to carry on their lives as Jews and as members of diverse ethnic, religious, voluntary or even national communities. But in a democracy, the state "belongs" to all its citizens.

✓ *Who can guarantee the well-being of Israeli Jews in a state with a Palestinian majority?*

First, if we accept the idea that there is already a single *de facto* state ruling over the whole area between the River and the Sea, then Israeli Jews are already a minority. And in claiming exclusive "ownership" over the whole of Palestine, and instituting an apartheid regime, Israel has put itself in a position of having to control the Palestinian majority by force. It is Israel that has created the conditions of insecurity that threaten the well-being of its own population. That is not a normal situation, and does not have to be.

The one-state initiative is premised on the view that the two peoples are not "enemies" in any preordained way or historically. Rather, their enmity arises out of a colonial situation of repression, inequality and the inability of the Palestinians to pursue *their* well-being, including their national self-determination.

In the one democratic state program presented in this book, a Constitution protects both the individual civil rights of all the country's citizens as well as the collective rights of all its ethnic, religious and national communities. As we've mentioned, the Constitution, enforced by the judiciary, will prohibit parliament from passing any laws or regulations that discriminate against any group or person. It will protect the right of all communities to their identity, associations, culture and institutions. The new state will also become a signatory to existing human rights conventions, adding yet other layers of protection. Finally, equality, integration and sharing in the daily life of the country will give rise to a new civil society in which old enmities and grievances will no longer have resonance or relevance.

Decolonization levels the playing field and addresses the fundamental injustices suffered by the Palestinians. It moves everyone into an inclusive post-colonial future, with no more inter-communal problems than any other country suffers from. The end of colonialism ensures the well-being of all the country's inhabitants. If the Palestinians can reconstitute themselves in their homeland under conditions of equality, dignity and full rights, then the process of decolonization can be brought to an end. In a post-colonial reality they may declare that Israeli Jews, now citizens of the new state and an integral part of its civil society, can now be accepted as a normal part of the population. The new country is free to move on to a better future.

✓ *Why should the Palestinians agree to this? If Zionism is a form of colonialism, shouldn't Palestine revert back to the Palestinians? What about the loss of land, the loss of generations of productive life? What about Israeli control over all of Palestine's resources?*

It is not "fair" that Palestinians must be asked to share their country with Israelis. The latter, after all, have denied their national rights and displaced them from their own country and lands – and continue to do so. But it is also an irreversible fact that an Israeli Jewish population will remain, albeit their "Israeli Jewish" identity incorporated into a broader civil one. That leaves the Palestinians with a challenge. For all the injustices done to them, can they envision a shared life with (former) Israeli Jews if a new society emerges based on restorative justice?

Can they agree to a shared life with Israeli Jews in a country that is transformed into something entirely different? A country in which colonial structures of domination and control are replaced by universal citizenship and vibrant democratic institutions. Where refugees and their descendants are brought home. Where resources and land are redistributed to give all citizens equal access. Where Palestinians receive compensation for loss of land and property, together with collective reparations for loss of life and productivity, for the effects of traumatization and for lost life opportunities extending over generations. Where robust programs of investment and affirmative action in the Palestinian sector are instituted.

While not erasing the injustice and suffering of the past, the prospect of restorative justice might well persuade the Palestinian people that an egalitarian post-colonial reality is possible and worth their support. It will be a protracted and difficult process, one that will require good faith and transparency as decolonization progresses.

✓ *Why not a confederation or a bi-national state?*

Different variations of a single state or Palestinian-Israeli (-Jordanian) confederation have been proposed. A confederation would be the easiest to "sell" to Israelis, since it would leave Israel and, to a degree, Israeli society and geography intact. It suffers, however, from the same reality as the two-state solution: the impossibility of carving out a viable Palestinian component in the West Bank and Gaza, including East Jerusalem. A bi-national state, too, would be marginally easier for Israelis to accept. But for Palestinians, who are ready to coexist with Israeli Jews, a formally bi-national state forces them to recognize Zionism and its historical crimes towards them as legitimate, which they are unwilling to do. Yet another variation in which the two peoples live in a single country but with two separate citizenships and parliaments is far too convoluted, possessing no real advantage over a more straightforward single state. Finally, all these options beg the most crucial question: who controls the military, the economy, natural resources and borders? None of the options except the one-state solution (in which the military and security forces are one set of integrated bodies under the central government) genuinely remove the military domination of Israel.

✓ *What about national self-determination?*

The Middle Eastern and North African (MENA) region is still reeling from its destructive colonial heritage and is still contending with Great Power neo-colonialism. Repressive regimes and corrupt, underdeveloped countries are only one symptom of this. Decolonizing needs to happen across our region, not only in Palestine. The Middle East and North Africa functioned for millennia as one huge market and cultural arena. Hundreds of peoples, tribes, religious and cultural communities, political movements and ideologies coexisted and comingled, no matter what empire or colonial power controlled parts of it at one time or another. We must ask, then, whether the creation of representative states is our final goal. Perhaps this is just a stepping stone to the interconnected and multicultural region that once existed. Perhaps we should begin thinking about national self-determination within this more fluid space rather than trapped in artificial, European-created states – a kind of ME/NA confederation not unlike the EU.

No state is really homogeneous. "Nation-states" do not exist in any pure form; all states contain diverse populations and peoples that spill messily across state borders. Few if any national groups enjoy self-determination in "their" own countries. Instead, they tend to transfer their "national" identities to that of their state, leaving their cultural identities as meaningful but somewhat subordinate. Palestinians and Israeli Jews are so intertwined that they cannot separate into discrete homogeneous states. Nonetheless, they can find as meaningful a degree of self-determination as strong national groups, religious communities or even language groups find in countries such as the UK, Belgium, Canada, Spain or many African countries. True, coexistence sometimes breaks down and has to be repaired. Some multinational states even break up, like Yugoslavia, Czechoslovakia and perhaps modern India. And evolution is always possible: our new state may ultimately integrate into a confederation with Jordan, or a Greater Syria might re-emerge, or a common ME/NA community. The point is that at this time the most equitable, just and workable arrangement for Palestinians and Israeli Jews is a single state that recognizes and protects the national, religious and cultural identities of all its citizens.

So while the issue of national self-determination is important, how it will be handled in a state that is pluralistic, bi-national or part of a confederation remains to be seen. The two-state solution might have offered another possibility, but Israel eliminated it.

✓ *Can the Palestinians achieve a genuine parity with Israelis? Isn't there a danger that they will become a permanent underclass to a wealthier, better educated, more powerful Israeli Jewish population?*

As we've discussed earlier, instituting a sustainable, equitable economy is a prime priority of the one-state initiative. Despite the debilitations of colonialism and occupation, the Palestinians possess strong economic advantages: a highly literate society, a functioning economy that has shown the potential for rapid growth when unleashed, and a wealthy Diaspora community that would invest in a strong Palestinian/Israel economy with access to the region and the world alike. Palestinians are capable of achieving parity with the Israelis in a relatively short period, especially given the leveling envisioned in our mixed socialist/regulated capitalist system.

✓ *Israelis will never agree to a one-state solution.*

Here we get into issues of strategy. There are cases where a population is unable to take responsibility for its choice of leaders, policies or actions. The Serbs are one example, the Whites in the American South are another, the Afrikaners in apartheid South Africa yet another. When Mandela's ANC began its struggle against the apartheid regime, it knew that nothing would convince the White population that apartheid was wrong and should be replaced. Rather than spend time trying to do the impossible, it instead developed a strategy to bypass them and the governments they elected. The ANC appealed directly to the people of the world, the international civil society. The goal was to cause the collapse of the apartheid regime regardless of the willingness of the dominant society to support it, and it succeeded.

This may well be the kind of strategy the Palestinians must adopt. Like the anti-apartheid struggle, the plan presented here is not waged against any population. It would be best, of course, if the Israeli Jewish population would willingly support the end of occupation and Israel's colonial policies, and take an active role in changing their system of government. If, however, they are unwilling to do so, then they forfeit their right to object if Palestinian and international actors endeavor to bring about just such change.

✓ *This is a very reasonable and rational approach to peace-making. But the Middle East is anything but rational, as the rise of radical Islam shows. Besides, no Middle Eastern countries have democracies as you envision.*

This criticism is not unique to the Middle East. Like other areas of the world, Muslim countries are still struggling with ongoing neo-colonialism and despotism. Muslim extremism, fanned in particular by Saudi Arabia's Wahabi Islam, is a product of that destabilization, corruption and despotism, not its cause. On the contrary, recent revolts by peoples throughout the Middle East, epitomized by the Arab Spring, demonstrate clearly that they demand democracy, not theocracy.

The ODSC program does not ignore or underestimate the difficulties and even dangers of decolonization – to all the parties. It is possible, however, to construct a process that offers protections during this challenging period. To begin with, we must keep the vision of what we are trying to accomplish constantly before us: a win-win prospect of a pluralistic democracy based on equal rights and restorative justice should be kept. It is a project fraught with perils, but no less one filled with potential for finally changing the lives of everyone in Palestine/Israel for the better.

Then, accompanied by international observers and teams of advisors, we must begin the process of institution-building. It must be a transparent and participatory process, but not a jump into the unknown. There are many models of constitutional democracy we may borrow from. The goal is to create a process in which all parties see where they are going and have opportunities to incorporate their concerns as the process of institution-building progresses in good faith.

Who will actually broker this new political reality? As of today, the only representative of the entire Palestinian people is the PLO, which must be resuscitated if it is to play the historic role for which it was created. This is the task of the Palestinian people, led by its progressive forces. And the only elected representative of the Israeli public is the Israeli government. It will have to be induced by external and internal pressures to play its own historic role, just as happened in South Africa. Decolonization calls for partnerships.

✓ *How could such a solution be effectively progressed? Is it really achievable?*

The campaign to decolonize Palestine is much further advanced than we realize. Grassroots resistance among Palestinians has succeeded in mobilizing major segments of the international civil society. Palestinians have become emblematic of oppressed peoples everywhere. Activists around the world advance the Palestinian cause through grassroots campaigns and systematic lobbying. They host international conferences, organize on university campuses and produce a wealth of books, articles, films, social media presentations and advocacy materials. As Israel's panic over the BDS campaign shows, Israel realizes it has already lost in the Court of Public Opinion, and is left only the shallow support of governments, Christian evangelicals and a diminishing Jewish Establishment.

What is lacking at the moment is a vision, a political end-game and an effective strategy. The ODSC program, together with other one-state initiatives, represents only the very start of the process of decolonization. Let's hope it falls on fertile ground.

A Last Word: Being Political

We can all become discouraged by the condition of the world, and in our case, decolonizing Zionism, liberating Palestine. People often ask me: How do you keep going? From where do you draw your hope? I have two answers. First, as a non-religious person, I don't deal in hope. I deal in struggle – political struggle. It's called "struggle" because that's what it is. The difficulties are built-in, and it should be clear that a struggle will be hard and long-lasting. If you understand that, if you approach the world *politically*, you don't need hope. You need analysis, a political program, comrades, organization, strategy (how to summon effective power). I never lose hope, but I do get discouraged when I see us, the Left and progressives in all our shades, acting little more than reactive, disorganized and turf-y, with little critical analysis or strategy. Just a bunch of siloed movements, activism with no plan or strategy, "actions" with no expectation they will really change anything, mere protest. When we're not being *political*, that's when I get discouraged.

My second answer relates to the first. What I learned from Myles Horton (I won't introduce him; Google him, or better, yet, read him) was that there are no easy fixes. His autobiography was entitled *The Long Haul*,[1] and that was the point. You're in for the long haul. If you choose a meaningful chunk of social justice – Horton took on unionizing the southern US, then the struggle for civil rights, all the while engaged in popular education in his Highlander School – then you know you're not going to see the end in the near future. Maybe, like Martin Luther King, you know you'll never see it; you might just see the mountaintops. Still, the point of the struggle *is* to see it through.

Decolonizing Israel, Liberating Palestine – I don't know if I'll live to see it (although I firmly believe that it is do-able in the not-too-distant future if we organize, plan, strategize and work seriously). But the point is not to "be there" when the glorious day comes, though that would be nice. The point is to do the best you can, to marshal all the political resources at your disposal and, as focused and effectively as possible, move the struggle that much forward. I do hope I'll live to see justice for Palestinians. Hopefully this book will contribute to that struggle. I don't expect to see a progressive Middle East – although I'm part of a movement for obtaining it – and I know I won't see the end of predatory capitalism. What sustains me is the knowledge that we're moving forward. What discourages me is when we're not being strategic, not thinking and acting *politically*.

In this book I've tried to address the issue of justice and peace in Palestine/Israel *politically*. Drawing on the work with my comrades in the One Democratic State Campaign and others, I have laid out some of the crucial elements of our struggle. This is critical since, after 53 plus years of occupation, 72 years after the Nakba (as of this writing), and 138 years after the Zionist settler "invasion," many Palestinians have, indeed, "lost hope," crippled as they also are by ineffective and often oppressive Palestinian leadership. Most Palestinians view both the two-state and the one-state solutions as utopian.[2] The people, who have never stopped resisting, have lost faith in any political activity or program. The slogan found on all the graffiti-filled walls of the OPT – "To exist is to resist" – can be read as a kind of fatalism. It understands that without resistance Palestinians will not survive, but it also divorces that resistance from any political horizon. We've lost, you often hear. We've been abandoned by the international community and our own leaders; Israel is too strong. All that's left is to hunker down, survive – and resist immediate attempts to take our land, force us to leave, destroy our lives.

The degree to which Palestinians *have* been able to sustain their struggle is admirable, of course, but the lack of political leadership and a political plan – together with the suffocating presence of a strategic and powerful foe – has led them into an impasse: resistance without hope of change. Renewing effective political struggle by convincing the Palestinian masses that, if organized and pursued strategically, the one-state option is not utopian, is a key task of all the political groups working towards a single democratic state, the ODSC included. Palestinians have never stopped struggling, but their struggle requires leadership and a political program if it is to succeed. The ODSC is endeavoring towards that effort.

In addition to offering an analysis and a pathway out of Zionist colonialism, this book is a plea to return to the political, to show how seemingly insurmountable obstacles can be reframed as challenges susceptible to effective strategies of overcoming them. Being politically effective is the only way I can redeem my settler status, can genuinely refuse to be colonial, can become truly a comrade to my Palestinian partners. My work has been an engagement in task-oriented "practical" as well as ideological politics, ranging from rebuilding demolished homes and engagement in the ODSC to what I call Global Palestine. In *War Against the People: Israel, the Palestinians and Global Pacification*,[3] I show how, on the one hand, Israel exports its occupation for profit and political influence, but how, on the other, the Palestinian struggle against Israeli colonialism supported by the great capitalist powers has galvanized oppressed peoples the world over. There are no separate issues, no siloes. All our struggles, from paying credit card bills foisted on an impoverished Palestinian people by neoliberal policies to liberating our country to shepherding in a new, more just and sustainable world economic system – they all are interconnected, as the ODSC program recognizes.

So as we work out how to decolonize a settler regime, how to collectively liberate Palestine, how to confront and defeat a powerful militarized and racialized regime through the targeted summoning of power, and how to build something just, inclusive, equitable and sustainable, we are contributing as well to the struggles of oppressed, poor, marginalized people everywhere. As we've mentioned earlier, neoliberalism, neo-colonialism and their militarized enforcement have colonized the lives of all of us. To the degree that I endeavor to be the colonist-who-refuses and comrade-in-struggle, I hope – no, I fight for – a time when we all become colonists of global capital who refuse. Liberating Palestine is but a step towards liberating Global Palestine.

Notes

Websites were last accessed July 2020.

Foreword

1. Albert Memmi, *The Colonizer and the Colonized* (London: Earthscan Publications, 2003), Kindle edition.

Introduction: The Colonist Who Refuses, the Comrade in Joint Struggle

1. Peter Beinart, "Yavne: A Jewish Case for Equality in Israel/Palestine," *Jewish Currents* (July 7, 2020).
2. Jewish Voice for Peace, "Our Approach to Zionism" (January 2019). https://jewishvoiceforpeace.org/zionism.
3. European Union External Action, "West Bank: Annexation is Not a Solution" (July 8, 2020). https://eeas.europa.eu/headquarters/headquarters-homepage_en/82481/West%20Bank:%20annexation%20is%20not%20a%20solution.
4. Stuart Winer, "Two-Thirds of Jewish Israelis Don't Consider West Bank Occupied – Poll," *Times of Israel* (June 4, 2017).
5. Gil Hoffman, "Extensive Survey: Israelis Vote on Security," *The Jerusalem Post* (March 26, 2019).
6. Al-Awda, "FAQs about Palestinian Refugees," n.d. https://al-awda.org/learn-more/faqs-about-palestinian-refugees.
7. Jeff Halper, *War Against the People: Israel, the Palestinians and Global Pacification* (London: Pluto Press, 2015).
8. Patrick Wolfe, *Settler Colonialism and the Transformation of Anthropology: The Politics and Poetics of an Ethnographic Event* (London: Cassel, 1999), 4.
9. Jeff Halper, *War Against the People; Between Redemption and Revival: The Jewish Yishuv of Jerusalem in the Nineteenth Century* (Boulder: Westview, 1991); *An Israeli in Palestine: Resisting Dispossession, Redeeming Israel* (London: Pluto Press, 2011); *Obstacles to Peace: A Reframing of the Israeli-Palestinian Conflict* (Jerusalem: ICAHD, several editions from 2001).
10. Uri Davis, *Apartheid Israel: Possibilities for the Struggle Within* (London: Zed Books, 2003), 185.
11. Albert Memmi, *The Colonizer and the Colonized* (London: Earthscan Publications, 2003), Kinde edition.
12. Ibid.

13. Quoted in Marcelo Svirsky and Ronnen Ben-Arie, *From Shared Life to Co-resistance in Historic Palestine* (London: Rowman and Littlefield, 2017), 160.

14. Clare Land, *Decolonizing Solidarity: Dilemmas and Directions for Supporters of Indigenous Struggles* (London: Zed Books, 2015), Kindle edition, "Introduction."

15. Ibid., 110.

16. Anaheed Al-Hardan, "Decolonizing Research on Palestinians: Towards Critical Epistemologies and Research Practices." *Qualitative Inquiry* 20, no. 6 (2014), 61–72.

17. Indigenous Corporate Training, Inc., *Indigenous Peoples Terminology Guidelines for Usage* (2016). www.ictinc.ca/blog/indigenous-peoples-terminology-guidelines-for-usage.

1. Analysis Matters: Beginning with Settler Colonialism

1. Abigail Jacobson and Moshe Naor, *Oriental Neighbors: Middle Eastern Jews and Arabs in Mandatory Palestine* (Waltham: Brandeis University Press, 2016), 8. See also Nur Masalha, *Palestine: A Four Thousand Year History* (London: Zed Books, 2018), 24–5.

2. Gershon Shafir, "Settler Citizenship in the Jewish Colonization of Palestine," in *Settler Colonialism in the Twentieth Century: Projects, Practices, Legacies*, eds. Caroline Elkins and Susan Pedersen (London, New York: Routledge, 2005), Kindle edition, Chapter 2.

3. Kelley, referencing the Black Marxist scholar Cedric J. Robinson, observes that the enactment of race in European colonialism – and, we would add, other ethno-national privileges – were already embedded in European culture and political life; they did not spring out suddenly from the encounter with the Other, though that encounter influences the specific forms such claims take. See Robin D. J. Kelley, "The Rest of Us: Rethinking Settler and Native," *American Quarterly* 69, no. 2 (June 2017), 273.

4. Shlomo Svirsky, "Notes on the Historical Sociology of the *Yishuv* Period," in *Israeli Society: Critical Perspectives* ed. Uri Ram (Tel Aviv: Breirot, 1993), 80.

5. Anne de Jong, "Zionist Hegemony, the Settler Colonial Conquest of Palestine and the Problem with Conflict: A Critical Genealogy of the Notion of Binary Conflict," *Settler Colonial Studies* 8, no. 3 (2018), 364–83.

6. Quoted in Rachel Busbridge, "Israel-Palestine and the Settler Colonial 'Turn': From Interpretation to Decolonisation," *Theory, Culture and Society* 35, no. 1 (2018), 91–115.

7. Honaida Ghanim, "The Dynamics of Elimination and Replacement under the Israeli Colonial Project," *Institute for Palestine Studies*, 24, no. 96 (2013), 118–39.

8. Patrick Wolfe, "Settler Colonialism and the 'Elimination of the Native'," *Journal of Genocide Research* 8, no. 4 (2006), 387–409.

9. Mahmood Mamdani, "Beyond Settler and Native as Political Identities: Overcoming the Political Legacy of Colonialism," *Comparative Studies in Society and History* 43, no. 4. (October 2001), 651–2.

10. See Adom Getachew, *Worldmaking after Empire: The Rise and Fall of Self-Determination* (Princeton: Princeton University Press, 2019); Margaret Kohn and Keally McBride, *Political Theories of Decolonization* (New York: Oxford University Press, 2011).

11. Wolfe, "Elimination."

12. Patrick Wolfe, *Traces of History: Elementary Structures of Race* (London: Verso, 2016).

13. Glen Sean Coulthard, *Red Skins, White Masks: Rejecting the Colonial Political of Recognition* (Minneapolis: University of Minnesota Press, 2014), Kindle edition, Introduction.

14. Lorenzo Veracini, *Settler Colonialism: A Theoretical Perspective* (Basingstoke: Palgrave Macmillan, 2010).

15. Ilan Pappe, "Zionism as Colonialism: A Comparative View of Diluted Colonialism in Asia and Africa," *South Atlantic Quarterly* 107, no. 4 (2008), 614.

16. Lorenzo Veracini, "Settler Colonialism and Decolonization," *Borderlands e-journal* 6.2 (2007), ro.uow. edu.au/lhapapers/1337.

17. Patrick Wolfe, *Settler Colonialism and the Transformation of Anthropology: The Politics and Poetics of an Ethnographic Event* (London: Cassel, 1999), 4, 213.

18. Clare Land, *Decolonizing Solidarity: Dilemmas and Directions for Supporters of Indigenous Struggles* (London: Zed Books, 2015), 110.

19. Marcello Svirsky, "Resistance is a Structure Not an Event, *Settler Colonial Studies* 7, no. 1 (2017), 23.

20. Marcelo Svirsky and Ronnen Ben-Arie, *From Shared Life to Co-resistance in Historic Palestine* (London: Rowman and Littlefield, 2017).

21. Svirsky, "Resistance," 25.

22. Lorenzo Veracini, *The Settler Colonial Present* (Basingstoke: Palgrave Macmillan, 2015), 5.

23. Svirsky, "Resistance," 29–30.

24. Ibid., 30.

25. Alissa Macoun and Elizabeth Strakosch, "The Ethical Demands of Settler Colonial Theory," *Settler Colonial Studies* 3, nos. 3–4 (2013).

26. Svirsky, "Resistance," 24.

27. Nahla Abdo and Nira Yuval-Davis, "Palestine, Israel and the Zionist Settler Project," in *Unsettling Settler Societies: Articulations of Gender, Race, Ethnicity and Class*, eds. Daiva Stasiulis and Nira Yuval-Davis (London: Sage, 1995), 291–318.

28. J. Kēhaulani Kauanui, "'A Structure, Not an Event': Settler Colonialism and Enduring Indigeneity," *Lateral: Journal of the Cultural Studies Association* 5, no. 1 (2016), 1.

29. Tim Rowse, "Indigenous Heterogeneity," *Australian Historical Studies* 45, no. 3 (2014), 297–310. See also Francesca Merlan, "Reply to Patrick Wolfe," *Social Analysis* 40 (1997); Busbridge, "Settler Turn"; Jean M.

O'Brien, "Tracing Settler Colonialism's Eliminatory Logic in *Traces of History*," *American Quarterly* 69, no. 2 (2017), 249–55.

30. Uri Ram, "The Colonization Perspective in Israeli Sociology," in *The Israel/Palestine Question: Rewriting Histories*, ed. Ilan Pappe (London: Routledge, 1999), 56–7.

2. Zionism: A Settler Colonial Project

1. Franz Fanon, *The Wretched of the Earth* (New York: Grove Press, 1963), 28.

2. Uri Ram, "Zionist Historiography and the Invention of Modern Jewish Nationhood: The Case of Ben Zion Dinur," *History and Memory* 7, no. 1 (1995), 91–124; Anita Shapira, "Ben-Gurion and the Bible: The Forging of an Historical Narrative?" *Middle Eastern Studies* 33, no. 4 (1997), 645–74; Zeev Sternhell and David Maisel, *The Founding Myths of Israel: Nationalism, Socialism, and the Making of the Jewish State* (Princeton: Princeton University Press, 1998); Oren Yiftachel, *Ethnocracy: Land and Identity Politics in Israel/Palestine* (Philadelphia: University of Pennsylvania Press, 2006).

3. Willi Goetschel and Ato Quason, "Introduction: Jewish Studies and Postcolonialism," *The Cambridge Journal of Literary Postcolonial Inquiry* 3, no. 1 (2016), 4–5.

4. Hans Kohn, *The Idea of Nationalism* (New York: Macmillan, 1961), 29–31, 45–6.

5. Uri Ben-Eliezer, *War Over Peace: One Hundred Years of Israel's Militaristic Nationalism* (Oakland: University of California Press, 2019), Kindle edition, Chapter 2.

6. Ibid., Chapter 1; Jeff Halper, *An Israeli in Palestine* (London: Pluto Press), 67–73.

7. Ben-Eliezer, *War*, Chapter 1; Sternhell and Maisel, *The Founding Myths of Israel*.

8. Anthony Smith, "Zionism and Diaspora Nationalism," *Israel Affairs* 2, no. 2 (1995), 1–19.

9. Quoted in Tom Segev, *One Palestine, Complete: Jews and Arabs under the British Mandate* (New York: Henry Holt, 1999), 47; see also Yakov Rabkin, *A Threat from Within: A Century of Jewish Opposition to Zionism* (London: Black Point and Zed Books, 2006).

10. Ilan Pappe, "Zionism as Colonialism: A Comparative View of Diluted Colonialism in Asia and Africa," *South Atlantic Quarterly* 107, no. 4 (2008)," 612; see also Rashid Khalidi, *The Hundred Years' War on Palestine: A History of Settler Colonialism and Resistance, 1917–2017* (New York: Henry Holt, 2020), 9, 245–6.

11. Yoav Peled, "Delegitimation of Israel or Social-Historical Analysis? The Debate over Zionism as a Colonial Settler Movement," in *Jews and Leftist Politics: Judaism, Israel, Antisemitism, and Gender*, ed. Jack Jacobs (Cambridge: Cambridge University Press, 2017), 107. For a discussion

of nationalism as a component of Zionist settlement, see also Rachel Busbridge, "Israel-Palestine and the Settler Colonial 'Turn': From Interpretation to Decolonisation," *Theory, Culture and Society* 35, no. 1 (2018), 91–115.

12. Gershon Shafir and Yoav Peled, *Being Israeli: The Dynamics of Multiple Citizenship* (Cambridge: Cambridge University Press, 2002), 37.

13. Busbridge, in "Turn," discusses the problematics of applying exclusively a settler colonial analysis with its emphasis on structures, an "inexorable" logic and an unbridgeable "settler/native" polarity to a "conflict" as complex, fluid and contingent on outside forces as that of "Israel/Palestine." In particular, she argues that the national element of Zionism must be taken into account, not only the Zionists as settlers. I address this below, and have addressed the issue of structure and agency in the last chapter. I accept her assertion on a practical level that "understanding Zionism's nationalist impulse is crucial to understanding its political strengths and continued affective resonance" (p. 15), but not the notion that Zionist nationalism alters the settler colonial analysis in any fundamental way.

14. See Teodora Todorova's discussion of this issue of Israeli perception, in "Reframing Bi-nationalism in Palestine-Israel as a Process of Settler Decolonisation," *Antipode* 47, no. 5 (November 2015), 1367–87.

15. Tuvia Friling, "What Do Those Who Claim Zionism is Colonialism Overlook?" in *Handbook of Israel: Major Debates*, eds. Eliezer Ben-Rafael, Julius H. Schoeps, Yitzhak Sternberg, Olaf Glöckner, Anne Weberling (Oldenbourg: De Gruyter, 2016), 851.

16. Quoted in Smith, "Zionism," 3.

17. Eve Tuck and K. Wayne Yang, "Decolonization is Not a Metaphor," *Decolonization: Indigeneity, Education & Society* 1, no. 1 (2012), 10.

18. Smith, "Zionism," 5–7.

19. Jehuda Reinharz and Yaakov Shavit, *Glorious, Accursed Europe: An Essay on Jewish Ambivalence* (Waltham: Brandeis University Press, 2010), 135. https://bir.brandeis.edu/bitstream/handle/10192/26155/Reinharz.pdf?sequence=1&isAllowed=y.

20. Quoted in Segev, *One Palestine*, 153.

21. Fanon, *Wretched*, 43, 250. Some of the examples are his, some I brought in from the Zionist discourse.

22. Fanon, *Wretched*, 38–9.

23. Lorenzo Veracini, *Settler Colonialism: A Theoretical Perspective* (Basingstoke: Palgrave Macmillan, 2010), 10, 23.

24. Busbridge, "Turn"; Robin D. G. Kelley, "The Rest of Us: Rethinking Settler and Native," *American Quarterly* 69, no. 2 (June 2017), 267–76.

25. Martin van Creveld, *The Sword and the Olive: A Critical History of the Israeli Defense Force* (New York: Public Affairs, 1998), 17; Rashid Khalidi, *Palestinian Identity: The Construction of Modern National Consciousness* (New York: Columbia University Press), 105–11.

26. Elia T. Zureik, *Israel's Colonial Project in Palestine: Brutal Pursuit* (London: Routledge, 2015); Hillel Cohen, *Good Arabs: The Israeli Security Agencies*

and the Israeli Arabs, 1948–1967 (Berkeley: University of California Press, 2010).

27. Quoted in Segev, *One Palestine*, 154.

28. http://en.jabotinsky.org/media/9747/the-iron-wall.pdf.

29. Yosef Gorny, *Zionism and the Arabs, 1882–1948: A Study in Ideology* (Oxford: Clarendon Press, 1987), 26–39.

30. Scott Lauria Morgensen, "The Biopolitics of Settler Colonialism: Right Here, Right Now," *Settler Colonial Studies* 1, no. 1 (2011), 52–76.

31. Patrick Wolfe, *Settler Colonialism and the Transformation of Anthropology: The Politics and Poetics of an Ethnographic Event* (London: Cassel, 1999), 163.

32. Fanon, *Wretched*, 35.

33. Mahmood Mamdani "When Does a Settler Become a Native? Reflections of the Colonial Roots of Citizenship in Equatorial and South Africa," Inaugural Lecture as A.C. Jordan Professor of African Studies, University of Cape Town, May, 13, 1998. https://citizenshiprightsafrica.org/wp-content/uploads/1998/05/mamdani-1998-inaugural-lecture.pdf.

34. Patrick Wolfe, "Settler Colonialism and the 'Elimination of the Native'," *Journal of Genocide Research* 8, no. 4 (2006), 402.

35. Ibid.; Sara Salazar Hughes, "Unbounded Territoriality: Territorial Control, Settler Colonialism, and Israel/Palestine," *Settler Colonial Studies* 10, no. 2 (2020), 1–18.

36. Julia Lerner, "'Russians' in the Jewish State: Blood, Identity and National Bureaucracy," *Ethnologie francaise* 2, no. 45 (2015), 365–74.

37. Steve Kaplan, "The Invention of Ethiopian Jews: Three Models," *Cahiers d'Études africaines* 132 (1993), 645–58.

38. Ella Shohat, *Taboo Memories, Diasporic Voices* (Durham: Duke University Press, 2006), 330–58.

39. Wolfe, "Elimination," 388; Veracini, *Settler Colonialism*, 8.

40. Hughes, "Unbounded," 1. See also Wolfe, "Elimination," 390–3 (italics in original).

41. Richard Sutch, "Introduction: Toward a Unified Approach to the Economic History of Settler Economies," in *Settler Economies in World History*, eds. Christopher Lloyd, Jacob Metzer and Richard Sutch (Leiden: Brill, 2013), xviii.

42. Christopher Lloyd and Jacob Metzer, "Settler Colonization and Societies in World History: Patterns and Concepts," in *Settler Economies in World History*, eds. Christopher Lloyd, Jacob Metzer and Richard Sutch (Leiden: Brill, 2013), 1.

43. Veracini, *Settler Colonialism*, 14.

44. Gideon Kouts, "From Sokolow to 'Explaining Israel': The Zionist *Hasbara* First 'Campaign Strategy Paper' and Its Applications," *Revue, Européeanne des Études Hébraïques* 18 (2016), 105.

45. Wolfe, "Elimination," 393.

3. Settler "Invasion" and Foundational Violence: The Pre-State Cycle (1880s–1948)

1. Lorenzo Veracini, *Israel and Settler Society* (London: Pluto Press, 2006), 73.
2. Lorenzo Veracini, *Settler Colonialism: A Theoretical Perspective* (Basingstoke: Palgrave Macmillan, 2010), 75.
3. Uri Ben-Eliezer, *The Making of Israeli Militarism* (Bloomington: Indiana University Press, 1998).
4. Jeff Halper, *War Against the People: Israel, the Palestinians and Global Pacification* (London: Pluto Press, 2015), 144–6.
5. Ben-Eliezer, *Militarism.*
6. Quoted in Uri Ben-Eliezer, *War Over Peace: One Hundred Years of Israel's Militaristic Nationalism* (Oakland: University of California Press, 2019), Kindle edition, Chapter 2.
7. Quoted in Anne de Jong, "Zionist Hegemony, the Settler Colonial Conquest of Palestine and the Problem with Conflict: A Critical Genealogy of the Notion of Binary Conflict," *Settler Colonial Studies* 8, no. 3 (2018), 364–83.
8. Veracini, *Settler Colonialism*, 34–50. 1. Ethnic transfer, in which the expelled cease being indigenous (refugees); 2. Transfer by conceptual displacement, denying their very indigeneity (Palestinians become "Arabs," interlopers); 3. Civilizational transfer, whereby the Indigenous are coopted and rendered neutral (Palestinian farmers and Bedouins as biblical remnants – thereby indigenizing Jewish settlers, who are also biblical descendants); 4. Perception transfer, where Natives disappear as part of the landscape; 5. Transfer by accounting; the Indigenous simply not counted or registered; 6. Transfer by means of "repressive authenticity," whereby present-day Indigenous are disconnected from "authentic" pre-existing Natives (Palestinians are really Arabs who belong in "Arab countries"); 7. Narrative transfer, where Natives and their claims are rendered irrelevant because "we live in modern times" and "the country has changed" (we "can't go back to 1948"). Recognize displacement, violence & even injustice but relegate them to the unrecoverable past); 8. Transfer by settler indigenization, when settlers claim to be Indigenous ("the Land of Israel was originally Jewish," "God gave this land to us") and the natives are turned into settlers (Arabs came here as migrants); 9. Multicultural transfer, when all meaningful cultural difference is flattened into a general (and settler-defined) "multiculturalism"; 10. Bicultural transfer, when an equivalency of cultures is asserted but defined by settlers (Indigenous culture is subsumed); 11. Transfer by coerced lifestyle change: sedentarizing Bedouin, reducing Palestinian agriculture, forcing urbanization and casual labor; 12. Administrative transfer, whereby Indigenous are transferred to another administrative unit by redrawing borders (OPT, Areas A, B & C of West Bank, closed military zones, nature preserves); 13. Diplomatic transfer, when Indig-

enous are placed under other political entities (Palestinian Authority); 14. Non-diplomatic transfer, when settlers control an Indigenous population but relinquish responsibility (Gaza); 15. Indigenous criminalization, when daily life is criminalized and sanctioned (e.g., house demolitions, "sneaking into Israel" for employment, voting or waving a Palestinian flag in East Jerusalem); 16. Transfer by performance, when settlers occupy Indigenous identities (early Zionist Guards dressed in kafiyas; *mistaravim*, soldiers who disguise themselves as Palestinians); 17. Transfer by name confiscation, changing the names of places ("Judaization" of place names); 18. Transfer by executive termination, whereby Indigenous are declared non-existent ("No such thing as a Palestinian;" Nakba Law); 19. Transfer of settlers into Indigenous spaces so as to eliminate them (Israeli settlements); 20. Transfer by Indigenous/national "reconciliation" (the two-state solution, whereby Palestinians give up claim to Israel and recognize a Jewish state).

9. Ben-Eliezer, *War*, Chapter 2; Ben-Eliezer, *Militarism*, 7–8.

10. Quoted in Benjamin Beit-Hallahmi, *Original Sins: Reflections of the History of Zionism and Israel* (London: Pluto Press, 1992), 72–3.

11. Rashid Khalidi, *Palestinian Identity: The Construction of Modern National Consciousness* (New York: Columbia University Press, 1997), 105–6.

12. Martin van Creveld, *The Sword and the Olive: A Critical History of the Israeli Defense Force* (New York: Public Affairs, 1998), 17.

13. Khalidi, *Identity*, 105–11; Benny Morris, *Righteous Victims: A History of the Zionist-Arab Conflict, 1881–1949* (New York: Knopf, 1999), 59–63; ibid., 17.

14. Fayez Sayegh, *Zionist Colonialism in Palestine* (Beirut: Research Center, Palestine Liberation Organization, 1965), 222.

15. Tom Segev, *One Palestine, Complete: Jews and Arabs under the British Mandate* (New York: Henry Holt, 1999), 48.

16. Ibid., 46.

17. Rashid Khalidi, *The Iron Cage: The Story of the Palestinian Struggle for Statehood* (Boston: Beacon Press, 2006); ibid., 43–50.

18. Sayegh, *Zionist Colonialism*, 222; Khalidi, *Identity*.

19. Quoted in Sayegh, *Zionist Colonialism*, 222.

20. Van Crevald, *Sword*, 31; Arnon Golan, "European Imperialism and the Development of Modern Palestine: Was Zionism a Form of Colonialism?" *Space and Polity* 5, no. 2 (2001), 127–43; Yoav Peled, "Delegitimation of Israel or Social-Historical Analysis? The Debate over Zionism as a Colonial Settler Movement," in *Jews and Leftist Politics: Judaism, Israel, Antisemitism, and Gender*, ed. Jack Jacobs (Cambridge: Cambridge University Press, 2017), 11–18.

21. Segev, *One Palestine*, 367.

22. Hillel Cohen, *Year Zero of the Arab-Israeli Conflict 1929* (Waltham: Brandeis University Press, 2015); Sayegh, *Zionist Colonialism*, 223.

23. Veracini, *Settler Colonialism*, 8, 81–3; Yosef Gorny, *Zionism and the Arabs, 1882–1948: A Study in Ideology* (Oxford: Clarendon Press, 1987), 16.

24. "Demographic History of Palestine." https://en.wikipedia.org/wiki/Demographic_history_of_Palestine_(region).

25. Sami Hadawi, *Land Ownership in Palestine* (New York: The Palestine Arab Refugee Office, 1957), 11–12.

26. Michel Foucault, *The History of Sexuality: An Introduction* (New York: Vintage Books, 1990).

27. Sarab Abu-Rabia-Queder, "The Biopolitics of Declassing Palestinian Professional Women in a Settler-Colonial Context," *Current Sociology* 67, no. 1 (2019), 141–58; Shira Robinson, *Citizen Strangers: Palestinians and the Birth of Israel's Liberal Settler State* (Stanford: Stanford University Press, 2013), 68.

28. Veracini, *Settler Colonialism*, 35.

29. Yossi Verter, "Israeli Election Results: With One Stroke of the Pen, Netanyahu Writes Off Half a Million Israelis," *Ha'aretz*, March 6, 2020; Ian Lustick, *Arabs in the Jewish State: Israel's Control of a National Minority* (Austin: University of Texas Press, 1980), 33.

30. Segev, *One Palestine*, 284–6.

31. Franz Fanon, *The Wretched of the Earth* (New York: Grove Press, 1963), 38–9.

32. Veracini, *Settler Colonialism*, 23.

33. Elspeth Huxley, *Flame Trees of Thika* (London: Chatto and Windus, 1959), 15.

34. Segev, *One Palestine*, 380.

35. Gershon Shafir, "Theorizing Zionist Settler Colonialism in Palestine," in *The Routledge Handbook of the History of Settler Colonialism*, eds. Edward Cavanagh and Lorenzo Veracini (London: Routledge, 2017), 345–6.

36. Eyal Weizman, *Hollow Land: Israel's Architecture of Occupation* (London: Verso, 2007), 101–2.

37. Segev, *One Palestine*, 379.

38. Shafir, "Theorizing Zionist Settler Colonialism," 343–8.

39. Baruch Kimmerling and Joel Migdal, *Palestinians: The Making of a People* (New York: Free Press, 1993).

40. Quoted in Morris, *Victims*, 91.

41. Segev, *One Palestine*, 405; Chaim Simons, "A Historical Survey of Proposals to Transfer Arabs from Palestine, 1895–1947." http://chaimsimons.net/transfer.html.

42. Morris, *Victims*, 138–44; Segev, *One Palestine*, 403–7; Simons, "Survey."

43. Theodor Herzl, *Complete Diaries*, ed. Raphael Patai (New York: Herzl Press, 1960), 88–9.

44. Chaim Simons, *Israel Zangwell*. http://chaimsimons.net/transfer07.html.

45. Segev, *One Palestine*, 406.

46. Ilan Pappe, *The Ethnic Cleansing of Palestine* (London: Oneworld, 2006), Kindle edition, Chapter 1.

47. Quoted in Nur Masalha, *The Palestine Nakba: Decolonizing History, Narrating the Subaltern, Reclaiming Memory* (London: Zed Books, 2012), 5.

48. Segev, *One Palestine*, 405.

49. Khalidi, *Iron Cage*, 13.

50. Segev, *One Palestine*, 171; Yehuda Meltzer and Oded Kaplan, *Jewish Economy and Arab Economy in Palestine: Production, Employment, and Growth in the Mandatory Period* (Jerusalem: Falk Center, 1990) [Hebrew]; Barbara Smith, *The Roots of Separation in Palestine: British Economic Policy, 1920–1929* (Syracuse: Syracuse University Press, 1993).

51. Howard M. Sachar, *A History of Israel: From the Rise of Zionism to Our Time* (New York: Alfred A. Knoff, 1979), 189–90.

52. Jewish Telegraphic Agency, "*Haavara* Winds Up Reich-Palestine Transfer Operations; Handled $35,000,000 in 6 Years," September 10, 1939. www.jta.org/1939/09/10/archive/haavara-winds-up-reich-palestine-transfer-operations-handled-35000000-in-6-years.

53. Sacher, *History of Israel*, 190.

54. Rashid Khalidi, *The Hundred Years' War on Palestine: A History of Settler Colonialism and Resistance, 1917–2017* (New York: Henry Holt, 2020), 8.

55. Khalidi, *Iron Cage*, 13–14.

56. Robinson, *Citizen Strangers*, 18–19.

57. Segev, *One Palestine*, 370.

58. Ibid., 426.

59. Ibid., 415, 428–9.

60. Ibid., 42–31; Van Crevald, *Sword*, 39–40.

61. Segev, *One Palestine*, 426–7.

62. http://en.jabotinsky.org/media/9747/the-iron-wall.pdf.

63. Quoted in Morris, *Victims*, 144.

64. David Ben-Gurion, *My Talks with Arab Leaders* (Jerusalem: Keter, 1972), 80.

65. For just a few examples of that support, see Segev, *One Palestine*; Khalidi, *Iron Cage*, 3–7.

66. Sharon Rothbart, "Wall and Tower: The Mold of Israeli *Adrikhalut*," in *Territories: Island, Camps and Other States of Utopia*, ed. Anselm Frank (Berlin: KW, Institute for Contemporary Art), 165.

67. Sachar, *History of Israel*, 334–5.

68. Nihad Boqa'i, "Palestinian Internally Displaced Persons Inside Israel: Challenging the Solid Structures," *Palestine/Israel Journal* 15/16, no. 3 (2008), 31–42.

69. Pappe, *Cleansing*.

70. Khalidi, *Iron Cage*, 105–40.

4. The Israeli State Cycle (1948–67)

1. Martin van Creveld, *The Sword and the Olive: A Critical History of the Israeli Defense Force* (New York: Public Affairs, 1998), 51–2.

2. Uri Ben-Eliezer, *The Making of Israeli Militarism* (Bloomington: Indiana University Press, 1998), 13–14, 194.

3. Ibid., 195.

4. Sabri Jiryis, *The Arabs in Israel* (New York: Monthly Review Press, 1976), 11–13; Shira Robinson, *Citizen Strangers: Palestinians and the Birth of*

Israel's Liberal Settler State (Stanford: Stanford University Press, 2013), 33–5.

5. Jiryis, *Arabs*, 16–20; Robinson, *Citizen Strangers*, 33–5.

6. Avi Shlaim, *Collusion Across the Jordan: King Abdullah, the Zionist Movement, and the Partition of Palestine* (New York: Columbia University Press, 1988); Ilan Pappe, *The Ethnic Cleansing of Palestine* (London: Oneworld, 2006).

7. Pappe, *Cleansing*, Kindle edition, Chapter 2.

8. Ibid., Chapter 2.

9. Ibid., Chapter 2.

10. Justin McCarthy, *The Population of Palestine: Population History and Statistics of the Late Ottoman Period and the Mandate* (New York: Columbia University Press, 1990).

11. Walid Khalidi, *All That Remains: The Palestinian Villages Occupied and Depopulated by Israel in 1948* (Washington, DC: Institute for Palestine Studies, 1992); Benny Morris, *Righteous Victims: A History of the Zionist-Arab Conflict, 1881–1949* (New York: Knopf, 1999), 256–7.

12. Jiryis, *Arabs*, 75–134; Uri Davis, *Apartheid Israel* (London: Zed Books, 2003), 36–49; Geremy Forman and Alexandre Kedar, "From Arab Land to 'Israel Lands': The Legal Dispossession of the Palestinians Displaced by Israel in the Wake of 1948," *Environment and Planning D: Society and Space* 22 (2004), 809–30. http://law.haifa.ac.il/images/documents/From%20Arab%20Land%20to%20Israel%20Lands.pdf; Baruch Kimmerling, *Land, Conflict and Nation-Building: A Sociological Study of the Territorial Factors in the Jewish-Arab Conflict* (Jerusalem: Hebrew University, 1976); Hussein Abu Hussein and Fiona McKay, *Access Denied: Palestinian Land Rights in Israel* (London: Zed Books, 2003), 67–76.

13. Robinson, *Citizen Strangers*, 31.

14. Abu Hussein and McKay, *Access Denied*; Meron Benvenisti, *Sacred Landscapes: The Buried History of the Holy Land since 1948* (Berkeley: University of California Press, 2002); Noga Kadman, *Erased from Space and Consciousness: Israel and the Depopulated Palestinian Villages of 1948* (Bloomington: Indiana University Press, 2015); Khalidi, *All That Remains*; Baruch Kimmerling, *Zionism and Territory: The Socio-Territorial Dimensions of Zionist Politics* (Berkeley: University of California Press, 1983); Ian Lustick, *Arabs in the Jewish State: Israel's Control of a National Minority* (Austin: University of Texas Press, 1980), 57–8; Oren Yiftachel and Avinoam Meir, eds., *Ethnic Frontiers and Peripheries: Landscapes of Development and Inequality in Israel* (New York: Routledge, 1998).

15. Quoted in Lustick, *Arabs*, 41.

16. Lustick, *Arabs*, 51.

17. Ibid., 58.

18. Davis, *Apartheid Israel*, 48.

19. Lustick, *Arabs*, 1–27.

20. Quoted in Walter Schwartz, *The Arabs in Israel* (London: Faber and Faber, 1959), 141.

21. Lustick, *Arabs*, 125–6.

22. Robinson, *Citizen Strangers*.

23. Shlomo Sand, *The Invention of the Jewish People* (London: Verso, 2009), Kindle edition, Chapter 2.

24. Khalidi, *All That Remains*.

25. See, for example, Sand, *Invention*.

26. Quoted in Sand, *Invention*, 2.

27. Uri Ram, "Zionist Historiography and the Invention of Modern Jewish Nationhood: The Case of Ben Zion Dinur." *History and Memory* 7, no. 1 (1995), 91–124; Anita Shapira, "Ben-Gurion and the Bible: The Forging of an Historical Narrative?" *Middle Eastern Studies* 33, no. 4 (1997), 645–74.

28. Ian Lustick, *Paradigm Lost: From Two-State Solution to One-State Reality* (Philadelphia: University of Pennsylvania Press, 2019), Kindle edition, Chapter 2.

29. Ram, "Dinur," 91–2; Yakov Rabkin, *A Threat from Within: Jewish Opposition to Zionism* (London: Black Point & Zed Books, 2006), 15–63; Michael Brenner, "Why President Trump's Executive Order to Fight Anti-Semitism is Dangerous for Jews," *Washington Post*, December 15, 2019.

30. Ilan Pappe, *A History of Modern Palestine: One Land, Two People* (Cambridge: Cambridge University Press, 2004), 68.

31. Pappe, *Cleansing*, Kindle edition, Chapter 1.

32. Ram, "Dinur," 91–124; Sand, *Invention*, 209–11.

33. Sand, *Invention*, 209.

34. Lorenzo Veracini, *Settler Colonialism: A Theoretical Perspective* (Basingstoke: Palgrave Macmillan, 2010), 52.

35. Ibid., 41–2.

36. Ibid., 45.

37. Ibid., 22.

38. Ibid., 47.

39. Ibid., 21.

40. Eric Zakim, *To Build and Be Built: Landscape, Literature, and the Construction of Zionist Identity* (Philadelphia: University of Pennsylvania Press, 2006).

41. Quoted in Ben-Eliezer, *Militarism*, 149–50.

42. Jonathan Cummings, *Israel's Public Diplomacy: The Problems of Hasbara, 1966–1975* (Lanham: Rowman and Littlefield, 2016), 1.

43. Lustick, *Paradigm Lost*, Kindle edition, Chapter 2; Howard M. Sachar, *A History of Israel: From the Rise of Zionism to Our Time* (New York: Alfred A. Knoff, 1979), 292–304.

44. M. M. Silver, *Our Exodus: Leon Uris and the Amercanization of Israel's Founding Story* (Detroit: Wayne State University Press, 2010), 100.

45. Jeff Halper, *An Israeli in Palestine: Resisting Dispossession, Redeeming Israel* (London: Pluto Press, 2011), 126–37; Amy Kaplan, "Zionism as Anticolonialism: The Case of Exodus," *American Literary History* 25, no. 4 (2013), 870–95.

46. Shlaim, *Collusion Across the Jordan*.

47. Ben-Eliezer, *Militarism*, 153–68.
48. Ibid., 153–68.

5. The Occupation Cycle (1967–Present): Completing the Settler Colonial Project

1. Benny Morris, *Righteous Victims: A History of the Zionist-Arab Conflict, 1881–1949* (New York: Knopf, 1999), 329.
2. Arliela Azoulay and Adi Ophir, *The One-State Condition: Occupation and Democracy in Israel/Palestine* (Stanford: Stanford University Press, 2013), 2, 275.
3. Avi Raz, *The Bride and the Dowry: Israel, Jordan and the Palestinians in the Aftermath of June 1967 War* (New Haven: Yale University Press, 2012).
4. Shlomo Gazit, *Trapped Fools: Thirty Years of Israeli Policy in the Territories* (London: Frank Cass, 2003), 8–11, 20–2.
5. Ze'ev Maoz, *Defending the Holy Land: A Critical Analysis of Israel's Security & Foreign Policy* (Ann Arbor: University of Michigan Press, 2006), 5.
6. Ibid., 30–41.
7. Dan Diker, ed., *Israel's Critical Security Requirements for Defensible Borders: The Foundation for a Viable Peace* (Jerusalem: Jerusalem Center for Public Affairs, 2011).
8. C. Wright Mills, *The Causes of World War Three* (New York: Simon and Schuster, 1958), 221–2.
9. Moshe Yaalon, "Introduction: Restoring a Security-First Peace Policy," in *Requirements*, ed. Diker, 11.
10. Ibid., 7.
11. Ibid., 8.
12. Ibid., 8.
13. Ibid., 11.
14. Ibid., 14.
15. Dore Gold, "Regional Overview: How Defensible Borders Remain Vital for Israel," in *Requirements*, ed. Diker, 60.
16. Yaalon, "Introduction," 140.
17. Ibid., 10.
18. Tom Abowd, "The Moroccan Quarter: A History of the Present," *Jerusalem Quarterly File* 7 (Winter 2000), 9–12.
19. Morris, *Victims*, 314.
20. Michael Oren, *Six Days of War: June 1967 and the Making of the Modern Middle East* (New York: Random House, 2002), 191.
21. Sara Salazar Hughes, "Unbounded Territoriality: Territorial Control, Settler Colonialism, and Israel/Palestine," *Settler Colonial Studies* (2020), 10, no. 2, 1–18.
22. Jeff Halper, *An Israeli in Palestine: Resisting Dispossession, Redeeming Israel* (London: Pluto Press, 2011), 141–73.
23. Meir Margalit, *Discrimination in the Holy City* (Jerusalem: International Peace and Cooperation Center, 2006).

24. Foundation for Middle East Peace, "Settlement Report: October 11, 2019." https://fmep.org/resource/settlement-report-october-11-2019; Halper, *Israeli*, 165–8.

25. Yehezkel Lein, *Land Grab: Israel's Settlement Policy in the West Bank* (Jerusalem: B'Tselem, 2002).

26. Ian Fisher, "Israel Passes Provocative Law to Retroactively Legalize Settlements," *New York Times*, February 6, 2017. www.nytimes.com/2017/02/06/world/middleeast/israel-settlement-law-palestinians-west-bank.html?_r=1.

27. Margalit, *Discrimination*.

28. Nir Hasson, "New Jerusalem 'Apartheid Road' Opens, Separating Palestinians and Jewish Settlers," *Ha'aretz*, January 10, 2019. www.haaretz.com/israel-news/.premium.MAGAZINE-new-apartheid-road-opens-separating-palestinians-and-west-bank-settlers-1.6827201.

29. Jeff Halper, "The Road to Apartheid," *News from Within* 16, no. 5 (May 2000), 1–7.

30. Halper, *Israeli*, 168–71; Shir Hever, *The Economy of the Occupation (# 11–12): The Separation Wall in East Jerusalem: Economic Consequences* (Jerusalem: Alternative Information Centre, 2007), 7; B'Tselem, "The Separation Barrier" (2017). www.btselem.org/separation_barrier; United Nations, *The Humanitarian Impact of the West Bank Barrier on Palestinian Communities* (Jerusalem: OCHA, 2005).

31. Who Profits, "Industrial Zones in the Occupied Palestinian Territory," n.d. https://whoprofits.org/dynamic-report/industrial-zones; B'Tselem, *Made in Israel: Exploiting Palestinian Land for Treatment of Israeli Waste* (Jerusalem: B'Tselem, 2017).

32. Eyal Weizman, *Hollow Land: Israel's Architecture of Occupation* (London: Verso, 2007), 12–16.

33. B'Tselem. *Water Crisis* (2017). www.btselem.org/water.

34. The Applied Research Institute – Jerusalem (ARIJ), "Israel Military Orders in the Occupied Palestine Territory." http://orders.arij.org; Jamil Rabah and Natasha Fairweather, *Israeli Military Orders in the Occupied Palestinian Territories, 1967–1992* (Jerusalem: Jerusalem Media and Communications Center, 1993).

35. Bimkom, "The Prohibited Zone: Israeli Planning Policy in the Palestinian Villages in Area C," n.d. http://bimkom.org/eng/wp-content/uploads/ProhibitedZoneAbstract.pdf; Jeff Halper, *Obstacles to Peace: A Reframing of the Israeli-Palestinian Conflict* (Jerusalem: ICAHD, 2018), 58–9.

36. Yaakov Amidror, "Winning Counterinsurgency War: The Israeli Experience," *Strategic Perspectives* 2 (2008), 1–41.

37. Hillel Cohen, *Army of Shadows. Palestinian Collaboration with Zionism, 1917–1948* (Berkeley: University of California Press, 2008); Hillel Cohen, *Good Arabs: The Israeli Security Agencies and the Israeli Arabs, 1948–1967* (Berkeley: University of California Press, 2010).

38. Salah Abdel Jawad, "The Classification and Recruitment of Collaborators," *The Phenomenon of Collaborators in Palestine: Proceedings of a Passia*

Workshop (Jerusalem: Palestinian Academic Society for the Study of International Affairs, 2001).

39. Jonathan Cook, "Spotlight Shines on Palestinian Collaborators," *Al-Jazeera English* 17 (2014).

40. Addameer, *Palestinian Political Prisoners in Israeli Prisons*, 2014. www. addameer.org/files/Palestinian%20Political%20Prisoners%20in%20 Israeli%20Prisons%20(General%20Briefing%20January%202014).pdf.

41. Shir Hever, *The Political Economy of Israel's Occupation: Repression Beyond Exploitation* (London: Pluto Press, 2010), 8–9.

42. Ibid., 10.

43. B'Tselem, "Settlements," n.d. www.btselem.org/topic/settlements.

44. Adam Hanieh, *Lineages of Revolt. Issues of Contemporary Capitalism in the Middle East* (Chicago: Haymarket Books, 2013), 100. See also Raja Khalidi and Sobhi Samour, "Neoliberalism as Liberation: The Statehood Program and the Remaking of the Palestinian National Movement," *Journal of Palestine Studies* 15, no. 2 (Winter 2011), 6–25.

45. Leila Farsakh, "Under Siege: Closure, Separation and the Palestinian Economy" (Washington, DC: MERIP, 2000). https://merip. org/2000/12/under-siege.

46. Ishac Diwan and Radwan Shaban, *Development under Adversity* (Washington, DC: World Bank, 1999).

47. C. Astrup and S. Dessus, *Trade Options for the Palestinian Economy* (Washington, DC: World Bank, 2000).

48. Worker's Hotline. www.kavlaoved.org.il/en/areasofactivity/palestinian-workers.

49. Linda Tabar and Omar Jabary Salamanca, "After Oslo: Settler Colonialism, Neoliberal Development and Liberation," in *Critical Readings of Development under Colonialism: Towards a Political Economy for Liberation in the Occupied Palestinian Territories* (The Center of Development Studies at Birzeit University, 2015), 11–33.

50. Hanieh, *Lineages*, 100.

51. Ibrahim Shikaki and Joanna Springer, "Building a Failed State: Palestine's Governance and Economy Delinked," *al-Shabaka* (April 21, 2015). https://al-shabaka.org/briefs/building-a-failed-state.

52. UNCTAD (United Nations Conference on Trade and Development), *Report on UNCTAD Assistance to the Palestinian People: Developments in the Economy of the Occupied Palestinian Territory* (Geneva, October 2019). https://unctad.org/meetings/en/SessionalDocuments/tdbex68d4_ en.pdf?user=46.

53. Tariq Dana, "The Symbiosis between Palestinian 'Fayyadism' and Israeli 'Economic Peace': The Political Economy of Capitalist Peace in the Context of Colonisation," *Conflict, Security & Development* 15, no. 5 (2015), 455–77.

54. Hanieh, *Lineages*, 116–17; Toufic Haddad, "Neoliberalism and Palestinian Development: Assessment and Alternatives, in *Critical Readings of Development under Colonialism: Towards a Political Economy for Libera-*

tion in the Occupied Palestinian Territories (The Center of Development Studies at Birzeit University, 2015), 51–2.

55. Hanieh, *Lineages*, 119; Shikaki and Springer, "Building."

56. Nathan Thrall, "Our Man in Palestine," *New York Review of Books* (October 14, 2010); Hanieh, *Lineages*, 117.

57. Shikaki and Springer, "Building."

58. Khalil Nakhleh, *Globalized Palestine: The National Sell-Out of a Homeland* (Trenton: Red Sea Press, 2011).

59. Middle East Monitor, "Abbas: Security Cooperation with Israel is 'Sacred'"(May 29, 2014). www.middleeastmonitor.com/20140529-abbas-security-cooperation-with-israel-is-sacred.

60. Mark Duffield, *Development, Security and Unending War* (Cambridge: Polity Press, 2007), Kindle edition.

61. International Labor Organization, *The Situation of Workers in the Occupied Arab Territories* (Geneva: ILO, 2018), 15.

62. UNCTAD, *Report on UNCTAD Assistance to the Palestinian People: Developments in the Economy of the Occupied Palestinian Territory* (Geneva, 2018), 7–10. https://unctad.org/en/PublicationsLibrary/tdb65_2_d3_en.pdf.

63. OEC (Observatory of Economic Complexity), *Palestine* (2016). https://atlas.media.mit.edu/en/profile/country/pse.

64. Jonathan Cummings, *Israel's Public Diplomacy: The Problems of Hasbara, 1966–1975* (Lanham: Rowman and Littlefield, 2016), 2.

65. Tom Segev, *One Palestine, Complete: Jews and Arabs under the British Mandate* (New York: Henry Holt, 1999), 471.

66. Ann Mosely Lesch, "Israeli Settlements in the Occupied Territories, 1967–1977," *Journal of Palestine Studies* 7, no. 1 (1977), 26–47.

67. Lorenzo Veracini, *Settler Colonialism: A Theoretical Overview* (Basingstoke: Palgrave Macmillan, 2010), 101.

68. Ibid., 30.

69. Ilan Pappe, *The Idea of Israel: A History of Knowledge and Power* (London: Verso, 2016), 299–301.

70. Rashid Khalidi, *The Hundred Years' War on Palestine: A History of Settler Colonialism and Resistance, 1917–2017* (New York: Henry Holt, 2020), 237–8.

71. Ibid., 2–8.

72. Fayez Sayegh, *Zionist Colonialism in Palestine* (Beirut: Research Center, Palestine Liberation Organization, 1965).

73. As just one example, Edward Said, "Zionism from the Standpoint of Its Victims," *Social Text* no. 1 (Winter 1979), 7–58.

74. George Jabbour, *Settler Colonialism in Southern Africa and the Middle East*, no. 30 (University of Khartoum, 1970).

75. Nahla Abdo and Nira Yuval-Davis. "Palestine, Israel and the Settler Zionist Project," in *Unsettling Settler Societies*, eds. Daiva Stasiulis and Nira Yuval-Davis (London: Sage, 1995), 291–322.

76. Jamil Hilal, "Imperialism and Settler-Colonialism in West Asia: Israel and the Arab Palestinian Struggle," *UTAFITI: Journal of the Arts and Social Sciences, University of Dar Es Salaam* 1, no. 1 (1976), 51–69.

77. Daiva Stasiulis and Nira Yuval-Davis, eds., *Unsettling Settler Societies* (London: Sage, 1995).

78. Uri Ram, "The Colonization Perspective in Israeli Sociology," *Journal of Historical Sociology* 6, no. 3 (September 1993), 327–50.

79. Gershon Shafir, *Land, Labor and the Origins of the Israeli-Palestinian Conflict, 1882–1914* (Cambridge: Cambridge University Press, 1989).

80. Ilan Pappe, "Post-Zionist Critique on Israel and the Palestinians," *Journal of Palestine Studies* 26, no. 2 (Winter 1997), 29–41.

81. Akiva Orr, Haim Hanegbi and Moshe Machover, "The Class Nature of Israeli Society," *New Left Review* (January–February 1971), 3–26.

82. Maxime Rodinson, *Israel: A Settler Colonial State?* (New York: Monad Press, 1973).

83. Khalidi, *Hundred Years*, 239, 240.

84. Ibid., 244.

85. Ibid., 254.

86. This criticism is echoed in Salamanca, Omar Jabary, Mezna Qato, Kareem Rabie and Sobhi Samour, "Past is Present: Settler Colonialism in Palestine," *Settler Colonial Studies* 2, no. 1 (2013), 1–8: "[S]ettler colonialism remains a descriptive category that does not move beyond sentiment and into strategy. While activists, both in Palestine and outside it, continue to push back against Zionist encroachment, intensify the demand for equal rights, and build a boycott, divestment and sanctions movement aimed at shaming and delegitimising Israel internationally, the creative offerings of the settler colonial studies paradigm remain underutilised. This lack of rigorous engagement has consequences for movement building. The historic response to settler colonialism has been the struggle for decolonisation; in the absence of a settler colonial analysis, Palestinian strategies have tended to target or might enable individuals to transform that reality to accommodate settler colonial outcomes rather than aiming to decolonise the structure itself."

6. Decolonization: Dismantling the Dominance Management Regime

1. Anna Johansson and Stellan Vinthagen, "Dimensions of Everyday Resistance: The Palestinian Sumūd," *Journal of Political Power* 8, no. 1 (February 2015), 1–31.

2. Rashid Khalidi, *Palestinian Identity: The Construction of Modern National Consciousness* (New York: Columbia University Press, 1997), 98–111.

3. Yitzhak Epstein, "The Hidden Question," quoted in *Prophets Outcaste: A Century of Jewish Dissident Writing about Zionism and Israel*, ed. Adam Schatz (New York: Nation Books, 2004), 39, 43.

4. Rima Hammami, quoted in Johansson and Vinthagen, "Everyday Resistance," 3.

5. Sophie Richter-Devroe, "Palestinian Women's Everyday Resistance: Between Normality and Normalisation," *Journal of International Women's Studies* 12, no. 2, 32–46; Jack Khoury and Hagar Shezaf, "Israel Turns a

Blind Eye, and Palestinians Revel in a Weekend at Jaffa Beach," *Ha'aretz*, August 8, 2020. www.haaretz.com/middle-east-news/palestinians/. premium-palestinians-revel-in-a-weekend-of-freedom-at-israeli-beaches-1.9059886; Jeff Halper, *An Israeli in Palestine: Resisting Dispossession, Redeeming Israel* (London: Pluto Press, 2011), 18–21, 36–59.

6. Stephanie J. Baele, "Lone-Actor Terrorists' Emotions and Cognition: An Evaluation Beyond Stereotypes," *Political Psychology* 38, no. 3 (June 2017), 449–68.

7. Uri Ben-Eliezer, *The Making of Israeli Militarism* (Bloomington: Indiana University Press, 1998).

8. Martin van Creveld, *The Sword and the Olive: A Critical History of the Israeli Defense Force* (New York: Public Affairs, 1998), 17.

9. Ibid, 17; Khalidi, *Identity*, 105–11; Benny Morris, *Righteous Victims: A History of the Zionist-Arab Conflict, 1881–1949* (New York: Knopf, 1999), 9–63.

10. Baruch Kimmerling, "Patterns of Militarism in Israel," *European Journal of Sociology* 34 (1993), 196–221.

11. See, for example, Fayez Sayegh, "Zionist Colonialism in Palestine," *Settler Colonial Studies* 2, no. 1 (2012/1965), 206–25; Rosemary Sayigh, *The Palestinians: From Peasants to Revolutionaries* (London and New York: Zed Books, 1979); Rashid Khalidi, *The Hundred Years' War on Palestine: A History of Settler Colonial Conquest and Resistance, 1917–2017* (New York: Henry Holt, 2020); Mazin B. Qumsiyeh, *Popular Resistance in Palestine: A History of Hope and Empowerment* (London: Pluto Press, 2011); Yezid Sayigh, *Armed Struggle and the Search for State: The Palestinian National Movement, 1949–1993* (Oxford: Oxford University Press, 1997); Mary Elizabeth King, *A Quiet Revolution: The First Palestinian Intifada and Nonviolent Resistance* (New York: Avalon, 2009); Ramzy Baroud, *The Second Palestinian Intifada: A Chronicle of a People's Struggle* (London: Pluto Press, 2006); Nasser Abufarha, *The Making of a Human Bomb: An Ethnography of Palestinian Resistance* (Durham: Duke University Press, 2009); and Caitlin Ryan, *Bodies, Power and Resistance in the Middle East Experiences of Subjectification in the Occupied Palestinian Territories* (London: Routledge, 2016).

12. Sayegh, *Zionist Colonialism*, 221; Qumsiyeh, *Popular Resistance*, 36–47.

13. Rashid Khalidi, *The Iron Cage: The Story of the Palestinian Struggle for Statehood* (Boston: Beacon Press, 2006), 107.

14. Marcelo Svirsky and Ronnen Ben-Arie, *From Shared Life to Co-resistance in Historic Palestine* (London: Rowman and Littlefield, 2017), 23, 41.

15. Ibid., 22.

16. Qumsiyeh, *Popular Resistance*, 38.

17. Khalidi, *Identity*, 119–44.

18. Mohammad Muslih, *The Origins of Palestinian Nationalism* (New York: Columbia University Press, 1988), 158–78.

19. Ibid., 204–10; Khalidi, *Iron Cage*, 42. See also Ann Mosley Lesch, *Arab Politics in Palestine, 1917–1939* (Ithaca: Cornell University Press, 1979)

and Ilan Pappe, *The Rise and Fall of a Palestinian Dynasty: The Husaynis, 1700–1948* (Berkeley: University of California Press, 2011).

20. Qumsiyeh, *Popular Resistance*, 45.

21. Muhammad Muslih, "Towards Coexistence: An Analysis of the Resolutions of the Palestine National Council," *Journal of Palestine Studies* 19, no. 4 (Summer 1990), 8.

22. George Bisharat, "Maximizing Rights: The One State Solution to the Palestinian-Israeli Conflict," *Global Jurist* 8, no. 2 (2008), 1–36; on p. 2, Bisharat lists many papers advocating for this approach.

23. Muslih, "Towards Coexistence," 12–14; "5th Palestine National Council is Held in Cairo," Palestinian Journeys Timeline. www.paljourneys.org/en/timeline/overallchronology?event=5498.

24. Leila Farsakh, "The One State Solution and Israeli-Palestinian Conflict: Palestinian Challenges and Prospects," *The Middle East Journal* 65, no. 1 (Winter 2011), 71.

25. Muslih, "Towards Coexistence," 16–17.

26. Ibid., 17.

27. Ibid., 22–3.

28. Mark Tessler, *A History of the Israeli–Palestinian Conflict* (Bloomington: Indiana University Press, 1994), 722.

29. Muslih, "Towards Coexistence," 24 (italics in original).

30. Uri Savir, *The Process: 1,100 Days That Changed the Middle East* (New York: Vintage, 1998), 37, 98–100.

31. Bisharat, Maximizing Rights," 4; Omar Dajani, "Shadow or Shade? The Roles of International Law in Palestine-Israeli Peace Talks," *Yale Journal of International Law* 32, no.1 (2007), 61.

32. Bisharat, "Maximizing Rights"; on p. 2, Bisharat lists many papers advocating for this approach; Omar Barghouti, "BDS: A Global Movement for Freedom and Justice," *al-Shabaka* (May 2010). www.bdsmovement.net/files/2011/02/alshabakaBrief.pdf; Nadia Hijab and Ingrid Jaradat Gassner, "Talking Palestine: What Frame of Analysis? Which Goals and Messages?" *al-Shabaka* (April 12, 2017). https://al-shabaka.org/commentaries/talking-palestine-frame-analysis-goals-messages.

33. Michael Dillon and Julian Reid, *The Liberal Way of War: Killing to Make Life Live* (London: Routledge, 2009), 87.

34. Lawfare Project, *Lawfare: The Use of Law as a Weapon of War,* 2010. www.thelawfareproject.org/what-is-lawfare.html.

35. United Nations, The Question of Palestine, "Conference of High Contracting Parties to the Fourth Geneva Convention: Statement," July 15, 1999. www.un.org/unispal/document/auto-insert-194091.

36. Francesca Merlin, "Indigeneity: Global and Local," *Current Anthropology* 50, no. 3 (2009), 304.

37. Birzeit Concept Note, quoted in Markus Gunneflo, "Settler Colonial and Anti-Colonial Legalities in Palestine," *Lund University Faculty of Law* (2019), 6.

38. Bisharat, "Maximizing Rights," 2.

39. Svirsky, "Resistance," 24; Alissa Macoun and Elizabeth Strakosch, "The Ethical Demands of Settler Colonial Theory," *Settler Colonial Studies* 3, nos. 3–4 (2013), 432.

40. Mona Lilja and Stellan Vinthagen discuss the relationship of resistance to power in "Sovereign Power, Disciplinary Power and Biopower: Resisting What Power with What Resistance?" *Journal of Political Power* 7, no. 1, 107–26. We return to this discussion later in Chapter 6 when we consider the dismantling of the Domination Management Regime.

41. Yezid Sayigh, "Armed Struggle and State Formation," *Journal of Palestine Studies* 26, no. 4 (Summer 1997), 17.

42. Muslih, "Towards Coexistence."

43. Ilan Pappe, "Israel and Palestine in 2018: Decolonisation, Not Peace," *Al Jazeera* (May 14, 2018). www.aljazeera.com/indepth/opinion/israel-palestine-2018-decolonisation-peace-180514073500781.html; Linda Tabar and Chandni Desai. "Decolonization is a Global Project: From Palestine to the Americas," *Decolonization: Indigeneity, Education & Society* 6, no. 1 (2017), i–xix.

44. Margaret Kohn and Keally McBride, *Political Theories of Decolonization: Postcolonization and the Problem of Foundations* (Oxford: Oxford University Press, 2011).

7. Constructing a Bridging Vision and Set of Acknowledgements

1. Farid Abdel-Nour, "Irreconcilable Narratives and Overlapping Consensus: The Jewish State and the Palestinian Right of Return," *Political Research Quarterly* 68, no. 1 (2015), 117–27. For a similar approach with applicable conclusions, see Sami Adwan, Dan Bar-On and Eyal Naveh, *Side by Side: Parallel Histories of Israel-Palestine* (New York: The New Press, 2012).

2. Ibid., 118.

3. Ilan Gur-Ze'ev and Ilan Pappe, "Beyond the Destruction of the Other's Collective Memory: Blueprints for a Palestinian/Israeli Dialogue," *Theory, Culture and Society* 20, no. 1 (203), 93–108.

4. South African History Online, "Significance of the Congress of the People and the Freedom Charter," n.d. www.sahistory.org.za/article/significance.

5. Eldred De Klerk, "South Africa's Negotiated Transition: Context, Analysis and Evaluation," in *Accord: Owning the Process: Public Participation in Peacemaking*, ed. Catherine Barnes (London: Conciliation Resources, 2002): 19 c-r.org/accord/public-participation; Fanie du Toit, *When Political Transitions Work: Reconciliation as Interdependence* (Oxford: Oxford University Press), 94–100.

6. Uri Davis, *Apartheid Israel: Possibilities for the Struggle Within* (London: Zed Books, 2003), 149.

7. Raef Zreik, "When Does a Settler Become a Native? (With Apologies to Mamdani)," *Constellations* 23, no. 3 (2016), 358, 360.

8. Marcelo Svirsky and Ronen Ben-Arie, *From Shared Life to Co-resistance in Historic Palestine* (London: Rowman and Littlefield, 2017), 9 (italics in original).

9. Hillel Cohen, *Year Zero of the Arab-Israeli Conflict 1929* (Waltham: Brandeis University Press, 2015), Kindle edition, Chapter 1, 1208; Jeff Halper, *Between Redemption and Revival: The Jewish Yishuv of Jerusalem in the Nineteenth Century* (Boulder: Westview, 1991); Abigail Jacobson and Moshe Naor, *Oriental Neighbors: Middle Eastern Jews and Arabs in Mandatory Palestine* (Waltham: Brandeis University Press, 2016), 55–73.

10. Lorenzo Veracini, *Settler Colonialism: A Theoretical Overview* (Basingstoke: Palgrave Macmillan, 2010), 3.

11. Cohen, *Year Zero*, Introduction, 75.

12. Quoted in Simha Flapan, *Zionism and the Palestinians* (London: Croom Helm, 1979), 168–9.

13. Willi Goetschel and Ato Quason, "Introduction: Jewish Studies and Postcolonialism," *The Cambridge Journal of Literary Postcolonial Inquiry* 3, no. 1 (2016), 5.

14. Mahmood Mamdani "When Does a Settler Become a Native? Reflections of the Colonial Roots of Citizenship in Equatorial and South Africa," Inaugural Lecture as A.C. Jordan Professor of African Studies, University of Cape Town, May 13, 1998. https://citizenshiprightsafrica.org/wp-content/uploads/1998/05/mamdani-1998-inaugural-lecture.pdf.

15. Ibid.

16. Kevin Bruyneel, *The Third Space of Sovereignty: The Postcolonial Politics of U.S.-Indigenous Relations* (Minneapolis: University of Minnesota Press, 2007); see also Zreik, "When Does a Settler Become a Native?" 352.

17. Taiaiake Alfred, *Peace, Power, Righteousness: An Indigenous Manifesto* (Toronto: Oxford University Press, 1999); Walter Mignolo and Catherine Walsh, *On Decoloniality: Concepts, Analytics, Praxis* (Durham: Duke University Press, 2018), Kindle edition; Glen S. Coulthard, *Red Skin, White Masks: Rejecting the Colonial Politics of Recognition* (Minneapolis: University of Minnesota Press, 2014).

18. Gur-Ze'ev and Pappe, "Beyond Destruction," 97.

19. Jeff Halper, *War Against the People: Israel, the Palestinians and Global Pacification* (London: Pluto Press, 2015), 3.

20. De Klerk, "Negotiated," 18–19.

21. Nelson Mandela, *Long Walk to Freedom* (London: Hachette Digital, 1994), Kindle edition, Chapter 40.

8. A Plan of Decolonization

1. Cherine Hussein, *The Re-emergence of the Single State Solution in Palestine-Israel: Countering an Illusion* (New York: Routledge, 2015), 94.

2. Virginia Tilley, *The One-State Solution: A Breakthrough for Peace in the Israeli-Palestinian Deadlock* (Ann Arbor: University of Michigan Press, 2005).

3. Mazin Qumsiyeh, *Sharing the Land of Canaan* (London: Pluto Press, 2004).

4. Ali Abunimah, *One Country: A Bold Proposal to End the Israeli-Palestinian Impasse* (New York: Henry Holt, 2006).

5. Ariela Azoulay and Adi Ophir, *The One-State Condition: Occupation and Democracy in Israel/Palestine* (Stanford: Stanford University Press, 2012).

6. Hani Faris, ed., *The Failure of the Two-State Solution: The Prospects of One State in the Israeli-Palestinian Conflict* (New York: I. B. Tauris, 2013).

7. Ghada Karmi, *Married to Another Man: Israel's Dilemma in Palestine* (London: Pluto Press, 2014).

8. Ofra Yeshua-Lyth, *The Case for a Secular New Jerusalem: A Memoir* (Tel Aviv: Nymrod Publishing, 2014).

9. Leila Farsakh, "The One State Solution and Israeli-Palestinian Conflict: Palestinian Challenges and Prospects," *The Middle East Journal* 65, no. 1 (Winter 2011), 65.

10. Blake Alcott, "What Kind of Palestinian State Do We Want?" *Counterpunch* (January 3, 2019). www.counterpunch.org/2019/01/03/what-kind-of-single-democratic-state-in-israel-palestine-do-we-want; Yousef M. Aljamal and Blake Alcott, "Which Democratic State?" *Mondoweiss* (August 4, 2018). https://mondoweiss.net/2018/08/which-democratic-state; Naji El_Khatib and Ofra Yeshua-Lyth, "One Democratic State: An Ongoing Debate," *Mondoweiss* (July 25, 2018). mondoweiss.net/2018/06/democratic-ongoing-debate.

11. Farsakh, "One State," 67.

12. Ibid., 57, 71.

13. As we have mentioned before, "sovereignty" in the context of settler decolonization has a different meaning than it does in "classic" decolonization, where state sovereignty devolves to the local population as the colonial power withdraws. In the case of settler colonialism, the Indigenous regain their sovereignty by gaining the power to assert their rights and claims over their land, their resources, their culture and their community life.

14. Muhammad Muslih, "Towards Coexistence: An Analysis of the Resolutions of the Palestine National Council," *Journal of Palestine Studies* 19, no. 4 (Summer 1990), 14.

15. "The Revision of the Third Draft of the Constitution of the State of Palestine," Palestinian National Authority, May 15, 2003. https://web.archive.org/web/20040325025809/http://www.mopic.gov.ps/constitution/english%20constitution.asp.

16. Pew Research Center, "Israel's Religiously Divided Society" (March 8, 2016). www.pewforum.org/2016/03/08/israels-religiously-divided-society; Pew Research Center, "The World's Muslims: Unity and Diversity" (August 9, 2012). www.pewforum.org/2012/08/09/the-worlds-muslims-unity-and-diversity-executive-summary.

17. Farsakh, "One State"; George Bisharat, "Maximizing Rights: The One State Solution to the Palestinian-Israeli Conflict," *Global Jurist* 8, no. 2 (2008), 1–36; Nadia Hijab and Ingrid Jaradat Gassner, "Talking Palestine: What Frame of Analysis? Which Goals and Messages?"

al-Shabaka (April 12, 2017). https://al-shabaka.org/commentaries/ talking-palestine-frame-analysis-goals-messages.

18. Bashir Bashir, "The Strengths and Weaknesses of Integrative Solutions for the Israeli-Palestinian Conflict," *Middle East Journal* 70, no. 4 (2016), 562.

19. Salim Tamari, "The Dubious Lure of Binationalism," *Journal of Palestine Studies* 117 (Autumn 2000), 83–7.

20. Bashir, "Strengths," 568.

21. Omar Barghouti, "What Comes Next: A Secular Democratic State in Historic Palestine – a Promising Land," *Mondoweiss* (October 21, 2013). https://mondoweiss.net/2013/10/democratic-palestine-promising; see also his article "A Secular Democratic State in Historic Palestine: Self-Determination Through Ethical Decolonisation," in *After Zionism: One State for Israel and Palestine*, eds. Antony Loewenstein and Ahmed Moor (London: Saqi, 2012), 174–89.

22. Ali Abunimah, "ICAHD Endorses One-State Solution, Warns Against 'Warehousing' of Palestinians," *The Electronic Intifada* (September 14, 2012). http://electronicintifada.net/blogs/ali-abunimah/icahd-endorses-one-state-solution-warns-against-warehousing-palestinians.

23. Farsakh, "One State," 63.

24. Meron Benvenisti, "The Case for Shared Sovereignty," *The Nation* (June 18, 2007); Yehuda Shenhav, *The Time of the Green Line* (Tel Aviv: Am Oved, 2010).

25. As'ad Ghanem, "Cooperation Instead of Separation: The One-State Solution to Promote Israeli Palestinian Peace," *Palestine-Israel Journal of Politics, Economics and Culture* 14, no. 2 (2007).

26. Azmi Bishara, "The Palestinians of Israel: An Interview with Azmi Bishara," in *The New Intifada: Resisting Israel's Apartheid*, ed. Roane Carey (London: Verso, 2001), 147–8.

27. "The Future Vision of the Palestinian Arabs in Israel" (2006). www.adalah.org/uploads/oldfiles/newsletter/eng/dec06/tasawor-mostaqbali.pdf.

28. The Haifa Declaration (2007). www.adalah.org/uploads/oldfiles/newsletter/eng/may07/haifa.pdf.

29. "One Land for All: Shared and Agreed Principles," n.d. www.alandforall.org/english-program/?d=ltr.

30. Aryeh Eliav, *Land of the Hart: Israelis, Arabs, the Territories and a Vision of the Future* (New York: Jewish Publication Society of America, 1974).

31. Daniel J. Elazar, *Two Peoples, One Land* (Jerusalem: Jerusalem Center for Public Affairs, 1991).

32. Mark LeVine and Matthias Mossberg, eds. *One Land, Two States: Israel and Palestine as Parallel States* (Berkeley: University of California Press, 2014).

33. Lev Grinberg, "Israeli-Palestinian Union: The 1-2-7 States Vision of the Future," *Journal of Palestine Studies* 39, no. 2 (Winter 2010), 46–53.

34. Abraham Weizfeld, *The Federation of Hebrew and Palestinian Nations* (Newcastle: Cambridge Scholars Publishing, 2018).

35. Israel/Palestine Confederation. http://ipconfederation.org/homepage-english.htm.

36. The Federation Plan. www.federation.org.il/index.php/en/the-federation-plan.

37. Raef Zreik, "When Does a Settler Become a Native? (With Apologies to Mamdani)," *Constellations* 23, no. 3 (2016), 357.

38. Barghouti, "What Comes Next."

39. See the discussion by Leila Farsakh, "One State," 63. See also Grinberg, "Israeli-Palestinian Union," 49.

40. Teodora Todorova, "Reframing Bi-nationalism in Palestine-Israel as a Process of Settler Decolonisation," *Antipode* 47, no. 5 (November 2015), 1380–1 (italics in original).

41. Wendy Brown, *Undoing the Demos: Neoliberalism's Stealth Revolution* (Brooklyn: Zone Books, 2015), Kindle edition, Chapter 1.

42. Guy Standing, *The Precariat: The New Dangerous Class* (London: Bloomsbury, 2014).

43. William Robinson and Yousef Baker, "Savage Inequalities: Capitalist Crisis and Surplus Humanity," *International Critical Thought* 9, no. 3 (2019), 376–93.

44. Andy Clarno, *Neoliberal Apartheid* (Chicago: University of Chicago Press, 2017); Mark Neocleous, *War Power/Police Power* (Edinburgh: Edinburgh University Press, 2014); Nandita Sharma and Cynthia Wright, "Decolonizing Resistance, Challenging Colonial States," *Social Justice* 35, no. 3 (2008), 120–38; Magid Shihade, "Settler Colonialism and Conflict: The Israeli State and Its Palestinian Subjects," *Settler Colonial Studies* 2, no. 1 (2012), 108–23; Eve Tuck and K. Wayne Yang, "Decolonization is Not a Metaphor," *Decolonization: Indigeneity, Education & Society* 1, no. 1, 1–40.

45. Ruba Salih and Sophie Richter-Devroe, "Palestine Beyond National Frames: Emerging Politics, Cultures, and Claims," *South Atlantic Quarterly* 117, no. 1 (2018), 1–10.

46. Ibid., 4–5.

47. Paul Chamberlain, "The Struggle Against Oppression Everywhere: The Global Politics of Palestinian Liberation," *Middle Eastern Studies* 47, no. 1 (2011), 25–41; Fayez Sayegh, *Zionist Colonialism in Palestine* (Beirut: Research Center, Palestine Liberation Organization, 1965), 51.

48. Omar Jabary Salamanca, Mezna Qato, Kareem Rabie and Sobhi Samour, "Past is Present: Settler Colonialism in Palestine," *Settler Colonial Studies* 2 no. 1 (2013), 5.

49. Salih and Richter-Devroe, "Beyond National Frames," 7–8.

50. Abdullah Öclan, *Democratic Confederalism* (London: Transmedia Publishing, 2011).

51. Michael Vincent McGinnis, ed., *Bioregionalism* (London: Routledge, 1999).

52. Murray Bookchin, *The Philosophy of Social Ecology: Essays on Dialectical Naturalism* (Montreal: Black Rose Books, 1996).

53. Hamid Dabash, *The Arab Spring: The End of Postcolonialism* (London: Zed Books, 2012).

54. For example, Glen S. Coulthard, *Red Skin, White Masks: Rejecting the Colonial Politics of Recognition* (Minneapolis: University of Minnesota Press, 2014).

55. Alex Khasnabish, *Zapatistas: Rebellion from the Grassroots to the Global* (London: Zed Books, 2010), 167.

56. Linda Tabar and Chandni Desai, "Decolonization is a Global Project: From Palestine to the Americas," *Decolonization: Indigeneity, Education & Society* 6, no. 1 (2017), 2.

57. Adom Getachew, *Worldmaking after Empire: The Rise and Fall of Self-Determination* (Princeton: Princeton University Press, 2019), 2.

58. John Collins, *Global Palestine* (New York: Columbia University Press, 2011).

59. Shimshon Bichler and Jonathan Nitzan, *The Global Political Economy of Israel* (London: Pluto Press, 2002).

60. Jeff Halper, *War Against the People: Israel, the Palestinians and Global Pacification* (London: Pluto Press, 2015).

9. Towards Post-coloniality

1. Chris McGreel, "Worlds Apart," *Guardian* (February 6, 2006).

2. Uri Davis, *Apartheid Israel: Possibilities for the Struggle Within* (London: Zed Books, 2003), 149.

3. Khalil Nakhleh, *Globalized Palestine: The National Sell-Out of a Homeland* (Trenton: Red Sea Press, 2011).

4. Robert Tignor, "Palestine and Israel: A Case of Incomplete Decolonization,"*Origins*(2002).http://origins.osu.edu/history-news/palestine-and-israel-case-incomplete-decolonization.

5. See, for example, the special edition of *Setter Colonial Studies* 7, no. 4 (2017) on "Pathways of Settler Decolonization."

6. Maya Kahanoff, Walid Salem, Rami Nasrallah and Yana Neumann, "Between Palestinian and Israeli NGOs: An Assessment" (Jerusalem: Jerusalem Institute for Israel Studies, 2007).

7. Mahmoud Mi'Ari, "Attitudes of Palestinians Toward Normalization with Israel," *Journal of Peace Research* 36, no. 3 (May 1999), 339–48; Palestinian Campaign for Academic and Cultural Boycott of Israel, "Israel's Exceptionalism: Normalizing the Abnormal," posted October 31, 2011. www.pacbi.org/etemplate.php?id=1749.

8. Uri Ben-Eliezer, *War Over Peace: One Hundred Years of Israel's Militaristic Nationalism* (Oakland: University of California Press, 2019).

9. Taiaiake Alfred, *Wasase: Indigenous Pathways of Action and Freedom* (Toronto: University of Toronto Press, 2009); Clare Land, *Decolonizing Solidarity: Dilemmas and Directions for Supporters of Indigenous Struggles* (London: Zed Books, 2015); Leanne Simpson, *Dancing on Our Turtle's Back: Stories of Nishnaabeg Re-creation, Resurgence, and a New Emergence* (Winnipeg: Arbeiter Ring Press, 2011).

10. Heribert Adam and Kogila Moodley, *Seeking Mandela: Peacemaking Between Israelis and Palestinians* (Philadelphia: Temple University Press, 2005), 71–2.

11. Mahmood Mamdani, "Beyond Settler and Native as Political Identities: Overcoming the Political Legacy of Colonialism," *Comparative Studies in Society and History* 43, no. 4 (2001), 661 (italics added).

12. Mahmood Mamdani, "When Does a Settler Become a Native? Reflections of the Colonial Roots of Citizenship in Equatorial and South Africa," Inaugural Lecture as A.C. Jordan Professor of African Studies, University of Cape Town, May 13, 1998. https://citizenshiprightsafrica. org/wp-content/uploads/1998/05/mamdani-1998-inaugural-lecture.pdf.

13. Walter Mignolo and Catherine Walsh, *On Decoloniality: Concepts, Analytics, Praxis* (Durham: Duke University Press, 2018), Kindle edition, Introduction.

14. Kevin Bruyneel, *The Third Space of Sovereignty: The Postcolonial Politics of U.S.-Indigenous Relations* (Minneapolis: University of Minnesota Press, 2007), 22.

15. Mamdani, "Beyond Settler," 652.

16. Lorenzo Veracini, *Settler Colonialism: A Theoretical Overview* (Basingstoke: Palgrave Macmillan, 2010); Robert Yazzie, "Indigenous Peoples and Postcolonial Colonialism," in *Reclaiming Indigenous Voices and Vision*, ed. Marie Battiste (Vancouver: University of British Columbia Press, 2000), 46.

17. Michael Vincent McGinnis, ed., *Bioregionalism* (London: Routledge, 1999).

18. Murray Bookchin, *The Philosophy of Social Ecology: Essays on Dialectical Naturalism* (Montreal: Black Rose Books, 1996).

19. Abdullah Öcalan, *Democratic Confederalism* (2017). http://ocalanbooks. com/downloads/EN-brochure_democratic-confederalism_2017.pdf.

20. For example, Glen S. Coulthard, *Red Skin, White Masks: Rejecting the Colonial Politics of Recognition* (Minneapolis: University of Minnesota Press, 2014).

21. Alex Khasnabish, *Zapatistas: Rebellion from the Grassroots to the Global* (London: Zed Books, 2010), 167.

22. Frantz Fanon, *The Wretched of the Earth* (Harmondsworth; Penguin Books, 1963), 97–144.

23. Ibid., 235.

24. Ibid., 235–40 (italics in original).

25. Ibid., 235.

26. Ibid., 237; Adom Getachew also discusses this "fall of self-determination" from the "worldmaking" visions and efforts of the early anti-colonial nationalists. See especially her Epilogue to *Worldmaking After Empire: The Rise and Fall of Self-Determination* (Princeton: Princeton University Press, 2019), 177–82.

27. Omar Barghouti, "What Comes Next: A Secular Democratic State in Historic Palestine – a Promising Land," *Mondoweiss* (October 21, 2013). https://mondoweiss.net/2013/10/democratic-palestine-promising.

28. Veracini, *Settler Colonialism*, 107.

29. Raef Zreik, "When Does a Settler Become a Native? (With Apologies to Mamdani)," *Constellations* 23, no. 3 (2016), 357.

30. Salman Abu Sitta, *Dividing War Spoils: Israel's Seizure, Confiscation and Sale of Palestinian Property* (London: Palestine Land Society, 2009). www.plands.org/getattachment/f1b0a7d9-0004-43f4-8bc4-1bb3beff8462/dividing-war-spoils.

31. Zochrot-Badil. "Study Visit to Cape Town," 2012. https://zochrot.org/en/article/54464.

32. "Economy of Israel," Wikipedia. https://en.wikipedia.org/wiki/Economy_of_Israel; Trading Economics. https://tradingeconomics.com/palestine/gdp.

33. Farid Abdel-Nour, "Irreconcilable Narratives and Overlapping Consensus: The Jewish State and the Palestinian Right of Return," *Political Research Quarterly* 68, no. 1 (2015), 117.

34. Abdel-Nour refers on this point to Ilan Pappe and Jamil Hilal, eds. *Across the Wall: Narratives of Israeli-Palestinian History* (London: I. B. Tauris, 2010).

35. Ilan Pappe, *The Idea of Israel: A History of Knowledge and Power* (London: Verso, 2016), 254–8.

36. Ibid., 280, 298–303.

37. See, for example, Peter Beinart, "The Failure of the American Jewish Establishment," *New York Review of Books* 57, no. 10 (June 10, 2010), 10–21.

38. Jewish Voice for Peace, "Our Approach to Zionism" (2019). https://jewishvoiceforpeace.org/zionism.

39. Linda Tabar and Chandni Desai, "Decolonization is a Global Project: From Palestine to the Americas," *Decolonization: Indigeneity, Education & Society* 6, no. 1 (2017), x–xi; Beshara Doumani, "Rediscovering Ottoman Palestine: Writing Palestinians into History," *Journal of Palestine Studies* 21, no. 82 (1992), 5–28.

40. Mamdani, "Beyond Settler, 651–64.

41. Barghouti, "What Comes Next."

42. Ron Kuzar, *Hebrew and Zionism: A Discourse Analytic Cultural Study* (New York: Mounton de Gruyter, 2001); Mazin Qumsiyeh, *Sharing the Land of Canaan: Human Rights and the Israeli-Palestinian Conflict* (London: Pluto Press, 2004); Marcelo Svirsky and Ronnen Ben-Arie, *From Shared Life to Co-resistance in Historic Palestine* (London: Rowman and Littlefield, 2017).

43. Veracini, *Settler Colonialism*, 115.

44. Barghouti, "What Comes Next."

45. Bruyneel, *The Third Space of Sovereignty*.

46. Mamdani, "Beyond Settler."

47. Adolo Alban Achinte, quoted in Mignolo and Walsh, *On Decoloniality*, Kindle edition, Introduction.

48. Mamdani, "Beyond Settler," 153.

49. Taiaiake Alfred, *Peace, Power, Righteousness: An Indigenous Manifesto* (Toronto: Oxford University Press, 1999); Lynne Davis, Jeff Denis and Raven Sinclair, "Pathways of Settler Decolonization," *Settler Colonial Studies* 7, no. 4 (October 2016), 393–7; Katie Boudreau Morris, "Decolonizing Solidarity: Cultivating Relationships of Discomfort," *Settler Colonial Studies* 7, no. 4 (October 2016), 456–73.
50. Land, *Decolonizing Solidarity*.
51. Ngũgĩ wa Thiong'o, *Decolonizing the Mind: The Politics of Language in Africa Literature* (London: James Currey, 1986).
52. Mandani, "Beyond Settler," 652.

10. Addressing the Fears and Concerns of a Single Democratic State

1. Yuval Evri, Personal communication; Marcelo Svirsky and Ronnen Ben-Arie, *From Shared Life to Co-resistance in Historic Palestine* (London: Rowman and Littlefield, 2017), 47–129; Abigail Jacobson and Moshe Naor, *Oriental Neighbors: Middle Eastern Jews and Arabs in Mandatory Palestine* (Waltham: Brandeis University Press, 2016), 19–53.

A Last Word: Being Political

1. Myles Horton, *The Long Haul* (New York: Teachers College Press, 1997).
2. Ines Gil, Khalil Shikaki and Rami Kukhun, "Interview with Dr. Khalil Shikaki: 'A Majority of Palestinians Believe that the Two-State Solution is No Longer Feasible Because of the Israeli Settlements'," *Les Cles du Moyen Orient* (May 28, 2020). www.lesclesdumoyenorient.com/Interview-with-Dr-Khalil-Shikaki-A-majority-of-Palestinians-believe-that-the.html.
3. Jeff Halper, *War Against the People: Israel, the Palestinians and Global Pacification* (London: Pluto Press, 2015).

Index